# Mary Surratt

*Mary Elizabeth Jenkins Surratt.* (Author's Collection)

# Mary Surratt
## An American Tragedy

ELIZABETH STEGER TRINDAL

PELICAN PUBLISHING COMPANY
Gretna 1996

*The word "Pelican" and the depiction of a pelican are
trademarks of Pelican Publishing Company, Inc., and are
registered in the U.S. Patent and Trademark Office.*

**Library of Congress Cataloging-in-Publication Data**

Trindal, Elizabeth Steger.
    Mary Surratt : an American tragedy / Elizabeth Steger Trindal.
        p.   cm.
    ISBN 1-56554-185-5 (hc : alk. paper)
        1. Lincoln, Abraham, 1809-1865—Assassination. 2. Surratt,
Mary
    E. (Mary Eugenia), 1820-1865.   I. Title
    E457.5.T85  1996
    973.7'092—dc20
    [B]                                                                95-50031
                                                                          CIP

*Cover art by Judy Earp-DeLaughter*

Manufactured in the United States of America

Published by Pelican Publishing Company, Inc.
1101 Monroe Street, Gretna, Louisiana 70053

*To*
*Mary Elizabeth Surratt*
*and*
*her descendants*

# Contents

# *Preface*

The author highly recommends that the reader not overlook the endnotes that appear in this book. To disregard them is to deprive oneself of vitally important information. The endnotes are not only informative, but interesting as well.

When I first heard of Mary Elizabeth Surratt, I became intrigued. Did the United States government commit a grievous wrong when a seemingly pious mother of three was hanged? I had to find out, once and for all. After fifteen years of research and writing, my book answers the question.

Johann Wolfgang Von Goethe (1749-1832), Germany's most famous writer, was correct when he wrote that it is easier to perceive error than to find truth. The former lies on the surface and is easily seen, while the latter lies in the depth where few are willing to search. After my many years of research and writing, I can say that I have journeyed to the depths in my quest for the true story of Mary Surratt.

My search, however, was far from lonely. Along the way I met many wonderful people who extended themselves to help me. They were the teachers, I was the eager student. To each I send my heartfelt thanks: John C. Brennan; the Reverend Robert Keesler; Michael W. Kauffman; Laurie Verge; Joan Chaconas; James O. Hall, an author of *Come Retribution*; Guy W. Moore, author of *The Case of Mrs. Surratt;* Betty Ownsbey, author of *Alias "Paine," Lewis Thornton Powell, the Mystery Man of the Lincoln Conspiracy,* and my editor in her area of expertise; Phyllis Luskey Cox; Dr. Richard Mudd; Louise Mudd Arehart; Susan Ketron; Margaret Bearden; Dr. Terry Alford; and Dr. Joseph George.

Others are: Helen Finotti Golembieski; Mary Donohoe Murry; Harold Wang; Vivian B. Edelen; Rev. James Surratt Seaman; Frances X. Flaherty-Knox; Matthew Neal; the Reverend Monsignor L.F. Hurley and Margaret McNeill, St. Ignatius Church; Mike Miller and Sandy O'Keef, Alexandria Library; Colonel Alton and Mary Bynum, Fort Leslie McNair; Nicholas Sheetz and Margaret H. McAleer, Special Collections, Georgetown University Library.

Words of appreciation must be extended to: Jefferson City Historical Society, Steubenville, Ohio; the Surratt Society, Clinton, Maryland; and the Dr. Richard Mudd Society, Bryantown, Maryland.

Also, Joseph William Trindal, son, computer expert, and lifesaver; my husband Wesley, legal advisor, editor, and fellow sufferer (what would I have done without you, dear?); dear friend, supporter, and general editor, Bonnie Ward; and Aileen Campbell, true friend, midwife to my book seeing the light of day, and author of *The Wee Scot Book.* Finally, but far from last, Pelican Publishing copyeditor, Jimmy Peacock, the best editor in all the world.

# Mary Surratt

## CHAPTER ONE

# *Mary Elizabeth Jenkins—Her Beginnings*

It has been said, "Thank God for the veil that hides our futures!"

Safe in the innocence of youth, Mary Elizabeth Jenkins had been blessed to have had her future veiled from her.

She was born to Elizabeth Anne and Archibald Jenkins on a Maryland farm in Prince George's County. The farm was located in what is now Clinton.

They were plain folks from hard-working stock. For generations they had tilled the Maryland soil. And, like their neighbors, tobacco was their primary crop.

Tragedy struck early when Mary's father died. Life was not easy for her forty-one-year-old mother after Mary's father had died in the fall of 1825.[1] Elizabeth Anne ("Bessie") and Archibald had been married only four years prior to his death.[2] In those four short years, three children were born to the couple: John Zadoc in 1822,[3] Mary Elizabeth in 1823,[4] and James Archibald in 1825.[5]

After the loss of her husband, Mary's mother, Bessie, became an astute business woman. She was not only able to keep the farm and eleven slaves, but in addition, purchased more land that she managed with equal competence.[6]

The property that Mary's mother inherited from Mary's father was part of Edward Calvert's original seven-thousand-acre estate known as "His Lordship's Kindness."[7] Years earlier, Bessie's father-in-law, Zadoc Jenkins, had been a tenant farmer on that same estate.[8]

Beyond the arduous work of managing and working a farm, the Jenkins lived relatively private lives. James Gibbs Webster, Mary's maternal grandfather,[9] was probably an important member of Mary's family. He knew all about farm management. For years he had been an overseer on the extensive Calvert estate.[10]

Mary had one aunt and four uncles from her mother's side of the family: Mary Ann and her husband, Thomas Meade of Prince George's County;[11] William and his wife, Ann;[12] Philip Lewin and his wife, Martha; John and his wife, Sarah Latham; and finally, James Gibbs, Jr., and his wife Harriet.[13]

Probably, Sarah Webster, Mary's maternal grandmother, had been Bessie's greatest inspiration. According to oral history, it was Sarah who had bequeathed Mary enough money to obtain a relatively good education.

Like most of their neighbors, the Websters were devout Anglicans. They attended the Episcopal church at Broad Creek.[14]

Presumably the Webster family disapproved when Bessie's brother, John, married Sarah ("Sallie") Latham, an Irish Catholic. The young couple were married at St. Mary's Catholic Church, Washington, D.C. (now Alexandria, Virginia), on June 21, 1817.[15]

In time, Sarah, Mary's Aunt Sallie, apparently not only gained approval of the Websters, but was able to exert some influence over them. This is apparent when, on November 26, 1835, Mary Elizabeth Jenkins was enrolled at the Academy for Young Ladies. The school was affiliated with St. Mary's Catholic Church in Alexandria. It was located at the corner of Duke and Fairfax Streets. The building has since been demolished for a church parking lot. On November 27, Superintendent Sister Bernadina signed a twenty-five-dollar receipt to cover three months' room, board, and tuition for Mary Jenkins.[16] She was taught by the Daughters of Charity from Emmitsburg, Maryland. The order was founded by Mary Elizabeth Ann Seton. Mother Seton was canonized to sainthood by the Catholic Church on September 14, 1972.

Eventually, Sister Eugenia Maginnis became Mary's favorite teacher.

*Academy for Young Ladies, Alexandria, Virginia, the school that Mary Elizabeth Jenkins Surratt attended.* (Author's Collection)

The sister had entered the order in Emmitsburg on January 6, 1829. She served at the academy during the school years 1836 and 1837.[17]

No doubt Mary was warmed by the presence of the Reverend John Smith, S.J., the pastor in charge at St. Mary's. He was said to have been an "eloquent, whole-souled Irish man." The priest was responsible for the Sisters of Charity establishing the Academy for Young Ladies in Alexandria. With the assistance of Brother John Brigdon, S.J., Reverend Smith built St. John's Academy for Boys. The reverend served as pastor from 1830 to 1837.[18]

The courses of instruction at the Academy for Young Ladies included English, French, orthography (spelling), grammar, composition, writing, rational arithmetic, geography, ancient and modern history, conversations and natural philosophy, chemistry, bookkeeping, and plain and fancy needlework.[19]

When Mary was able to visit home, she crossed the wide Potomac River by ferry from Alexandria to Maryland. Unless there was a winter freeze-up, the river was always busy. Tall ships from the world over brought merchandise to the noisy, busy, Port of Alexandria. They left with furs, tobacco, flour, and leather.

During the warm months, small skiffs, laden with produce and handmade items, raced under full sail from Maryland to Alexandria. There, on market days, farmers sold their goods.

Mary's Uncle John and Aunt Sallie Webster lived near the academy and St. Mary's Church. Her Uncle John was a tanner at Smoot's Tannery on Washington Street.[20]

Mary was not the only student from Southern Maryland. Ann Elizabeth Ellen Mudd attended the academy as well. Ann was eighteen years old, six years older than Mary. Many years later, Ann Mudd's daughter, Mary Elizabeth Wildman Queen, would play an important role in Mary Jenkins' darker days.[21]

Mary Jenkins was brought up during the confusion over slavery. As early as the 1830s, the question both in the North and in the South was far from clear-cut concerning the subject. A consensus of opinion in either section was not to be found. Cotton Mather, the Boston preacher and slave dealer, had no problem in justifying slavery. He believed that in taking blacks out of Africa, he was taking their "heathen souls" to salvation via the Christendom road. In America they would hear the message of salvation and gain eternal life.[22]

The plight of the Northern textile workers did not go unnoticed by the South. Two-fifths of the Boston textile workers were children between the ages of six and seventeen.[23]

In time, Mary left the faith of her forefathers and joined the Catholic Church. Church doctrine would have been overwhelming and perhaps frightening to a young mind. The priests, she was told, were God's living representatives on earth. The sisters were the brides of Christ. Both the priests and the sisters were to be treated with reverence. Catholics were never to cease to endeavor to live lives of sanctity. The sisters, Father Smith and his sermons, and the confessional were ever-present measures to enkindle the aspirants to perfection. The confessional was dreaded. But it was necessary in order to gain the gates of heaven. Once a week, Catholics had to confess their sins to the priest. Every thought, word, and deed had to be acknowledged. After a sincere promise to "sin no more" and then effectuate the proper penance, the Catholic could be assured of a spotless soul and the love of God. In the church and in the academy, statues and holy pictures were ever-present reminders of what the ladies were to aspire to. All the while, the devil rode on one shoulder while an angel rode on the other. Hell was only a step away. One had to be careful. One had to be Catholic to insure salvation, so they were told.

It is not known when Mary Elizabeth Jenkins became Catholic. It is known that from that period to the end of her life, she was a devout convert to her faith.

On August 20, 1838, when Mary Jenkins was fifteen years old, she was named as the sponsor at the baptism of her nephew, Henry Randolph Webster. He was the eleven-month-old son of her Uncle John and Aunt Sallie Webster. Henry was baptized at St. Mary's Catholic Church in Alexandria. Mary was identified on the child's baptismal record as Maria Eugenia Jenkins.[24] It is generally believed that Mary chose Eugenia for her confirmation name to honor Sister Eugenia Maginnis.

Mary attended the academy for four years. In 1839, two years after Reverend Smith was transferred to the Diocese of New York, the Academy for Young Ladies closed.[25]

With the closing of the school, a new life would start for Mary Elizabeth Jenkins.

# CHAPTER TWO

# *Her Early Marriage to John Surratt—*
# *Their Children*

Mary Elizabeth Jenkins was only sixteen years old when she met her future husband.

John Harrison Surratt, ten years her senior, was a colorless, thin man with a questionable background. No one knew who his parents were. He had been raised by Richard and Sarah Neale. Sarah was much younger than her husband, a wealthy man who owned an extensive farm known as "Pasture and Gleaning." It was located in Washington County, Washington, D.C. When John Surratt reached his majority, Neale began to relinquish some of his land and other holdings to his young charge.[1]

John and Mary's early relationship in 1839 was probably a rocky one. A year before, in June 1838, John had had an illegitimate child by Caroline Sanderson. The child was named John Harrison. At the age of two years, John Harrison Sanderson was baptized at St. Peter's Catholic Church in Washington, D.C. The Reverend Van Hosligh officiated.[2] More than likely, Mary Surratt was responsible for the Sanderson child's baptism.

Another problem arose when the young couple learned that they could not be married in the Catholic Church. John Surratt was not Catholic. A church wedding would have been impossible.

On August 6, 1840, John Surratt and Mary Jenkins obtained a marriage license in Washington, D.C. At the same time, Joseph Goodyear and Eleatha Meade obtained their license to marry.[3]

Research indicates that Eleatha Meade and Mary Jenkins were distant relatives. Eleatha was the sister of Debora, who was the wife of James Boiseau. James Boiseau was the son of Ann Jenkins. Ann Jenkins' first husband was Joseph Boiseau.[4] He had been a well-known confectioner in Alexandria.[5] Enock and Ann Clarvo Jenkins were Ann Jenkins Boiseau and Mary Jenkins' great-grandparents. Ann Jenkins was the sister of Thomas Jenkins.[6] Thomas Jenkins would ultimately play an important role in Mary Jenkins' life. Eventually, Ann Jenkins Boiseau would marry Mitchell Smoot. She would become the godmother of two of Mary's children.

Mary and John were probably married the last of August or the first part of September. It is not known if Joseph Goodyear and Eleatha Meade were married at the same time. It appears, however, that John and Mary were married at the Boiseau home on Good Hope Road, in Prince George's County.[7]

John Surratt took his bride down the Livingston Road to Oxon Run. There they forded the willow-shaded stream, turned left, and passed the gristmill that belonged to John Surratt. Beyond, on a small rise, stood the miller's frame house. Here is where the young couple lived while John operated his mill.[8]

On Wednesday, June 2, 1841, Mary gave birth to Isaac. He was baptized on September 13, 1841, by Rev. Van Hosligh at St. Peter's Catholic Church in Washington, D.C. Ann Smoot was chosen as the sponsor or godmother to the child. At that time, Mary chose to use Eugenia, her confirmation name, on the baptismal record.[9] Isaac would grow into a handsome young man resembling his mother. When he was nearly two years old, his sister, Elizabeth Susanna ("Anna") Surratt, was born on New Years Day, 1843.[10]

At the beginning of the year, John Surratt initiated a dangerous precedent. The habit of charging for services rendered began, and in time it would cause him and his family a great deal of grief. From that point on, and for the rest of his life, debt would be his constant companion. Literally, it would eventually contribute to the death of Mary Surratt.

On February 27, then on March 4, and again on April 7, 1843, Dr. John Bayne attended a sick "black girl" for John Surratt. For the next year and a half the doctor made numerous calls to the Surratts without remuneration. Finally, on demand, the indebtedness was paid in July 1848.[11] By then John had accumulated more debts to different people.

Dr. Bayne had had a very sad life. The community of Broad Creek/Oxon Hill had not forgotten what had happened to him nine years earlier. The doctor's two sons, ages seven and five, had suddenly died at the same time. The mounds of the children's graves had barely settled when a third small casket was lowered into the ground. His little daughter, only seven months of age, had mysteriously died. Arsenic poison was discovered when the baby's stomach was analyzed. A fourteen-year-old servant girl confessed to having not only killed the baby, but the other children, as well.[12]

*Isaac Douglas Surratt, oldest son of John Harrison and Mary Elizabeth Surratt.* (The David Rankin Barbee Papers, Georgetown University Library, Washington, D.C.)

*Elizabeth Susanna ("Anna") Surratt, daughter of John Harrison and Mary Elizabeth Surratt.* (Author's Collection)

The year 1843 ushered in other changes. By then, John, for a nominal amount of money, had purchased 236 additional acres of land from Richard Neale. The property was known as "Foxall." It lay in both Maryland and Washington, D.C.[13]

That same year on April 13, 1843, Zadoc, Mary's favorite brother, married Mary Debora Ridgeway. They were married at St. John's Episcopal Church at Broad Creek.[14]

Frequently, in sizable families, a birth and a death or a death and a birth would follow each other. So it was with the birth of Anna and the death of Richard Neale (John's stepfather). After Anna's birth in January 1843, Richard Neale died that same year in September.

He was buried at St. John's Church, Broad Creek.[15] Apparently, Neale died quietly without the medical services of Dr. Bayne.

The death of the elderly man probably affected John deeply. Richard Neale had been the only father that John had ever known. Now, at the age of thirty, John was a father of two children, responsible for Mrs. Neale, and the master of a sizeable farm. This was a lot of responsibility for one just out of his twenties.

Even though John had not paid Dr. Bayne for his visits or the medicines for the family, the doctor loaned John $450 on October 25, 1843.[16] The day before, John had entered into an arrangement to pay William and Henrietta Kerby of Prince George's County $800 for 119 additional acres of the "Foxhall" land.[17] John repaid Dr. Bayne the loan in December 1847.[18]

In October 1843, Mary was well aware that she was expecting another child. No doubt, she had the services of Patty, one of the Neale servants. She was legally given to the Surratts on May 6, 1845, when Mrs. Neale conveyed her title and interest to the tract of land known as "Pasture and Gleaning."[19]

On December 19, 1843, two-year-old Anna Surratt was baptized at St. Peter's Catholic Church. As with Isaac, Fr. Van Hosligh officiated.[20]

It is not known what day in April 1844 it was that Mary presented her husband with his namesake. According to Dr. Bayne's ledger, on the night of April 10 he made a night visit to the Surratts. There, he claimed to have paid "particular attention to Mrs. Surratt." His charge was ten dollars. John Surratt, Jr., would always claim April 13 as his birth date. According to the doctor's ledger, he had visited Mrs.

*John Harrison Surratt, Jr., youngest son of John Harrison and Mary Elizabeth Surratt.* (Author's Collection)

Surratt on April 13, at which time he gave her six anodyne pills. Anodyne was used for pain or sleep or both. The doctor charged two dollars. This would indicate that John Jr. was born on April 10, since the charge was more for that visit than the visit on April 13. No date of birth is indicated on John Surratt, Jr.'s, baptismal record.

Between Mary's brother Zadoc's marriage to Mary Debora Ridgeway and the baptism of their first child, "Zad" had become a Catholic. Margaret Elizabeth Jenkins was born in May 1844. She was baptized at St. Mary's Catholic Church, Alexandria, D.C. (Virginia).[21]

History was not only being made in the Jenkins-Surratt families during the spring of 1844, but in Maryland and the nation, as well. "What hath God wrought" became an often-repeated slogan. Samuel F.B. Morse, working with an appropriation from Congress, conducted telegraph experiments at "Riversdale," the Charles Calvert plantation in Prince George's County, Maryland. On April 9, 1844, Morse's first message was sent from "Riversdale" to Washington, D.C. It was on May 13 that the celebrated message, "What hath God wrought," traveled the wires between Washington and Baltimore, Maryland. That was the first telegraph message sent between two American cities.[22]

The telegraph probably interested Mary, but she had other things on her mind. Between visits to Mary and Mrs. Neale, Dr. Bayne became a frequent caller at "Pasture and Gleaning" for the remainder of 1844.

The year 1845 did not bring any better health to Mrs. Neale. If anything, Dr. Bayne's visits became more frequent. By May, the fifty-three-year-old lady must have felt that she didn't have long to live. On May 27, she relinquished her remaining interested in "Pasture and Gleaning" to John Surratt.[23]

With the decline of Mrs. Neale's health, Mary probably took on more of the domestic responsibilities. In addition to that, she had the care of her three young children and an elderly woman in need of near constant attention.

James and Sara Barrett, their baby William, and William Chinn, a miller, probably Sara's brother, took over the operation of the mill. John was finally able to become a full-time planter.[24]

With the appearance of the miller and his family, the Surratts logically vacated their home at the mill and moved to the larger home at "Pasture and Gleaning."

Apparently, Mary was able to convince Mrs. Neale that she should become a Catholic. On June 27, 1845, Fr. Charles Stonestreet came from Alexandria and baptized Sarah Neale, daughter of Thomas Talbot and Hester Soper. The priest made a notation on the record of baptism that, since Mrs. Neale had been an Episcopalian, her baptism was only conditional. He indicated that Mary was the sponsor.[25]

Toward the last of July, Dr. Bayne began to visit Mrs. Neale more often. She required frequent tapping to relieve the congestion in her lungs.[26]

The physician's last visit to the ailing woman was on August 6, 1845.[27] The death of John's stepmother, no doubt, was a terrible shock. The only family that he had ever had was gone. Now, the future was in his hands.

CHAPTER THREE

# *St. Ignatius Church*

Perhaps not all of John's family was a mystery to him. He may have known about his cousin Mary Anne Surratt Seaman. She lived with her family in Washington, Pennsylvania. Samuel Sarratt was Mary Anne's father, who was the brother of John's father.[1] There were nine brothers and one sister. The names of two of the brothers still remain a mystery. It is generally believed that John Surratt's father was one of the nameless brothers. All of the known Sarratts were from Prince George's County. All of them spelled their names S*a*rratt. But, for some reason, Mary Anne spelled her maiden name S*u*rratt.[2] The same spelling as John Surratt's.

Samuel had fought in the War of 1812. His military service ended in 1813. Sometime after that, he left Prince George's County for Washington County, Pennsylvania.[3] Coincidentally, John Harrison Surratt was born the same year that Samuel was discharged from the military. In 1819, Samuel married Isabella Houston of Washington, Pennsylvania. After his marriage, he operated a tavern that had belonged to his father-in-law. Samuel named it the S. S*u*rratt's Inn.[4] (Notice the spelling.) Interestingly, John Harrison Surratt opened a similar type of an establishment in 1852. He named his establishment

*Reverend Father Joseph Maria Finotti, founder of St. Ignatius Catholic Church, Oxon Hill, Maryland, and a friend of Mary Surratt's.* (Courtesy of St. Ignatius Catholic Church)

the Surratt House and Tavern. Years later, Mary Anne Surratt Seaman and her daughter, Mary Belle, were caught up in the assassination of President Abraham Lincoln.

We learn nothing more about Mary Surratt until September 20, 1847. For some reason, Mary waited until her son John Jr. was three years old before he was baptized.[5] This was most unusual for a Catholic. According to the teachings of the Church, should death claim an unbaptized child, the child would spend eternity in a place called Limbo. Obviously, the delay in having her son baptized would not have been of Mary's choosing.

According to oral history, John Surratt, Sr., had little use for the Catholic church. Perhaps it angered him when Mrs. Neale was baptized Catholic shortly before her death. Perhaps Mary feared for Mrs. Neale's eternal soul and went behind her husband's back to have the dying woman baptized. *And perhaps* John had measured out a mite of suffering to Mary by refusing to have his son and namesake baptized a Catholic. Perhaps he eventually relented.

For the next few years, Mary's interest turned to the construction of a Catholic church in Oxon Hill, Maryland. The new church would serve her well. She would no longer have to travel to Washington, D.C., or Alexandria to attend Mass. The land for the church was donated by Major Edelen and Dr. Folsum. Both men were Episcopalians.[6]

Mary Surratt and Christina Edelen, the wife of Major Edelen, rode the Maryland countryside collecting money for the church.[7] To this day, Mrs. Surratt is still remembered fondly for her part in the formation of the church.

The little church was eventually named St. Ignatius Catholic Church. Saint Ignatius Loyola was the founder of the Jesuit Order. A Jesuit priest first served the church. The cornerstone was laid in 1849.[8]

Until the church was built, Mass was celebrated at the home of Christina Edelen. Mrs. Edelen, who at an appointed time, had her carriage waiting at the ferry to meet the priest from St. Mary's Catholic Church in Alexandria. The priest would come on Saturday, spend the night, and say Mass on Sunday.[9]

One of the priests to make the long ferry ride from Alexandria to Mrs. Edelen's waiting carriage was the Jesuit priest, the Reverend Joseph Maria Finotti.

The Reverend Mr. Finotti was born in Ferra, Italy, on September 21,

1817.[10] The Finottis were wealthy and owned a well-staffed villa in Italy. The senior Finotti was a judge on the Italian Supreme Court of Appeals.[11]

The Reverend Joseph Maria Finotti was an extremely intelligent man, but very eccentric.[12] Apparently his eccentricities did not detract from his "very good heart."[13] He was an extraordinarily handsome man who likely bewitched the women with his liquid, jet eyes, and black, wavy hair. He spoke with a Romanesque accent that, no doubt, mesmerized everyone.

The hearts of the parishioners were probably warmed when they learned how much he loved and missed his beautiful mother, Rosina. She had been brought up in an Ursaline convent where she had lived until her marriage. Her flowers were her passion. At one time she had more than four thousand plants. In addition to her interest in horticulture, she was extremely talented with the artist's brush and the embroidery needle.[14]

The congregation would have been delighted when they learned that Father Finotti's older brother, Gustavus, was seriously considering leaving Italy and joining his brother in Alexandria.[15] If he came, certainly Reverend Finotti would not return to Italy. He had come to St. Mary's Catholic Church in 1850.[16] That same year, St. Ignatius Catholic Church in Maryland was completed.[17]

Mary Surratt would have been one of many in the congregation who would have disliked losing the priest from Italy.

A number of things probably drew Father Finotti and Mrs. Surratt together. By now, Mary likely needed spiritual help and guidance. It was about this time that her husband was beginning to show signs of alcoholism. Then there were the coincidences. They were minor things perhaps, but they may not have gone unnoticed to the homesick priest. Reverend Finotti had a sister by the name of Eugenia,[18] the same as Mary's confirmation name. The other coincidence had to do with Mary's married name and Saint Ignatius. The Surratts had originated from the south of France.[19] Saint Ignatius once prayed at the Shrine of Our Lady of Montserratt in France.[20] This bit of trivia would probably have been meaningful to the two Catholics since Saint Ignatius was the patron saint of the Jesuits, and Reverend Finotti was a Jesuit.

St. Ignatius church was dedicated on May 2, 1850. Nearly one hundred of the faithful were in attendance.[21]

Approximately two years after the dedication, St. Ignatius Church built a school for girls.[22] According to the announcement, the school was located approximately two and a half miles from the Alexandria Ferry. It was described as being elevated and in an airy location overlooking a delightful and extensive valley. If at all possible, Mary would have sent her nine-year-old Anna to "St. Ignatius Female Institute."

# CHAPTER FOUR

# *The Fire*

It was a Maryland "dog day" in August when the bespectacled Gustavus Finotti came to worship in St. Ignatius Church for the first time. In spite of his deficiency with the English language, his courtly manner was no doubt well received.[1] Eventually, Gustavus would win the hand of Emily Hill who lived with her parents at "Prospect Hill."[2]

Had it not been for the gathering clouds of war, the remaining days of 1850 would have passed uneventfully. Innocent debates frequently erupted into fisticuffs that repeatedly ended life-long friendships. The manipulation of minds in order to justify wars had begun. Preachers and newspapers aroused the country's unrest. Congressional representatives in Washington dug themselves deeper into sectional and political trenches.

To avert war, New York-born, President Millard Fillmore signed the Compromise of 1850. It did no more, however, than to postpone the inevitable crisis. From mid-August to mid-September, Congress passed four important bills. The Texas borders were changed. The territories of California, Utah, and New Mexico were admitted into the Union as being either slave or nonslave, depending on their *own* constitution.

The Compromise of 1850 enacted stringent fugitive slave laws. It became unlawful for the District of Columbia to further deal in the slave trade.

As a consequence, California came into the Union as a free state, but sent mostly proslave representatives to Washington. The territories of Utah and New Mexico joined the Union on the side of slavery.

While the Compromise of 1850 ended the transportation of slaves into the District of Columbia, it did not prohibit the buying and the selling of slaves within the confines of the District itself.

The continuance of the Fugitive Slave Law became volatile. The dilemma of runaway slaves or those held in servitude was addressed in Article IV, Section 2, of the Constitution. It stipulated that any person, "held to Service or Labour in one State," who fled to another, "shall be delivered up on Claim of the Part to whom such Service or Labor may be due." This law covered indentured servants, as well.

The 1850s would be the decade that divided the country and became the preamble to war. Slaves were not always being returned to the claimants. In fact, runaway slaves were helped to escape by way of the Underground Railroad to Canada. Even though the railroad was not as extensive as embellishments indicated, it angered Southerners that their rights, under the U.S. Constitution, were being violated. Moderates in both the North and the South breathed a sigh of relief when President Fillmore announced that the Compromise was "a final and irrevocable settlement" of regional differences.[3]

The Compromise of 1850 appeared favorable to the Southern states. On the other hand, the tariff presented more difficulties. In essence, Southerners felt as though they were being treated no better than the American colonies had been treated by England prior to the War for American Independence.

The South, primarily an agricultural economy, depended on the industrial North for its farm implements. The prices for the implements, including Northern-imposed tariffs, became so high that they could be purchased from England for less money. In spite of the Compromise of 1850, the North was politically more powerful than the South. The North used its power to regain Southern trade by imposing costly tariffs on all products from England that were primarily needed in the South. Southerners became infuriated over the tariffs that forced them to pay even more for their much-needed farming implements. In time, Northerners began to stair-step the prices of their products with those from England. Consequently, the implements manufactured in the North would always be a little less expensive than those manufactured in England. In time, the cost of replacing the most minor tool must have became prohibitive at "Pasture and Gleaning."

However, the Surratt family was faced with another worry that made the tariff problem seem minuscule by comparison. It was approximately 1851 when fire destroyed the home at "Pasture and Gleaning." Generally it is believed that a disgruntled slave was responsible.[4] Since he was never apprehended, perhaps the suspect fell into the hands of Nat Butler. Nat was a enterprising free-black Marylander who sold fugitive Negroes to Southern traders.[5]

After the fire, Mary Surratt and her three children moved in with Cousin Thomas Jenkins, his wife Charity, and their six children.[6] As previously mentioned, Thomas Jenkins and Ann Jenkins Smoot were Mary's cousins.

But John Surratt did not rebuild the home at "Pasture and Gleaning." Like his Uncle Samuel Surratt, John decided to become a tavern keeper. Being land poor, he needed money in order to enter into his new enterprise. John Surratt and a friend, David Barry, formed a contracting company to work on the extension of the Orange and Alexandria Railroad.[7] Research indicates that they were active in building the middle section of the railroad to Culpeper Courthouse, Virginia, from Alexandria. This section was scheduled for completion by January 1, 1852.[8]

For Mary, the year 1851 proved to be the beginning of her road to ruin. Until the home-tavern combination was built, she and the children were completely dependant on the kindness of Thomas Jenkins and his family. To Mary, the future must have looked bleak. The thought of her children being raised in an atmosphere of hard-drinking and hard-living men must have tormented her. She needed all the moral support and spiritual wisdom that she could find. Consequently, she turned to her priest.

Reverend Finotti was celebrated for his piety and his concern for the young.[9] It would be only natural that his concern for the young would extend to Mary's children. It became a historic fact that the handsome priest saw enough of Mrs. Surratt to provoke a few raised eyebrows.[10]

Only briefly was attention drawn from the gossip to the marriage of

Gustavus Finotti to Emily Hill on June 18, 1851. "Gus," as he was affectionately called, had already purchased a small farm from David Barry. It was located opposite Colonel Dangerfield's "Wood-Cut Estate," and about a mile from St. Ignatius church. Gus named his farm "Italian Hill."[11]

It was around January 1, 1852, when John Surratt purchased 187 acres of farmland from Charles B. Calvert. The land was located at the intersection of the Marlboro-Piscataway and New Cut Roads, Prince George's County, Maryland.[12] This was near Mary's mother's farm and her brother Zadoc's farm.

In the meantime the gossip concerning Mary Surratt and Father Finotti persisted. Eventually the priest received notice that he was being transferred to Brookline, Massachusetts. A delegation of approximately fifty-five men assembled at the Provincial of Jesuits and begged that Reverend Finotti's transfer be canceled. Another committee traveled to Baltimore to entreat the intervention of Archbishop Kenrick.[13] Both efforts proved futile.

On Holy Saturday, 1852, Father Finotti arrived at his new post in Massachusetts.[14] The priest never returned to Maryland or to Virginia. Initially, he wanted to return to Italy. He stated in his memoirs that he had had "enough of America at that point." In looking back over his life, he wrote that if he had, at times, withheld his opinions and censures, it was so that he might save himself some "heartburnings." Then he made the thought-provoking statement by writing that he "had nought to regret on that score."[15] Perhaps he had censured the gossip mongers too enthusiastically, but on second thought, he was glad that he had.

For Mary, her unsettled life continued. By April 23, 1852, the Surratt House and Tavern was only partially completed. On that day Jeremiah Townshend, the builder, received $170.80 from John Surratt as part payment on the building. It was agreed that Townshend would receive the sum of $600.00 on completion of his work.[16] It wasn't until October 15, 1852, that John Surratt gave Jeremiah Townshend a promissory note for $279.21.[17] Apparently Surratt had paid Townshend $320.79, leaving a balance of $279.21. It was around this date that the house and tavern were completed.

The dwelling was far from pretentious. It was a simple, nine-room building with five rooms on the first floor and four on the second. The kitchen was an attached room on the right of the house. As humble as it was, in time, it would become quite famous.

Before life returned to any semblance of normalcy, Mary and the children would experience the loss of her Grandfather Webster. He died in December 1852.[18]

By 1853, Mary and the children had left the Jenkins home and had returned to "Pasture and Gleaning."[19] Most likely, they were living in vacated servant's quarters. Perhaps Mary had found that life with her cousins had become too tedious. Yet, for some unknown reason, they had returned to "Pasture and Gleaning," instead of moving to their new crossroads home.

On April 12, 1853, Mary begged for help from Reverend Father John P. Donelan.[20] Perhaps it was the priest's way with the unrepentant that had inspired Mary to enlist his help for her husband who refused to attend church. For years, an awesome story had circulated concerning Father Donelan. The incident happened in Alexandria when the wife of a man by the name of Magraw called on Father Donelan for help. Her husband, a professed heretic, lay dying. Just to mention priests or religion would send the man into a rage. Mrs. Magraw, being a devout Catholic, was sure that her husband would be condemned to eternal damnation when he died. When the priest visited Mr. Magraw, he asked a favor from the dying man. He requested that Magraw, since he was dying anyway, recite the Memorare prayer along with him. After much persuasion, Magraw finally recited the prayer. When he had finished, a remarkable change occurred. Magraw asked Father Donelan to baptize him! At the same time, the priest gave the repentant sinner Holy Communion and administered Extreme Unction.[21]

Apparently Father Donelan was successful in inspiring John Surratt to attend church three times in two months! Mary disclosed this fact in a letter to her friend, Father Finotti. At the same time, she assured the priest that she had been attending to her children's education, "both of soul and body." She added that she had been suffering from violent headaches, of late. Finally she mentioned that she had heard that Father Finotti planned to return to Maryland to visit his brother Gustavus.[22]

On May 10, 1853, John sold "Pasture and Gleaning" and part of "Foxhall" to Benjamin F. Middleton and Benjamin Beall. At that time, in order to collect the money owed them, Benjamin L. Jackson, William B. Jackson, and Dr. John Bayne were present at the land transfer.

*Early rendition of the Surratt House and Tavern and out buildings.* (Author's Collection)

Beneath the signature of her husband's, Mary dutifully signed her confirmation name, Mary Eugenia, to the lengthy document.[23]

On December 6, 1853, for four thousand dollars, John Surratt acquired what eventually became the ill-fated house on H Street in Washington, D.C.[24]

According to Washington, D.C., Land Records, by December 6, 1853, the entire Surratt family had moved to their Maryland crossroads home.[25] By then, John was well stocked for his new enterprise. From the distributer, Jackson, Brother, and Company, he had purchased 77 and 3/4 gallons of several brands of whiskey, 10 gallons of brandy, 5 gallons of wine, and approximately 550 cigars.[26]

It wasn't long after Mary and the children had moved into the house that life became an interminable string of hectic days. At times it must have been overwhelming. Every form of transportation pulled by mules, oxen, and horses found its way to the crossroads station. Horses and mules needed shoeing. Coaches frequently broke down and had to be repaired. The wheelwright and blacksmith, whom John had hired, worked in the barn across the lane from the front of the house. While a coach was being repaired, no doubt the passengers fretted in Mary's parlor. Undoubtedly she saw to it that mothers, babies, and children were given every comfort possible. She fed them and bedded them down. Then there were those who were too sick to continue their journeys. Logically, then, either Dr. John T. or William W. Hoxton[27] was called to see them. No doubt, at times, "Surratt's Villa," as Mary insisted on calling it, was inundated with screaming children, crying babies, and tired, unnerved adults, in addition to the sick of all ages. Yet, meals had to be prepared and a thousand and one other things had to be attended to in order to run a wayside inn. No doubt Patty, the servant girl, had come from "Pasture and Cleaning." Perhaps ten-year-old Anna helped to set and wait on tables.

In every way, the crossroads establishment became an island of comfort for travelers. The local farmers in need of repairs came to the wheelwright or the blacksmith for help.

The tiny tavern room that was entered from the side porch was filled with men, smoke, and booze. John Surratt's place was very popular with the local tipplers. In time, though, John became his own best customer.

Mary's life of endless drudgery, probably, kept her from either visiting her mother or brother Zadoc and his growing family. According to Mary's descendants, Mary held prayer services in the parlor for her family and any travelers who wished to attend. A traveling priest could always be prevailed upon to say Mass.

## CHAPTER FIVE

# *Surratt House and Tavern*

In an undated letter, probably written in 1854, Mary Surratt wrote once again to Reverend Finotti. In the letter she mentioned that, up until recently, she had not spoken to her husband for ten or twelve days. She had been up with John until three o'clock that morning. "I thought I would see if he intended to retire or not. His company had all left him and he was spread out at his full length, beastly drunk in the bar room." Mary continued her letter by asking the priest for his help in trying to find a Catholic boarding school for her daughter Anna. She explained that she was not in a position to pay very much tuition.[1]

Eventually, Anna was enrolled at St. Mary's Female Institute in Bryantown, Maryland.[2] Two sisters by the names of Mary and Winfred Martin operated the school.[3] With Anna gone, Mary was able to concentrate on finding a school for the boys.

In the meantime, the Surratt House and Tavern began to take on an air of respectability. The newly designated Ninth Election District was named by the Maryland General Assembly. According to Section 3 of the law, the voting place for the district would, henceforth, be held at the "Surratt hotel."[4]

John Surratt's establishment became even more reputable when he was appointed postmaster in October 1854.[5] It wasn't long before Mary began to serve in that capacity when the position became too difficult for her husband.[6]

With this added responsibility, Mary Surratt saw more of her neighbors, and their lives began to touch her own. She learned who had died and who had given birth. She knew what had happened to the children who no longer lived at home. Some were in the service, some were attending school, while others had married and moved away.[7]

On Saturday morning, December 30, 1854, the stagecoach from Washington clattered and bounced to a stop in front of the Surratt House and Tavern. A pleasant-looking, rotund middle-aged priest alighted. He walked briskly into the house, down the hall, and into the dining room where he looked around, selected a table, and sat down.

He was Father Nota from Georgetown College, Washington, D.C. He was on his way to Bryantown to baptize two girls who attended St. Mary's Female Institute. This, of course, is where Mary's daughter, Anna, was attending school.

Mary confided in the priest concerning her worries about her sons, John Jr. and Isaac. By then Isaac was fourteen years old and John was eleven. She asked the priest for his help in finding a place to send her boys away to school. But as with Anna, she couldn't afford the full tuition.

Reverend Nota promised that when he returned to Georgetown, Washington, D.C., where he lived, he would write Rev. Bernardine Wiget. Reverend Wiget was the Father Superior at St. Thomas Manor at Chapel Point near Bryantown, Maryland. Perhaps Father Wiget could use his influence in getting the boys enrolled at that school.[7]

When Father Wiget received Father Nota's letter, he wrote his superior, Fr. Charles Stonestreet. Mary had known Father Stonestreet when he was pastor at St. Mary's Catholic Church in Alexandria. Arrangements were made and Isaac and John were enrolled at St. Thomas Manor.[8]

By 1855, all of the children had left home. Probably Mary found herself less tense and her headaches not as frequent. Conceivably, she felt freer to visit her mother and to attend St. Mary's Catholic Church at Piscataway.

While she attended that church, Mary became friends with Susannah Bryan. She was the mistress of "Bryan Hall," two miles southwest of the Surratt House and Tavern.[9] Her husband had died and she was left to raise seven children: Pliny, Bob, William Pike, Buddy, Bayne, Samprona, and Eleanor.[10] Having Susannah as a friend undoubtedly did much to elevate Mary's status in the community.

The brick church at Piscataway was twenty-four years old. It nestled serenely in the center of town and only a few feet from the wharf on Piscataway Creek.[11] The delightful little hamlet was an important seaport town located fourteen miles south of Washington, D.C. But, like many small port towns in Maryland and Virginia, it was slowly being strangled out of existence by the encroachment of river silt.

About fifty yards to the right of the church stood a lovely weeping willow tree. Under it were two marble obelisks. There, Susannah's husband had been buried on July 1, 1853.[12]

Susannah would have visited her husband's grave after Mass and while her children attended Sunday school. Barely able to endure her friend's sadness, Mary probably ambled through the churchyard reading the headstones while she waited for her friend. Behind the church were graves enclosed by an iron rail. It was Capt. Bennett Gwynn's family plot. Captain Gwynn was a neighbor of Mary's and a patron of the Surrattsville post office.

Perhaps she read George and Alice Edelen's headstones. They had been mere children when they died the year before. No doubt Mary would have thought of her children and how devastating it would be to lose them.

Probably the inscription above the church door gave Mary and Susannah some peace. The message was from Matthew 11:28, "Come to me all ye that labor and are heavy laden and I will refresh you."[13]

Mary was indeed "heavy laden." According to her letter to Father Finotti, dated January 15, 1855, "Mr. Surratt has be come so that he is drunk on evry occation and are more and more dis-agreeable evry day. I think some times I would give the world if you could come in and give him a good lecture for me. Father John [Donelan?] calls to see us often but he is affread to say any thing to him."[14]

It would have been nice, when things were so hard for Mary, that she received the replacement "keepsake" from Father Finotti that she had requested. The original had burned in the home at "Pasture and

Gleaning." Whenever she received the small black book entitled *The Month of May Consecrated to the Mother of God*, signed by the priest, it would have been cherished.[15]

The days and seasons passed in a blur of hard work with little else. November 4, 1856, came in cold and clear. It was the first time that the Ninth Election District polling place at Surrattsville was used in a presidential election. The voters of District Nine agreed with the majority of the nation and helped to elect the Democrat James Buchanan to succeed President Franklin Pierce.

The platform of the Democratic Party restated the state's rights planks of Jefferson and Jackson, reaffirmed the Fugitive Slave Law, accused the newly formed Republican Party of being abolitionists in disguise, and endorsed territorial sovereignty.[16]

The Republican Party had nominated John C. Frémont as their champion. It was a poor choice, since Frémont's mother was a member of the, then, unpopular Catholic Church and he had been married by a Catholic priest. What popularity that he did enjoy was won by his Western explorations and his role in California's revolt against Mexican rule. The Republican Party made a fatal mistake when they allowed young members of their party to march in large torchlight parades that promoted sectionalism over the issue of slavery. This furnished the Democratic Party with more ammunition. They accused the Republicans of promoting disunity in the country and being traitors to their own race.[17] The Democratic Party fought a hard-fisted fight and James Buchanan won. Once again, war was averted.

On December 31, 1856, John Surratt advertized in the *Planter's Advocate* that he had 120 acres for sale with two log houses. One of the houses was "very comfortable." He identified the property as being within three miles of the Navy Yard Bridge in Washington, D.C., and a little east of the Piscataway Road leading from the bridge. This would indicate that he was selling more of his "Foxhall" property.[18]

The following year, in the spring of 1857, John Surratt had improved his farm with a carriage house, corn house, and granary.[19] A hog pen was built toward the end of 1857. About a year later a "tobacco house" and a "pigeon house" were constructed. The tobacco house was used for curing the tobacco that was grown on the farm. The pigeons were, no doubt, part of the bill of fare.[20] In spite of John's drinking, it would appear that he was still able to maintain the house and tavern and to make improvements on the farm.

# CHAPTER SIX

# *The South Secedes*

In 1857, Mary had more on her mind than the hammering and sawing of John's buildings being erected. St. Thomas Manor had closed.[1] Father Bernardine Wiget had been transferred to Baltimore the year before.[2] His replacement, Fr. Robert D. Woodley, wrote: "The people want the school but do not pay, did not meet expenses last year."[3] When the academy was discontinued, approximately twelve paying students were transferred to the College of the Holy Cross in Worchester, Massachusetts.[4] The Surratt boys were not among them.

In mid-January 1858, Mary dashed off a frantic letter to Father Wiget. She confided that, almost every day, her husband was in a drunken condition. She begged the priest to find a job for Isaac in a dry goods store "or some other place that would be fit for him."[5] Again Mary rescued one of her children from their unfortunate environment when Isaac was sent to Baltimore to work.

Nine months later, Mary admitted in a letter to Father Finotti how desperate she was. She asked the priest if he would use his influence to have Johnnie enrolled at Boston College for two years. Again, she had to ask for charity as she could not pay the full tuition. It seemed, according to Mary, that Johnnie was now looking more to his father for guidance.[6]

Apparently, Father Finotti was unable to help. It was not until September 2, 1859, when John Jr., now age fifteen, enrolled at St. Charles College near Ellicott's Mill, Maryland. There young John began his studies for the priesthood. The discipline was rigid and the studies were difficult. The students were not allowed to be distracted by the outside world.[7] John flourished in the strict environment. He became an outstanding student and a member of an elitist group known as the Society of Angels.[8] In time he met and befriended Louis Weichmann. Calvinists would say that the futures of the two young men were predestined. As it turned out, the Calvinistic assertion would not have fallen on infertile soil.

Once again, Mary's children were away from home and doing well. However, her husband's circumstances became progressively worse. Again he had gone into serious debt. For ten dollars an acre, he had to sell a hundred acres of his Surrattsville farm. Seventy-five acres were purchased, on time, by John Nothey,[9] a neighbor, and a man who would, eventually, become important in Mary Surratt's life. Francis Lawson Goddard purchased the remaining twenty-five acres.[10]

If Mary's prayers for her husband were not being answered, her prayers for her children were. Anna was doing splendidly at school. She had made many friends and had become an accomplished pianist. Louise Stone, Dr. William H. Stone's daughter, became Anna's special friend. Anna was probably a frequent visitor at the Stones, since the doctor became quite fond of his daughter's friend.[11] Anna was an exemplary student. She wrote well and spoke fluent French. She turned into a loveable young lady and a loyal friend.[12] Music recitals gave Mary special pride since Anna wore the blue sash that identified her as an outstanding student and a member of the "Enfant de Marie Society."[13]

It may have been at a school recital where Mary met a friend of her daughter's. The friend was Mary Elizabeth Wildman, the daughter of Anna Elizabeth Mudd Wildman. Anna Elizabeth was six years older than Mary when, in 1835, they attended the Academy for Young Ladies in Alexandria.[14] Since then, Anna Elizabeth had married and died. At the time, Mary Elizabeth was living in Alexandria with her widowed father, Cornelius, and her numerous brothers and sisters.

Apparently, Mary Elizabeth Wildman visited and spent time with her Mudd relatives near Bryantown. Anna probably met Mary Elizabeth through the Stones, who were good friends with the Mudds.

Four years hence, the three Elizabeths—Mary Elizabeth Surratt, Elizabeth Susanna ("Anna") Surratt, and Mary Elizabeth Wildman—would share in a tragedy that would traumatize the nation. Beyond that, the three would share a personal nightmare that would send shock waves for generations to come. But there were chapters yet to be written before that *fateful moment* was reached.

There was scarcely anyone who had not heard of John Brown. Few could not recognize the wild-looking, white-bearded man. His face had glared out at them from every publication. In 1856, Brown and his five sons, in far-off Kansas, had killed five proslavery settlers.

According to eyewitness accounts, "Brown went crazy" when he learned about the caning of Sen. Charles Sumner of Massachusetts by Sen. Preston Brooks of South Carolina.[15] Sumner had just finished a long tirade against the South in the U.S. Senate, when Brooks jumped to his feet and nearly caned the senator to death.

Since his bloody escapade in 1856, Brown preached his Calvinist fanaticism. "Without the shedding of blood there is no remission of sins,"[16] he ranted. In time, he became convinced that he was the chosen one to carry out God's will against slavery and the caning of Senator Sumner. Brown devised an amazing scheme to insure that blood would flow. He went South to unleash what he was convinced was "God's" wrath. He chose the little town of Harpers Ferry, Virginia (now West Virginia), as his staging place. There, he planned to lead a raid on the Federal arsenal so he could arm thousands of slaves that he would recruit from the lowland plantations. Their "holy" mission was to murder slave holders and to burn the planters' farms. Brown tried to induce Frederick Douglass, the famous black leader, to join him. To Brown's astonishment, Douglass refused and tried to persuade the insurgent to abandon his insane campaign.

On October 16, 1859, Brown and twelve men captured the unguarded arsenal, rifle works, and armory at Harpers Ferry. Then he waited impatiently for the local slaves to be brought to him by a small band of his own men. Other than a few frightened slaves and some captive whites, Brown's wait was in vain.

The news of the raid at Harpers Ferry spread far and wide. On

October 17, the militia and local citizens mobilized and drove the raiders out of the arsenal, the rifle works, and the armory. Ironically, one of the first to be killed in Brown's ill-fated attack was a free black! Two local men, two of John Brown's sons, and several of Brown's men were also killed. Then Brown and the rest of his raiders were driven into the firehouse. It was there that they "made their last stand for God." During the night, 106 U.S. Marines, commanded by Col. Robert E. Lee and Lt. J.E.B. Stuart, stormed the firehouse, after Brown refused to surrender. Brown was wounded and two of his raiders killed. He and six of his captured cohorts were jailed and put on trial.

On October 25, John Brown was indicted for murder, treason, and instigating a slave insurrection. He pleaded "not guilty" and the trial began two days later. Brown lay on his cot in front of the courtroom during the entire proceedings. The attorney for the defense tried to save Brown's life on the grounds of insanity. The plea was rejected and the trial proceeded.

Witness after witness recounted the frightening details of the raid at Harpers Ferry. The insurrectionist was found guilty on October 31.

On December 2, at eleven-thirty in the morning, John Brown was hanged in Charles Town, Virginia (now West Virginia). As he dangled at the end of a rope, a military officer shouted, "So perish all such enemies of Virginia! All such enemies of the Union! All such enemies of the human race!"[17]

In the ranks of those who heard the words and witnessed the death throes of John Brown, stood a handsome young actor by the name of John Wilkes Booth![18]

It was at this time that "Aunt" Rachel and her children appeared at the Surratt House and Tavern.[19] She had been hired to Mary by Cornelius Wildman, the father of Mary Elizabeth Queen, née Wildman.[20] In time, Rachel and Mary became very devoted to each other.

By the time that 1859 had ended and 1860 had started, the dark clouds of war were thickening. John Brown's name was being heard everywhere when Congress convened for the 1860 winter session. Brown's take-over of Harpers Ferry and his later execution had further divided the Union. To some, his act was an exquisitely noble one. To others, he was no more than a crazed traitor. Benign senatorial discussions erupted into arguments and threats of disunity. Political and sectional differences led to bitter personal animosities. In both Houses of Congress, violent quarrels came just short of physical attacks. Some representatives felt it necessary to arm themselves and be escorted to and from the Capitol.

The divisive unrest in Washington had its effect on Mary. Thoughts of a possible war no doubt plagued her. The North became sympathetic toward John Brown and many Northerners pronounced him a martyr. They demanded that the institution of slavery be ended immediately. Many in the South lashed back that Brown had been no more than an insane butcher. Slavery was an important part of agriculture. To end it would mean the ruination of the entire nation.

No doubt Mary reeled in disbelief when she heard that the North accused those who had slaves of being enormously wealthy. She was testimony to the fact that not all slave holders lived in opulence. The great majority were like her, Zad, and her mother, all barely able to scratch out an existence. Certainly, they could never afford to pay their help in money. And if they could, how would the workers pay for their own housing, food, clothing, and medical expenses? What would happen to the old and the disabled? If the blacks were freed, what then? Would they be any better off, presuming that they could pay their own way?

As it was, many slaves earned money on their own. Some raised chickens and vegetables and sold them to the local grocers. Many purchased their freedom that way. Most people were convinced that there would be no winners if the slaves were freed. It was unthinkable to go to war over slavery. If, in fact, that was the real issue. For the South, it was the tariff. For the North, it was maintaining a united nation. If Northerners were really concerned about slavery, why had they not done something to improve the unspeakable working condition of their factory workers?

If things were not unsettled enough, 1860 was also a presidential election year. Three important events had transpired, since the 1856 election, that helped to fracture the Democratic Party. First, of course, was the John Brown incident. His fellow Calvinists in the North revered the man as a saint. Their sanctimonious preaching about their martyred comrade began to filter to the adherents of the other denominations. This enraged the Southern Democrats. The second indignity to the South came when a western North Carolinian, by the name of Rowan Helper, wrote *The Impending Crisis of the South.*

The book was so inflammatory that the author couldn't find a Southern publisher. On the other hand, Helper had no problem in finding a Northern publisher.[21] Eventually the book would be viewed by its readers as a holy call to war against slavery.[22] The third crisis was caused by another writer, by the name of Harriet Beecher Stowe. Her book, *Uncle Tom's Cabin*, electrified both the North and the South. It stirred the North to righteous indignation. The South was furious that a Northerner could write such a book while at the same time tolerating the atrocities that were being committed daily in Northern factories. Such hypocrisy!

In addition to the slavery issue, outrageously high tariffs were still being imposed by the United States on foreign goods, goods that the South needed badly. Southerners began to react to what they perceived as unjust treatment by the North. In order to save the Democratic Party, the Southern Democrats insisted that certain addenda be added to the 1856 National Democratic platform prior to the Charleston, South Carolina, National Democratic Convention.[23]

The convention was convened on April 23, 1860. At that time, the Committee on Resolutions met. It was composed of both Northern and Southern delegates. The resolutions that the committee proposed were found to be unacceptable to the remainder of the Democratic Party. An alternative platform was offered. It was unsatisfactory to the Southern delegates.[24] The Cotton States withdrew from the delegation. The border states remained, with the hope of effecting a settlement to the problems, when it was agreed to have another convention on June 18, in Baltimore.[25]

In June, all hope for a united Democratic Party met its demise in Baltimore. A compromise could not be struck. All of the border slave states, with the exception of Missouri, withdrew from the convention. Hence, the Southern Democratic Party was born![26]

With little dissention, the new party nominated the current vice president, John Cabell Breckinridge of Kentucky, for the presidency. Joseph Lane of Oregon was nominated for vice president. Oregon had only known statehood for a year.

What remained of the Northern Democratic Party nominated Stephen A. Douglas of Illinois for president and Herschel V. Johnson of Georgia for vice president.[27]

In June, the Republican Party nominated Abraham Lincoln of

Illinois for president and Hannibal Hamlin of Maine for vice president. It was the split of the Democratic Party that caused the Republican nominee to be elected.[28]

The country was obviously on the threshold of war. Few would escape its dire consequences, including the Surratts. Both Northerners and Southerners were filled with animosity. A number of times Rachel was offered sanctuary away from her "brutish slave holders." Each time she declined, saying that she was perfectly happy where she was.[29]

Political pulpitry did not escape the churches, both North and South. If Father Donelan were typical, his sermons became fiery when he hammered away on the political issues. Southern priests and ministers took the biblical stand. The Bible wasn't against slavery! In fact, the Good Book exhorted that they be treated with kindness. To strengthen their proslavery arguments, the clergy, no doubt, quoted passages from: Genesis, Exodus, Deuteronomy, Samuel, Kings, Chronicles, Job, Proverbs, and Revelation!

On February 27, 1860, Abraham Lincoln gave a lengthy speech at the Cooper Institute in New York City. The speech did much to secure his nomination. The future president was very conciliatory toward slavery. He assured his listeners that: "This is all Republicans ask—all Republicans desire—in relation to slavery. As those fathers [framers of the Constitution] marked it, so let it be again marked, as an evil not to be extended, but to be tolerated and protected only because of and so far as its actual presence among us makes that toleration and protection a necessity."[30]

Meanwhile, in Southern Maryland, Zadoc Jenkins became a zealot for the Union.[31] Perhaps it was Lincoln's speech at the Cooper Institute that had decided Zad to remain loyal. After all, didn't Lincoln say that slavery would be protected? But there were others in Southern Maryland who were not so easily persuaded.

The sky was dark and ominous,[32] on November 9, when the vote for the presidency was cast. After the votes were counted, Abraham Lincoln and the Republican Party were at the helm of the ship of state.

An unheard of seventy percent of Maryland's electorate had cast their ballots.[33] Lincoln received only 2,294 votes, while Douglas received 5,873, and Breckinridge received 42,497.[34] Abraham Lincoln had been overwhelming defeated in that state. After the election, anger's heavy breath began to breathe over Maryland. Secession no longer became unthinkable. Could this mean war? A mother of military-age sons would have had cause to worry.

On December 20, 1860, the first of the primal fires of bloodshed was lighted when South Carolina seceded from the Union. The state demanded that all forts within her perimeter be vacated by the United States troops that occupied them. No doubt the audacious Southern move gave both the proprietor and the customers at the Surratt House and Tavern something more to chew on besides food and tobacco. Innumerable pints of spirits would have washed their insides as they sat and glared at every suspicious-looking traveler who chanced to walk past them on the way to the public dining room.

Would the young once again be sacrificed because a government had failed to keep the peace? As a little girl Mary Surratt would have remembered the blackened ashes of farm buildings that had been burned during the War of 1812. This was when the English troops marched through Maryland on their way to Washington where they burned and sacked the Capitol and the White House. Mary would have heard the old folks' talk. They told about other things, things that had happened to unfortunate girls and women. Things that were worse than death itself, they said. Mary's thoughts would have surely turned to Anna and Mary would have shuddered.

It was true that the makers of wars became heroes and were cast in stone, while the little people, who did the fighting, made feasts for ravens. If another war came, Mary knew that, once again, blood would flow on Maryland soil.

CHAPTER SEVEN

# *War Comes to Maryland and Virginia*

By the 1860 Christmas season, the inevitability of war had drawn even closer. Before the strains of "O Come, All Ye Faithful" had faded, John Floyd, the secretary of war, had resigned. He left his post on December 28 and returned to his home in Mississippi. The secretary's resignation was the prologue to Southern secession and the birth of the Confederacy. By February 2, 1861, seven states had left the Union!

The Virginia legislators sent invitations for a "peace convention" to the legislators of the remaining Union states. They, in turn, were requested to send delegates to meet on February 4, at Willard's Hotel in Washington, D.C. Governor Thomas H. Hicks of Maryland appointed state senator Reverdy Johnson as one of the men to represent Maryland at the convention. Former president John Tyler was appointed as the chairman. The Virginians knew that if war developed, most of the fighting would take place on Virginia soil. Unfortunately, nothing was resolved at the convention and the meeting was adjourned.

By February 9, 1861, Jefferson Davis had been elected president of the Confederate States of America. The Confederate constitution was adopted soon after.

As a show of protest against the election of President Lincoln, Mary's son, Isaac, returned from Baltimore on March 4, Inauguration Day, to say goodbye. He was going to Texas. Eventually, he would join the Thirty-Third Texas Cavalry, Capt. James Duff's Company, Texas Partisan Rangers, Confederate States of America.[1]

Conversely, Mary's brother, Zad, had spent his own money and worked tirelessly to get President Lincoln elected.[2] Her family was typical of many families. The coming of war divided the country and sadly divided families, as well.

In mid-March, as a conciliatory overture to regain South Carolina, President Lincoln and his cabinet agreed to withdraw the troops stationed at Fort Sumter, which lay in Charleston Harbor. Two weeks later, Gen. Winfield Scott suggested, in a note to the president, that Fort Pickens, off the coast of Pensacola, Florida, be evacuated, as well. The president's cabinet disagreed with General Scott. To give up two forts was unthinkable.[3]

On March 15, Justice John A. Campbell, of the U.S. Supreme Court, and a moderate Southerner, told Secretary of State William H. Seward that he was writing a letter to Confederate president Jefferson Davis. He asked the secretary, "as one good friend to another," what he should tell Davis concerning Fort Sumter.

"You tell him," said Seward, "that before that letter reaches him, the telegraph will have informed him that Sumter will have been evacuated."[4] Yet, that very day, President Lincoln had gone to his cabinet and asked them for their written opinions concerning the advisability of sending supplies to Fort Sumter.[5] Naturally, Seward, as a cabinet member, was present at President Lincoln's cabinet meeting! Yet, Seward told his friend to tell Jefferson Davis that Fort Sumter would be evacuated! It was years later when Campbell wrote that he finally realized that Seward had been "deliberately and intentionally false."[6]

On April 1, Governor Francis W. Pickens of South Carolina was assured by Secretary Seward, through Justice Campbell, that Fort Sumter would not be reinforced without first giving notice to the governor. No one knew if the president had concurred or not. If he had, the message should have gone through Secretary of War Simon Cameron.[7]

On April 4, President Lincoln called Gustavus Fox, a former naval officer, back to duty to take provisions to Fort Sumter. Then the president sent a message to Governor Pickens saying that no troops would be used if the governor did not interfere with the delivery of the provisions. Major Robert Anderson, the commanding officer of Fort Sumter, was alerted much later that provisions were on the way.[8]

The entire expedition to resupply the fort was bound to be viewed with suspicion by President Davis and Governor Pickens. After all, with all of the mixed messages that they had received, who was to know what President Lincoln was planning to do with Fort Sumter? It was feared that more than food would be coming from the North!

Major Anderson had not been completely trusted by his superiors, since the major was of Virginia ancestry and had been born in Kentucky. His wife was from Georgia.[9] When he was finally told the fort was going to be provisioned, he wrote to the War Department saying that he thought Washington should have told him earlier. "I fear that its results cannot fail to be disastrous to all concerned," wrote Major Anderson, "though I frankly say that my heart is not in the war which I see is thus to be commenced."[10]

So, the stage was set. Former captain in the United States Army and the late superintendent of the United States Military Academy at West Point, Pierre G.T. Beauregard was placed in charge of the Southern defenses at Charleston. He held the rank of brigadier general. General Beauregard knew that if he fired on an innocent-appearing supply ship, it would look to all the world that the South had fired on the North while it was in the process of performing a mission of mercy.

Before Fox and his ship of mercy with soldiers on board arrived in Charleston, Secretary of the Navy Gideon Welles had sent three warships to the entrance to Charleston Harbor and the Treasury Department had supplied a revenue cutter.[11]

Obviously, the game plan had changed! Originally, a single supply ship was to go to Fort Sumter. Governor Pickens must have been surprised when he was otherwise officially notified. With the notification came a warning that the warships would open fire if the supply venture was met with interference.[12] To any casual observer, it would appear that there was more than food being supplied to the fort.

On April 11, General Beauregard sent a message to Major

Anderson, his former artillery instructor at West Point, to surrender the fort. He said that "there was reason at one time to believe that such would be the course pursued by the Government of the United States."[13]

Major Anderson declined the general's request to evacuate.[14]

General Beauregard sent another message to Anderson on the same day, asking again that the fort be evacuated. Three men of prominence had been selected to carry the notes to Fort Sumter. This time, the major received the second request with no answer at all.[15]

The final decision as to what to do about Fort Sumter was made by the three men. Together they sat down and penned a reply in front of the major. In essence, the note read that the Charleston batteries would open fire on Sumter within the hour.[16] This momentous occasion occurred at three-thirty on the morning of April 12.

With sadness in his heart, Major Anderson escorted the Confederates to the wharf of the fort. They shook each others' hands and, with resignation, said their goodbyes.

Two days later, on April 14, a surrender flag flew over Fort Sumter. Four thousands shells had been fired without a loss of a single life![17] The incident had ended, but the war had begun!

On April 17, 1861, the Virginia Convention met and passed an Act of Secession. No doubt Mary wondered if Maryland, the plum of the Union and a plum for the Confederacy, would be the next state to secede. It would not have seemed possible that Virginia, the state where she had attended school and where her Webster relatives lived was now in another country.

The days passed, and the tempo at the Surratt House and Tavern increased. Old men bragged while young men left for Richmond and the Confederacy.

Soon after Virginia seceded, Arthur Barry, a neighbor's son, joined the army of the Confederacy as a doctor. He had recently graduated from the University of Georgetown.[18] Mary had known the young man for most of his life. As youngsters, he and Isaac had been good friends. Arthur was a fine, bright young man whom, perhaps, Mary would have chosen for a son-in-law. He enlisted in Capt. Francis B. Shafeffer's National Rifles. This Confederate unit consisted primarily of Maryland and District of Columbia youths.[19]

Most Southern Marylanders were on the side of secession. Like the South as a whole, they didn't want war. All they wanted was to be allowed to peacefully leave the Union and form their own government. As it was, they felt cast aside without representation.

According to the United States Constitution, there had to be thirty thousand voters for every representative in Washington, D.C. Consequently, the states with the largest number of voters wielded the most power. The representatives made the bills and cast their votes on behalf of their own states. The population centers were in the North because that is where the immigrants settled—and in time they became voters. Consequently, the North had complete sovereignty over the South.

It wasn't long after Arthur Barry left that a riot occurred in Baltimore. At ten o'clock, on the morning of April 18, a train carrying the Sixth Regiment, Massachusetts Volunteer Militia, pulled into the President Street Railroad Station in Baltimore. The troops were being sent South to suppress the infant Confederacy. A hostile, pro-Southern crowd waited for the soldiers. The troops were to be transferred in railroad cars, pulled by teams of horses, across the city, to the Cameron Street Railroad Station. At that time, rail service from the North did not connect with the southbound rail service running from Baltimore to the nation's capital. At the Cameron Street Station, the cars would be connected to another locomotive and the troops would continue their journey to Washington.[20]

The malevolent crowd gathered along the path of the railroad cars carrying the soldiers between the stations. Insults, rocks, and bricks were hurled at the troops. A gun was fired by a soldier or a civilian and a full-scale riot ensued.[21] By the time the outbreak was subdued, twelve citizens and four soldiers had been killed and an unknown number injured.[22]

Baltimore was not the only place in Maryland that was beginning to experience hostilities. That same month, in April, St. Thomas Manor, the school that John and Isaac had attended, became a Union encampment and remained so until the end of the war. According to Brother Vorbrinck, "Nothing could be done except to look on and see the property destroyed." Even the tombstones were shot down in the graveyard. The inventory of the troops plundering throughout the war at the manor was staggering. General Philip H. Sheridan's cavalry had done the most damage.[23]

Approximately fifteen miles from St. Thomas Manor, Anna was still attending St. Mary's Female Institute. On April 23 she wrote a letter to her friend Louise Stone. In it, she said that the thoughts of war that day had distracted her so much that she was unable to study. She ended her letter by saying: "Poor Isaac! I never expect to hear from him anymore. I wish Texas had been annihilated before he thought of going there."[24]

The reality of war came to Mary Surratt in another way when a New York infantry regiment, under order of Colonel McCarthy, tore down Thomas Jenkins' home. That was the home where Mary and the children had stayed after the fire at "Pasture and Gleaning." The lumber from the house was needed to build officers' quarters at Fort Snyder.[25]

More sadness came to Mary when Bob, William ("Bill"), and Pliney Bryan left to join the Confederacy. Susannah had lost her husband. Now would she lose her three sons, as well?[26]

The incursion of the Union troops did not escape "Italian Hill." They camped on Gustavus Finotti's property and tore down his fences for firewood.[27]

On April 24, 1861, Gustavus, with the approval of the state of Maryland, visited President Lincoln. The purpose of his mission was to "mediate Maryland between the North and the South." To Gustavus' disappointment, the only way that the president would accept the mediation would be with Maryland and Virginia together.[28]

Susannah Bryan and her family soon felt the effects of the Union onslaught into Maryland. Her slaves had packed up and left to settle around one of the many Union forts that ringed Washington. In addition, most of the Bryan livestock was driven off.[29]

Probably it was John Surratt's enterprises that were his saving grace. The services at the Surratt House and Tavern, the wheelwright, and the blacksmith were valuable to the Union troops. Consequently, the Surratts were left relatively unscathed. Aunt Rachel Seavers would testify later during the trial of the conspirators that "Mrs. Surratt has fed Union soldiers at her house, sometimes a good many of them; and I know that she always tried to do the best for them that she could, because I always cooked for them. She always gave them the best she had and very often she would give them all she had in the house, because so many of them came . . . I never knew her to take any pay for it."[30]

By now, the North had lost many of its noted military leaders to the

Confederacy. One was Lt. Col. Robert E. Lee. He resigned his U.S. commission and became the commander of Virginia's armed forces. The Southerners saw his resignation as significant. Mrs. Robert E. Lee was the step-granddaughter of George Washington. Considering that General Washington, the Father of the Country, had had no children of his own, Mrs. Lee was one of his closest living relatives. Would this imply that the general, himself, would have approved of Colonel Lee's resignation? Probably so, Southerners reasoned, since General Washington had fought to throw off English oppression, just as the South was now attempting to rid itself of Northern repression.

On May 14, 1861, the Federal occupation of Baltimore began. One day later, Mary's relatives in Alexandria were facing the *Pawnee*, one of the U.S. Navy's sloops-of-war, that had helped to provoke the firing on Fort Sumter.

On May 24, and within a matter of hours, news spread across the Potomac that Union troops were in possession of Alexandria! On that day, three regiments of the Eleventh New York Volunteers, under the command of Col. Elmer E. Ellsworth, marched up King Street. The Confederate flag was still flying from the Marshall House. When Ellsworth saw the flag, he ran into the hotel and tore the flag from its mounting outside the third-story window. When the colonel returned to the street, James Jackson, the proprietor of the hotel, rushed out the door and shot the colonel. In turn, Cpl. Francis Brownell killed James Jackson.[31] Now, the first blood of Virginia had been spilled in the name of independence.

# CHAPTER EIGHT

# *Mary Surratt Becomes a Widow*

The Union disaster on July 21, 1861, at Bull Run, Manassas, Virginia, would have brought jubilation to the Confederate sympathizers around Surrattsville. Zad Jenkins, however, in a show of outraged patriotism, hoisted Old Glory to the top of a flag pole. When a number of Rebel sympathizers threatened to haul it down, Zad sent for help. A band of twenty to fifty Union men stood guard all night to keep the banner flying.[1]

In August 1861, Maryland governor Thomas H. Hicks and numerous Maryland legislators became alarmed at the growing sentiment for the Confederacy within their own ranks. They were convinced that when the legislature convened in Frederick, Maryland, the following month, an ordinance for secession would be introduced and passed. Neither the government in Washington nor the Maryland Unionists could allow this to happen. Northern "spies" had previously identified the "bad men" within the Maryland legislature and had informed President Lincoln and the War Department.[2]

The secretary of war, Simon Cameron, issued an order to Major General Banks in Darnestown, Maryland, that, in order to prevent

Maryland from seceding, "all or any part of the Legislative members must be arrested."[3]

By the darkness of night in Baltimore, on September 12 and 13, all known Southern sympathizers in the Maryland state legislature and certain prominent citizens were rounded up and incarcerated at Fort McHenry.[4]

By September 19, the hunt for the Southern sympathizers had ended with the imprisonment of fifty-one people, both Maryland citizens and state legislators. Governor Hicks was delighted at the outcome. The *Annapolis Gazette* and the *Baltimore American* newspapers both applauded. The Unionists prevailed, and the democratic system of government breathed its last breath in Maryland.[5]

Henceforth, Marylanders who adhered to the ideology of secession had to look to their neighbor, Virginia, to fight for Southern independence. Since the First Battle of Bull Run, war in all its fury was being fought in the Old Dominion. Little-known places such as Newport News, Martinsburg, and Phillipi, Virginia, began to appear in the headlines. Both the hither-to names of the renowned and unrenowned leaders became familiar to everyone through the newspaper accounts of the war.

As in any war, there would be many more whose names would only be honored by their families and in their hometowns. Two such men would probably have been Dr. Arthur Barry and Clarence Gwynn. Both men had been neighbors of the Surratts. Dr. Barry was sent to Manassas where he ministered unceasingly to the wounded at the First Battle of Bull Run.[6] Clarence Gwynn was Bennett Gwynn's seventeen-year-old son. Early in 1861, Clarence ran away from his school in Alexandria and enlisted in the Confederate army. He was later killed at Munson Hill in Fairfax County, Virginia.[7]

By now, Anna had graduated from school and had returned to her home in Surrattsville.[8] She was eighteen years old, well polished, and well schooled. Sadly, it was Anna's lot to have to now live in an environment "not befitting" a young lady.

It was in secretive places around Surrattsville where the local news was whispered. Whose son had been wounded, killed, or captured? What neighbor had suddenly been snatched away and incarcerated in Old Capitol Prison in Washington, D.C.? Who was in such desperate straits that he had to take the Oath of Allegiance to the Federal government in order to receive his veteran's pension? It was only the tried and the true who were trusted to be included in these gatherings. Others were treated with caution.

Voting day, at the polls, in November 1861, was a frightening experience for most Marylanders. It was a foregone conclusion who their state and local representatives would be, since those of Southern persuasion had been sent to prison. On their way to the ballot boxes, voters had to walk between Union soldiers with fixed bayonets. To the anger of most, the soldiers were under orders to vote in the Maryland election even though they came from distant states. At the same time, many Marylanders were deprived of the right to vote.[9]

When the elections were over, Dr. John H. Bayne, the Surratt's doctor at "Pasture and Gleaning," became a state senator for the state of Maryland. At the same time he served as a physician, with the rank of a Union colonel. He was assigned to care for the troops at Fort Foote and Fort Washington.[10]

For some, at least, the Christmas season would start on a happy note. On December 10, 1861, a fine new theater opened for business in Washington, D.C. It would become the famous Ford's Theatre where President Lincoln was shot.

Feelings of anger ran high around Surrattsville when, at four o'clock on the morning of January 8, 1862, Bennett Gwynn was arrested by a detachment of the Eighty-Fifth Pennsylvania Infantry Volunteers.[11]

A force of two hundred men, under the command of Col. J. B. Howell, left Fort Good Hope, D.C., for the purpose of arresting the thirty-nine-year-old man for disloyalty. When the soldiers arrived at "Auburn," Gwynn's farm, they searched his home. There, according to the report, an "amount of clothing and military stores designed for the rebels" was found and confiscated. The arrest must have angered the Surratts, since Bennett Gwynn was a special friend.[12]

It was, perhaps, soon after the arrest that John's former mill was completely burned by Union troops.[13]

When President Lincoln discontinued mail service between the North and the South, John Surratt entered into another enterprise. The Surratt House and Tavern became a receiving station for Confederate couriers coming from and going to the North. It was extremely dangerous work. Major William Norris, from Baltimore

County, Maryland, was chief of the Confederate Signal Service.[14] He knew how to pick his men, and sometimes women, to carry the mail. Not infrequently they carried what had been declared as contraband by the United States government. These were medical supplies and clothing needed by the Southern troops.

From Confederate agents and civilians in Canada and the United States, the couriers carried pouches filled with ordinary mail, secret dispatches, and contraband. By night, with heads bent low over their fleet-footed horses, the couriers dashed South, collecting and dropping off messages on their way to Richmond.[15] Out of the South, other couriers raced with secret messages from agents and letters from loved ones serving in the Confederacy. Such places as Surrattsville, T.B., and Bryantown were important mail drops and, no doubt, places where a fresh horse could be had when needed. The Surratt House and Tavern was a strategic point both to the North and to the South. Local mail along with Northbound mail brought from the South by couriers would receive the Surrattsville frank then be sent by U.S. mail service to the North.[16] In the evening between five and six o'clock, John Bartlett, driving the Union stage, picked up the mail on his return trip from T.B. back to Washington. He had started his round-trip run from Washington at eight o'clock in the morning.[17]

If oral history is correct, Anna Surratt would have been especially interested in the mail from the South. Hearing from Dr. Arthur Barry would have brought starlight to her eyes.[18] No doubt he would have written and told her when he became assistant surgeon at Chimborazo Hospital in Richmond.[19]

In January 1862, President Lincoln appointed Edwin Stanton as secretary of war. Stanton, in turn, appointed Zadoc's friend, Col. William Wood, as the superintendent of Old Capitol Prison.[20] Ironically, Colonel Wood, a Marylander, would be in charge of many lifelong friends who were currently "guests" of the prison.

On Monday evening, August 20, 1862, the Surratts were entertaining a gentleman from Alexandria. John "was more animated than usual." The family, including Anna, stayed up late "discussing politics and other things." The friend had given them "great encouragement."[21]

Perhaps they discussed the fact that Washington, D.C., had only recently freed 3,100 of its slaves.[22] Such hypocrisy would have upset

John, considering the fact that slavery in the South was given as a reason for the Civil War. Perhaps this is when he said, "The glorious banner of Southern liberty will be unfurled and planted upon the shores of Maryland."[23]

In Anna Surratt's letter to her friend, Louise Stone, Anna told her friend that, at dawn the following morning, her father had died. At first, the family believed that he was paralyzed. Doctors (probably Drs. John and William Hoxton) were called and examined the body. According to Anna, the doctors found it difficult to acknowledge that John Surratt was dead. Of course, neither John Jr. nor Isaac was present at the time. The family still had not heard from Isaac.[24]

Mary sent for John Jr. at St. Charles College in Ellicott's Mill. As soon as John Jr. arrived home, John Surratt, Sr., was buried at St. Mary's Catholic Church cemetery in Piscataway.[25]

John, now eighteen years old, abandoned his studies for the priesthood. On September 1, 1862, he was appointed the postmaster of the Surrattsville post office.[26]

An accounting of John Surratt's estate was made between November 28 and December 3, 1862. There were only two middle-aged male servants remaining, each valued at two hundred dollars.[27] Certainly, there were too few to work over a hundred acres of the Surrattsville farm, which was still mortgaged. There were both bills that could not be paid and debts that had not been collected. John Sr. had left his family in desperate straits.[28]

During all of Mary's problems, the war still continued. Another battle had been fought at Bull Run. Again, the Federals had been defeated.

On July 29, 1862, Belle Boyd, the famous female Confederate spy, had been captured near Warrenton and sent to Old Capitol Prison. And the Peninsular Campaign was now history. In Western Maryland, the Battle of Antietam had been fought. And Williamsburg, Virginia, had fallen to the Union.

On September 2, 1862, United States gunboats were in the Potomac River facing Alexandria. They had been ordered to shell the town if the threat of a Confederate take-over materialized.

Washington, D.C., had been alerted that it, too, was in danger of attack from the Confederates. The Unionists declared that before they would allow that to happen, they would destroy the city!

On September 23, 1862, President Lincoln issued his proclamation
to emancipate the slaves. It would become effective on January 1,
1863. Strangely, the proclamation was not intended for the states
under Federal control! Maryland and Delaware would continue being
slave states! Nonetheless, the proclamation became a clarion call to
freedom. Slaves left the South by the thousands and headed for
Washington. Zad's "people" were among them. As a result, he and
many of President Lincoln's supporters felt betrayed. After all, didn't
the president promise that slavery would go unmolested? From that
period on, Zad Jenkins cast his lot with the South.[29]

President Lincoln's Emancipation Proclamation made someone
else angry. "Aunt" Rachel was infuriated! Many years later she would
say, concerning her husband, Tom Seavers, that he had left Walter P.
Griffin for Washington. She made the remark that he was "a lazy and
good for nothing." She added that she "would rather stay there
[meaning the Surratt House and Tavern] and work for my children
than to come here [Washington] and suffer with him."[30]

It was perhaps in the fall of 1862, when Mary finally received the
long-awaited letter from Isaac. He was serving the Confederacy in
Matamoros, Mexico.[31]

# CHAPTER NINE

# *The War and the Widow*

January 1, 1863, was the effective date for the abolishment of slavery. Southern Marylanders probably winked and nodded at each other when Lord Palmerston of Great Britain remarked that President Lincoln had undertaken to abolish slavery where he had no authority. Yet, the president protected slavery where he had the power to crush it.[1]

It was estimated that the U.S. government was spending two million dollars a day to finance the war.[2] Certainly, this was more than enough, the South reasoned, to compensate slave holders for releasing their slaves, thus enabling them to pay for help. With but a few exceptions, the planters and farmers did not have the liquidity required to pay wages and at the same time remain solvent. Just about every cent earned was reinvested back into their farms.

Two years after the conflict had started, feelings against the war began to surface among the common folk in the North and in the Midwest during the summer of 1863. Armed gangs roamed the Northern city streets, beating Negroes and murdering military draft officials.[3] It was the poor and the foreign born who bore a disproportionate burden of conscription. Yet, those same people, the factory workers and the unskilled laborers, had the most to lose when the jobless blacks from the South migrated North in search of work.[4] It was for this reason that, on July 13, in New York City, bands of Irishmen and women burned draft offices and looted and burned the homes of prominent Republicans. While chanting "kill the naygers," the mob swarmed into the black districts. There, they lynched no less than a dozen blacks and burned the Colored Orphan Asylum.[5] Four days later, police, with the help of several regiments of soldiers fresh from the Gettysburg campaign, rushed into the fracas and put down the rioters. Wild estimates of the number of people killed ranged from 120 to 1,200.[6] Such riots brought hope to Southerners. Perhaps "Yankeedom" was turning on itself and the war would soon end, they reasoned.

Even though President Lincoln's Emancipation Proclamation did nothing to free the Maryland slaves, it did add unspeakable hardship to the people in Southern Maryland. Many slaves, who did not join their brothers in the North, resorted to lawlessness. Yet, there were those who remained faithful to their planter families.

Prior to the New York riots, the South had defeated the Army of the Potomac at Chancellorsville, near Fredericksburg, Virginia. But with that welcomed victory came a loss that did much to demoralize the Confederacy. The mighty "Stonewall" Jackson, hero of many battles, had been killed! The South would not entirely recover from the loss of their hero general.

Messages smuggled from prisoners held in the Northern prisons to their loved ones in the South were often filled with alarming news. Accounts of unspeakable sufferings that Confederate prisoners endured in Northern prisons added to the travail of the homefolk. Stories told how sickness, starvation, executions, brutal winters, and the lack of sanitation were taking their toll on the helpless prisoners. When fat salt pork, shins, and rice were not forthcoming, rats became the staple food. Prisoners begged for clothing, as theirs was worn to tatters. During the winter, frozen, bootless, feet were amputated. Such amputations often led to infections, gangrene, and death.

In time, John Surratt became intrigued with the Confederate courier service and joined its numbers. Perhaps it was for the purpose of carrying dispatches out of Washington that he began to go to the public market in Washington to sell fresh vegetables from the family farm.[7]

*Louis J. Weichmann, friend of John Surratt, Jr., and a boarder at Mrs. Surratt's boardinghouse.* (The David Rankin Barbee Papers, Georgetown University Library, Washington, D.C.)

How simple it would be for dispatches and letters to be slipped into John's wagon to begin their journey Southward.

It was on one of these trips to the public market in the spring of 1863 that John returned to Surrattsville with Louis Weichmann, a former school chum from St. Charles College.[8] The day was damp and overcast. It had been raining and the roads were muddy. When the two young men entered the parlor, a fire was blazing in the fireplace.[9]

Louis Weichmann would have been considered far from attractive to the opposite sex. He was paunchy and bespectacled. His head was crowned with curly hair and he spoke with a lisp. Young women would have giggled at his dapperness. Older women would have felt maternal toward him. His banal manner seemed to pose no threat to anyone. He appeared sexless, safe for a daughter to be around. Like

John, Lou had studied for the priesthood at St. Charles College. One would wonder why he had abandoned his studies for the priesthood. Being a priest would probably have been the only way that the young man would have ever been taken seriously.

Currently, Lou Weichmann was living in Washington and teaching at St. Matthew's Institute for Boys. He had come to realize that teaching wasn't his forte. He told the Surratts that he would like to secure a government position.[10]

The morning after Louis Weichmann arrived, the sound of music stirred the young visitor to wakefulness. The rest of the household had been up attending to the members of the U.S. Marine Band. The band had come from Washington to Surrattsville the night before for the purpose of serenading a newly elected county official.[11]

In the assemblage was a young man who was no stranger to Surrattsville. He was twenty-three-year-old David Edgar Herold, more commonly known as Davey. He was the sixth of eleven children born to Adam and Mary Porter Herold. Two brothers had died in the 1830s, leaving him the only boy in a family of eight girls. The Herolds resided in a large brick house just outside the main gate of the Washington Navy Yard. They were well to do and highly respected. They counted among their friends the family of the later-to-be famous Marine Corps Band leader, John Philip Sousa.[12] In 1863, young Sousa would have been nine years old.

The Herolds were natives of Maryland. David and his father used to hunt partridge in the woods around Piscataway. The young man once bragged that he had spent several months out of every year in that pursuit.[13] Consequently, David Herold was very familiar with the Maryland countryside. This was an aptitude that would eventually become his undoing.

David had studied pharmacy at Georgetown College. Currently, he was working for Dr. Bates, a pharmacist, near the Navy Yard. Within reach of the young pharmacist were medicines, such as quinine, that the Confederacy so desperately needed.[14]

Yet, with all of his attributes, there was something quite lacking in David Herold. The frowzy-headed young man was generally regarded as immature and unreliable.[15]

Little did Lou Weichmann, Davey Herold, and the Surratts realize that the random parts of their destinies were beginning to come together.

On Holy Thursday, April 2, 1863, John and Lou Weichmann visited St. Charles College, their former school at Ellicott's Mill. There they spent a couple days before they traveled to Ellengowan, or Little Texas, Maryland. At Ellengowan they met Father Mahoney and his friend, Henri Beaumont de Sainte-Marie.[16] The latter would become a "Judas" in the life of John Surratt.

Before the spring of 1863 had ended, Sainte-Marie moved in with Weichmann and joined his friend in teaching at St. Matthew's Institute. Mysteriously, though, he disappeared soon after he started teaching![17]

Back in Surrattsville, the Union soldiers, who were stationed nearby, were an unhappy looking lot when Maj. Gen. Ambrose E. Burnside failed to take Fredericksburg, Virginia, and his replacement, Maj. Gen. Joe Hooker, lost at Chancellorsville. Needless to say, their moral didn't improve when the uninspiring, scholarly looking Gen. George Gordon Meade took over General Hooker's command.

Surrattsville was nearly traumatized in hushed expectancy when, on July 1, the campaign in Gettysburg, Pennsylvania, had started. Whatever the outcome, it would be a decisive battle. The South was finally waging war on Northern turf. If the Southerners won at Gettysburg, the scenes of war would shift to the North. Then it would be only a matter of time until Confederate troops would be marching victoriously down Pennsylvania Avenue. By then, most Southerners reasoned, the South would be free of the United States, just as the United States had freed itself from England!

On July 4, volley after volley of cannon fire thundered in the distance. This was it! General Lee had licked the Yankees at Gettysburg. Now the Confederate troops were moving on to Washington, or so it was generally believed. How foolish the Marylanders must have felt when they learned that the thundering cannon they had heard was in celebration of Independence Day.

A double blow came the following day when news arrived that General Grant had taken Vicksburg, Mississippi, and General Lee had lost at Gettysburg, Pennsylvania. Washington was in ecstacy over the victories. Cannons boomed and church bells rang incessantly. Thousands surged on the White House and serenaded President Lincoln. From there, the crowd trooped to Secretary Stanton's home and serenaded him.

A few days later, Anna may have received a secreted, short message from Arthur Barry. As delicately as he could, he would have told her about the fighting at Gettysburg.[18] He would have told her how discouraging it was to try to minister to the injured soldiers when there was so little medicine.

During the summer of 1863, a search party of soldiers invaded the Surratt House and Tavern. They were looking for John. They had some questions to ask him. Mary was hot and tired. Her patience must have worn thin with the continual intrusions of the military.

When the soldiers had finally searched the house and were about to leave, Mary was waiting for them. She was at the back of the house standing in the hall. "Now, I insist that you look in here for my son," she said, indicating a small closet under the front stairs. "If you don't, I must tell your commander that you did a poor job in searching this establishment!"[19]

Sheepishly, no doubt, the soldiers slunk to where Mary had directed. After they had glanced into the closet, they quickly left the house without uttering another word.

The inhabitants in and around Surrattsville would not soon forget voting day, November 1, 1863! It was the first general election since 1861.[20] As before, voting would be held at the Surratt House and Tavern. This time it would be a gubernatorial election.

At this particular election, there were no Union soldiers present with fixed bayonets to make sure that only Northern sympathizers voted and to discourage any fighting. At this election, Zad and his friends took it upon themselves to make sure that no one would be accosted at the polls, that is, until Zad and his son did some accosting of their own.

Zadoc's sixteen-year-old son became infuriated over something a Mr. Ridgeway had said. In a fit of temper, the young man threatened to shoot the older man and some members of the pro-Union Robey family. Later that day, Zad involved himself in the ruckus and threatened to cut the heart out of Andrew Robey, the son of T. B. Robey. When Union soldiers appeared, Zad went so far as to threaten their hearts with a knife. If that wasn't bad enough, Zad roared at the top of his voice, ". . . no one but a damn rascal would hold office under him."[21] Everyone knew that he was referring to President Lincoln. Needless to say, Zad was hauled off to the Old Capitol Prison. There he cooled his heels until his friend, Col. William Wood, superintendent of the prison, released Zad after the polls had closed.[22]

The local hero of the day turned out to be old Dr. Hoxton (probably John Hoxton). Nothing, not even the uproar at the poll, distracted him from his job. All day he had quietly helped the voters.[23]

Seventeen days later, on November 17, John Surratt was relieved of
his position as postmaster. Twenty-seven-year-old Andrew Robey
became the new postmaster.[24] That meant that the post office, even
though still in the Surratts' tavern, was now in Union hands. No
longer would the Northbound courier mail from the South be
franked at the post office and combined with the regular mail and
sent North. Now, John Surratt would have to hand carry the mail in
and out of "Yankeedom."

Apparently, after his father had died, John began to correspond
with his cousin, Mary Belle Seaman. Belle was the daughter of Mary
Anne Surratt Seaman of Washington, Pennsylvania.[25] In turn, Mary
Anne was the daughter of Samuel Sarratt, who had been the brother
of the senior John Surratt's unknown father.[26]

In mid-December 1863, Anna visited the Sarratts in Ohio and the
Seamans in Pennsylvania. She traveled by rail from the Baltimore and
Ohio Railroad Station in Washington, D.C. to Steubenville, Ohio.
There she visited Joseph Huston Sarratt and his family.[27] Joseph was
Mary Anna Sarratt Seaman's brother and Belle Seaman's uncle. No
doubt, Anna was impressed with her cousin Joseph's occupation as a
jeweler and his lovely home on South 4th Street.[28] The regional con-
victions concerning the war were very conspicuous. Joseph had been
an early abolitionist in that section of Ohio. He promoted the
Underground Railroad that managed the escape of many fugitive
slaves into Canada.[29] No doubt, Anna's visit with her cousin, Joseph
Sarratt and his family, would have been a difficult one.

After visiting with the Sarratts, Anna traveled by stage to visit the
Seamans in Washington, Pennsylvania.[30] There, as well, was an entirely different view of the war than Anna was used to. Belle Seaman had
an uncle whom she adored. Major James Fleming Sarratt, U.S. Army,
was a thirty-five-year-old bachelor.[31] From an early age, Belle had cor-
responded with her Uncle Jim. No doubt, Belle's love for her uncle
and Anna's cousin convinced Anna that not all Yankee soldiers were
bad. After all, her cousins were her relatives on her father's side, and
Anna had too few of those.

# CHAPTER TEN

# *A Change of Scene*

It was a cold winter day in January 1864 when John Surratt returned to Washington. Perhaps, he was picking up Confederate mail and dispatches from the North to take South. Unfortunately, no one knows if John told Lou Weichmann his true mission to Washington when they dined together at the boardinghouse where Lou was staying. It would seem that John would have trusted his long-time friend who had declared his allegiance to the South. Or did John no longer trust Lou after his friend told him that he had secured a job with the United States government? Or was it a private joke between the two men when Lou told John that he had to swear his loyalty to the United States in order to obtain his clerical position with the War Department?[1] In any case, Weichmann was now working in the office of the commissary general of prisons under the secretary of war, Edwin Stanton. For swearing his loyalty to the North, Weichmann earned forty-two dollars more a month than he had previously earned teaching at St. Matthew's Institute.[2]

During their mid-day meal, Lou introduced John to Gen. Albion Paris Howe, U.S.A. He was one of a number of Union officers who boarded at the same establishment where Lou lived. Ironically, one and a half years later, this same general would serve on the Military Commission that would try and convict John's mother![3]

In March, the *Evening Star* newspaper began to sing the praises of Lt. Gen. Ulysses S. Grant. The middle-aged general had covered himself with laurels at Vicksburg and Chattanooga. That same month, President Lincoln appointed Grant general-in-chief of the Union armies.

But back in Surrattsville, the responsibilities for the farm and the tavern had begun to fall more heavily on Mary's shoulders. To her concern and chagrin, John was making more frequent trips between Washington and Richmond.

Mary had seen to it that the fields had been plowed in February and that the ice had been cut from ponds and hauled to the ice house. She saw to it that the corn and other vegetables had been planted in April and that the sheep had been sheared in May. This was in addition to running a public business during the harrowing times of Union occupation. At the same time, her son was operating clandestinely for the Confederacy. Meanwhile, Union man Andrew Robey, the same man whose heart Zad had threatened to cut out, had taken over the operation of the post office in the tavern itself. No doubt, every move that John and the rest of the family made was being observed by Robey. Life must have become inordinately dangerous and stressful for Mary and for the rest of the family.

That summer the long-awaited Confederate invasion of Maryland was proceeding according to General Lee's plans. In July 1864, Gen. Jubal Early was under orders to capture Frederick, Maryland, and, from there, to take Washington, D.C. After Washington was occupied by Confederate troops, General Early was to seize the Federal prison at Point Lookout, Maryland, and free the Confederate soldiers being held there. There was just one snag. Unfortunately for the South, a Richmond newspaper learned of the plan and leaked the details in its publication.[4]

Even though General Early's expedition failed, it served to shake Washington from its complacency. Afterwards, all male clerks from the various bureaus of the War Department were trained to defend Washington in case of a Confederate invasion. Louis Weichmann became a member of Company G of the War Department Rifles.[5]

When John asked Lou if he would shoot a Rebel, if Washington were invaded, his friend answered that he would never fight on the Northern side! Weichmann again assured John that he was an avowed Southern sympathizer. Furthermore, Weichmann confided that he wished that he could secure a clerical position in Richmond.[6]

Yet, there were lighter moments. On August 1, John sat in the parlor writing a letter to his cousin, Belle Seaman. From his letter we are treated to the young man's sense of humor. He teased her by saying that it was an extremely hot day, and that it was heat like this that "makes us Rebs. so savage, cruel and disagreeable." He continued by saying that "it is so hot, that we can neither eat, sleep, sit down, stand up, walk about, and in fact, to sum the whole in a nutshell, it is too warm to do anything."[7]

In Belle's previous letter to John, she must have mentioned to him that he had a great amount of "assurance." In his return letter of August 1, he thanked her, but said that he actually was "bashful, and perfectly unsophisticated, as very few ladies take a fancy to me."[8]

In answering Belle's question as to why he had not married, John said that he hadn't found anyone who would have him. "Often they have vowed, yes." Then John quoted Lord Byron, "But—This record will forever stand—Woman, thy vows are traced in sand." Apparently, in spite of John's alleged unfortunate experiences with womankind, he still had faith in the gentler sex, by saying, "If you know of any lovely angel, in human form, desirous of a matrimonial correspondence, just tell her to indite a few lines to your humble cousin and I can assure her she will not be sorry for it."[9]

John continued his letter ten days later. He said that he had been on a visit of a week's duration. Then John proceeded by treating his reader to a bit of domesticity. "Ma and Anna are sitting in the hall enjoying the evening breeze, whilst I am sitting over my desk, almost cracking my brain in order to find something to fill these pages."[10]

The following paragraph of the same letter to Belle is interesting; it demonstrates that John felt no animosity toward his cousin, Maj. James Sarratt, U.S.A., John asks, "Have you heard from your Uncle James lately? There has been some very hard fighting out West recently, and you know, Cousin Bell, that the foe has very little regard where he directs his bullets. May God preserve him, and grant that he may see the end of this unholy war without harm."[11]

In John's final paragraph he tells Belle that, "everything looks like starvation." Then he adds that Ma and Anna send their love. He continues by saying, "I wish you knew Ma, I know you would like her. Neither of us is like her. My brother resembles her very much. He is the best looking of the family." Then John gives us a view of Anna. Apparently, she had come in from the hall and had started playing the song "Hindoo Mother" on the piano. He mentioned that the piece is beautiful and that he advised Belle to get the sheet music. John ended his letter with another witticism. "To whom shall we Grant the Meade of praise? Ha! Ha!"[12]

Even though Mary probably had not heard from Fr. Joseph Finotti directly, no doubt she was saddened when the priest's last ties were broken with Southern Maryland. This happened when Gustavus Finotti, his wife Emily, and their seven children moved to Brookline, Massachusetts. They would have left Maryland when the war had started, but Emily didn't want to leave her elderly parents. Now that they both had died, the Finottis were free to move North and to be near Gustavus' brother.[13]

Then, there was politics as usual. Four years had passed since the last presidential election. The Washington newspapers were filled with the usual candidates' campaign speeches. Promises and condemnations of the presidential aspirants for the Democratic Party went on unceasingly. Finally, on August 29, 1864, the party nominated retired general George B. McClellan and George Pendleton for president and vice president.

Much of the North was beginning to wonder if President Lincoln was incapable of defeating the Confederacy. Northern carnage was high and Northern victories few. McClellan and his "Peace Platform" became more appealing as an alternative to the war that seemed would never end. The platform denounced the United States government policy of "arbitrary military arrests," suppression of freedom of speech for the citizenry and the press, and a complete disregard of state's rights. The platform further espoused that after three years of failure to restore the Union with "the experiment of war" that the immediate cessation of hostilities was imperative.[14]

Meanwhile, back in Maryland, Mary Surratt had made a decision. It would be easier, she decided, to lease her house and tavern and move into Washington. Once there she could take in permanent paying

guests at her town house on H Street. Then if John could get a paying position, he wouldn't have time for the dangerous courier business that he was in. Besides, it was about time that he started to earn
some money. The family could certainly use it.

When Louis Weichmann paid a second visit to the Surratt House
and Tavern, in September, John told him about his mother's plans
and asked him if he would like to board with the family when they
moved into Washington. Weichmann cheerfully accepted.[15]

Mary didn't have to wait long to find someone to lease the Surratt
House and Tavern. The lessee was John Lloyd, a large man and a
Roman Catholic. He had married the former Virginian, Mary
Elizabeth Mahoney. What children they eventually had, all died of
smallpox at a young age.[16]

*The Boston Globe*, May 15, 1865, described Lloyd as ". . . a poor white
man raised in a slave region. He was a blatant Democrat, and came
here [Washington, D.C.] during the Buchanan Administration to
serve on the police force, which was disbanded when Congress established a metropolitan police. When the war broke out he became a
blockade-runner, and was at one time arrested, but pardoned. He
leased the Surratt Tavern [Surratts' Villa] with the evident expecta-
tion of making it a rendezvous for blockade-runners and carriers of
the underground mail to Dixie, as he agreed to pay $500 a year rent."

It would not be beyond belief that the Surratts knew of John Lloyd's
activities before they leased the house and tavern to him. After all, the
South was not exclusively involved in the courier service and block-
ade-running. In fact, such services were considered brave and roman-
tic by both sides.

Nevertheless, the changes that were about to transpire in the lives
of the Surratts were minuscule compared to the changes happening
in the Deep South.

After four months of bitter fighting, on September 2, 1864, Union
general William Tecumseh Sherman invaded and occupied Atlanta.
Confederate general John B. Hood had withdrawn from the city the
day before. It was Sherman's aim to make the city his military base of
operation. From Atlanta, he would march his troops to the sea. "Any
Southerner who gets in my way, will quickly be changed into topsoil,"
he had said. Logistically, Sherman was forced to expel all of the civilian population from the city. He said he didn't want the burden of

feeding and protecting them or guarding against the spies and the guerrillas among them. Yet, to the South, Sherman's actions were deplorable. Long lines of women, children, elderly, and lame wearily trudged the hot, dusty roads in their forced marches to God knows where. Stories of looting, burning, starvation, rape, and murder told of the horrors of the hellish times that civilians had to endure. From Atlanta, General Sherman and his "bummers," as he called them, expanded their path of death and destruction until they spent themselves on the shores of the Atlantic Ocean.

That same month, in September 1864, Union general Philip H. Sheridan began to lay waste to the resources of the Shenandoah Valley. Virginia and North Carolina both depended on this "land of milk and honey" for food and iron.

At the same time, Petersburg, the doorway to Richmond, was continually being hammered by Gen. Ulysses S. Grant and his forces.

Militarily, the prospects for the South looked very bad. After three years of war, Southerners were tired and they were starving and they were running out of the implements of war. Their only hope now lay with the Democratic candidate, General McClellan and his "Peace Platform." A Confederate Secret Service agent in Canada sent to Richmond a report on the Northern Democrats: "The platform means peace, unconditionally . . . McClellan will be under the control of the true peace men . . . At all events, he is committed by the platform to cease hostilities and to try negotiations . . . An armistice will inevitably result in peace. The war cannot be renewed if once stopped, even for a short time."[17]

By October 1, Mary and Anna had moved to their Washington townhouse at 541 H Street, N.W. (currently 604 H Street, N.W.). Aunt "Rachel" remained at the Surratt House and Tavern to work for John Lloyd. Since Lloyd had no need for Rachel's little girl, Mary took the child with her to Washington.[18] John Surratt remained at the farm until Lloyd physically took over the operation of the establishment in December.[19]

Mary's Washington house was conveniently located. It wasn't far from Ford's Theatre on Eleventh Street, the National Hotel at Sixth and Pennsylvania Avenue, and the Herndon House at Ninth and F Streets. All of these establishments would eventually figure as important places in the lives of the Surratts.

*Mary Surratt's H Street boardinghouse, Washington, D.C.* (Courtesy of James O. Hall)

Mary, being a devout Catholic, must have been thankful that she could walk to St. Patrick's Catholic Church, at F Street between Ninth and Tenth Streets. Father Jacob Ambrose Walters was the pastor at the church.

Father Bernardine Wiget, formerly superior of St. Thomas Manor and instrumental in having John and Isaac enrolled at the school, was now president of Gonzaga College, which was located between Ninth and Tenth Streets.

Annie Ward, who had been an assistant teacher at St. Mary's Female Institute in Bryantown when Anna attended the school, was now teaching at the Academy of the Visitation. The school was in the same block as St. Patrick's Church.

Hugh B. Sweeny, banker, lived in the house that joined the Surratts'. He had been instrumental in working out the land deal when John Surratt, Sr., became the owner of the H Street house. Dr. Evans' home joined Sweeny's. Not far away from Mary, at 494 Massachusetts Avenue, lived detective William Wallace Kirby, who Mary later claimed was a family connection.

City living must have been hard for Mary, coming from the country. Fresh air, trees, and fields were no longer part of her life. Mary's townhouse was located between a dirty, narrow alley and Sweeny's home. The smells of city sewage, and the droppings from horses and oxen, permeated the air. The family's well was located in a small, board-fenced backyard. In front, a maple sapling struggled for a root hold between the walk and the street.

The house had three stories with an English basement under the front steps and stoop. From the street-level entrance, a long hall extended the length of the building along the right, inside wall. It passed the public sitting room, the dining room, and the kitchen in the back. The stairs to the second floor were approximately halfway down the hall.

On the second floor, another hall ran the length of the building above the hall below. The family sitting room, with a fireplace, was located at the front of the house, with a parlor behind. Two doors to two identical bedrooms faced the parlor. Mary choose one of these bedrooms for herself. Each of the two bedrooms had an outside window that looked out on the rear porch.

On the third floor, a hall duplicated the two below. The third floor had a foyer and two bedrooms. Later on, John and Louis Weichmann would share the back bedroom when the two men moved into the house.

In the attic and under the two outside dormers were two bedrooms that faced H Street.[20] Anna chose one of these rooms when her cousin, Olivia Jenkins, Zad's daughter, visited. Otherwise, Anna occupied one of the first-floor bedrooms. The attic would have been stifling in the summer.

Even during the war years, Washington was an awakening city. The Capitol building stood as a glorious centerpiece above the streets and buildings that radiated in all directions from its edifice. Thomas Crawford's "Statue of Freedom" topped the building and looked down on the city and the Potomac River below. The Washington Monument was not completed and cattle grazed contentedly on the grounds, oblivious of their fate. The elegant facade of the Smithsonian Institution resembled a European castle. The handsome Greek Revival architecture of the Patent Office building was under construction. Currently, it was being used as a hospital for injured soldiers. The massive, Greek Revival building of City Hall gave everyone a reason to pause to admire. The splendid edifice of the White House sat secluded, yet very much the heartbeat of the Union. Both military personnel and civilians, filled with their own self-importance, beat a path to the Executive Office. The Treasury and Department of State buildings looked out from their grandeur onto Pennsylvania Avenue. But there were other buildings of every description that paraded cheek and jowl up and down the filthy streets. Everywhere the "haves" and the "have nots" struggled. The teeming masses of whites and blacks, Westerners and Orientals, old and young (and not so young), Northerners and Southerners, spies and counterspies, angels and sinners, the hopeful and the hopeless, all crowded into Washington to live or die, in one way or another.

Mary Surratt had also come to Washington to make a better life for herself and for her family. As soon as possible, she had to fill the spare rooms of her home with paying guests.

On Thursday, October 6, nineteen-year-old Honora Fitzpatrick came to the Surratts to make her home.[21] Honora's father was a collector for several banks in Washington.[22] He was quite elderly with long white hair.[23] Honora was a plain, shy young lady.[24]

John visited his mother and sister several times before he finally moved to the townhouse. On one of his visits from Richmond, no doubt he told his family about the terrible sights that he witnessed there. At this time a limited number of prisoners from the Northern and Southern prisons were being exchanged. Many of the young Confederates were brought to Richmond in flag-of-truce ships. Many were so weak that they had to be carried, others had to be helped, still others managed to shuffle along. Many were no more than yellow skin stretched over bones. Their terrified, bloodshot eyes looked out beseechingly to everyone who stood staring at them in shocked silence. Some of the soldiers were so depleted from famine that their faces had shrunken into atrophied grimaces. Unless those being carried on stretchers moved or moaned, it was uncertain if they were dead or alive.[25]

Newspaper accounts printed ad nauseam accounts of how terribly Northern soldiers were being treated in Southern prisons. John and the other sickened onlookers would have witnessed the other side of the story. Everyone suffered in Southern prisons because there was little food left in the South. Southern ports had been blockaded, the crops had been burned, and the livestock had been either killed or stolen. The North, on the other hand, wanted for little. Northerners had the means to feed their prisoners, but chose not to. The North did not go lacking in its own Andersonvilles.

When John had finished telling about the atrocities that he had witnessed in Richmond, perhaps Mary remembered the ample meals that she had served the Union soldiers at the Surratt House and Tavern.

CHAPTER ELEVEN

# *The Boardinghouse*

On November 1, 1864, Louis Weichmann moved into the H Street boardinghouse. He paid thirty-five dollars a month for his food and lodging.[1] He earned eighty dollars a month, where he was employed, at the War Department.[2]

Eight days after Weichmann moved in with the Surratts, President Lincoln defeated General McClellan and his "Peace Platform." The president's reelection dashed any hope of the South that the war would end amiably. With the reelection of President Lincoln, the conflict would continue until the South was defeated. The Confederate States of America would be forced to reenter the Union after being whipped to their knees.

On November 24, Maryland freed its slave population.[3] Many of the former slaves headed for Washington. The city and its suburbs were already inundated with Negro camps. The Negroes had left the South and had migrated to Washington, D.C., and to the North in quest of their promised land. One of the camps was on North Twelfth Street in Washington, D.C. It was so crowded that tents had to be erected beyond its confines. The smallpox hospital in the camp was overrun with the sick. Those who died were carelessly interned in a graveyard on Boundary Street.[4]

The thousands of former slaves were disappointed when they found themselves unwelcomed in the capital city. They were stoned and cursed. Even their churches were not free from attacks. Not all of the abusive treatment came from hoodlum whites. Some of the abuse came from long-time free black residents of Washington.

One day, Mary opened the door to a familiar face. It was John, a former runaway slave of her mother's. Before he ran away, he had insulted Mary's mother, who had always been very kind to the man. The incident had been very painful for Mary. Yet, she treated John with kindness and gave him food. He returned several times after that.[5]

The rent money that Lou Weichmann and Honora Fitzpatrick paid was still not enough to meet the expenses of operating the boardinghouse. On November 30, December 8, and December 27, Mary advertised for lodgers in the *Washington Star* newspaper.[6]

Christmas of 1864 for the Surratts must have been scanty, if they depended on turkey to round out their holiday feast. By then, turkeys sold for fifty to one hundred dollars apiece. Perhaps when John moved to the H Street house he brought with him a fine wild turkey from Maryland that he had killed. Christmas was, indeed, a meager celebration for most everyone during those desperate times.

But something transpired before Christmas that brought excitement to the inhabitants of the boardinghouse.

During Christmas eve breakfast, John and Lou, no doubt, captivated everyone when they told them that they had met the famous actor, John Wilkes Booth, the night before. Dr. Samuel Mudd of Bryantown, Maryland, had introduced the actor to the two young men. Booth had wasted no time in inviting them to have refreshments in his room at the National Hotel.[7]

Dr. Mudd had met Booth for the first time on November 20, 1864, after church services at St. Mary's Catholic Church in Bryantown, Maryland. John Thompson of Baltimore and Booth were visiting Dr. William Queen, a neighbor of Dr. Mudd's. When John Thompson saw Dr. Mudd, he introduced him to the famous actor. Booth claimed that he had made a great deal of money in oil and was interested in purchasing some land or a farm. He added that he would also like to purchase a horse. Dr. Mudd indicated that he was thinking about selling his farm and offered to show it to the actor. Booth spent the night at Dr. Mudd's, but strangely said no more about purchasing the farm. According to Dr. Mudd, Booth indicated that he wanted to look around the area more and mingle with the people.

The actor seemed particularly interested in Southern Marylanders' political views. He was very curious about the contraband trade that existed between the North and the South in that area. The obscure back roads that bordered the Potomac River especially interested him. Before the actor left the following morning to return to Washington, he had purchased an old horse that was blind in one eye. He had procured it from a neighbor of Dr. Mudd's. A blind, aged horse? A strange choice for so elegant a man. Booth's incessant questions about the area, the people, and the couriers left Dr. Mudd highly suspicious of the young actor. He wondered if Booth was actually a U.S. government detective.[8] As it turned out, unbeknown to Dr. Mudd until William Bowman, a neighbor, later told him, Booth had returned several times to Southern Maryland. Sometimes he stayed with Dr. Queen, other times he stayed with William Bowman.[9]

The next time that Dr. Mudd saw John Wilkes Booth was on December 23. The doctor had gone to Washington to do some last-minute Christmas shopping. That night, the city church bells were pealing the messages of Peace on Earth, while at the same time newspaper boys pranced the streets and shouted that Savannah had been evacuated. When the doctor neared Seventh Street, he heard someone call his name. There, standing under a gaslight, was Booth's arresting figure. He mentioned to Dr. Mudd that he was still gathering information about the counties to the south of Washington so he could better "select a good locality for a country residence." Booth had apparently heard of John Surratt in his travels around Southern Maryland and asked the doctor to introduce him to the young man. Booth added that Surratt had moved with his family to H Street, not far away. It was when they were on their way to the boardinghouse that the two men saw John Surratt and his companion, Lou Weichmann, walking past the Odd Fellows' Hall at Seventh and Pennsylvania Avenue.[10] This is when Dr. Mudd introduced Surratt to Booth, and Booth invited them to his room at the National Hotel for refreshments.

Outside of Booth's room, Mudd quickly took John Surratt aside and told him that he knew very little about Booth, expressing to him his suspicions that the actor might be a U.S. government agent.[11]

After the men had settled themselves in the actor's room, Booth mentioned that he had been in lower Maryland and had gotten lost. He took an envelope from his pocket, drew some lines, and asked Surratt to tell him more about the roads. There was nothing secretive about the inquiry according to Dr. Mudd's sworn statement that he made later in prison. Lou Weichmann had heard everything that had been said between John Wilkes Booth and John Surratt.[12] Yet, Weichmann stated to the contrary in his book, *A True History of the Assassination of Abraham Lincoln and of the Conspiracy of 1865*.[13] Again, according to Dr. Mudd's statement, he did not have a secret conversation with either Booth or Surratt separately or together except when he took Surratt aside and warned him that Booth could be a U.S. government agent.[14] This, too, was counter to what Weichmann stated in his book.[15]

Both Dr. Mudd and Lou Weichmann did agree that the meeting at the National Hotel was of short duration. From the National Hotel, the foursome adjourned to the Pennsylvania House, where Dr. Mudd was staying. In the public room at the hotel, Dr. Mudd and Lou Weichmann sat together on a settee, while the other two men sat apart, talking by a roaring fire in the fireplace. Weichmann wrote in his book that Booth and Surratt had a "jolly time" together. Weichmann was sure that that evening Surratt had become captivated by the famous actor.[16]

One week later, on December 30, John Surratt began to work for the Adams Express Company. As it turned out, he did not stay long in their employment.

On the evening of January 1, 1865, the doorbell rang at the boardinghouse. Mary, Anna, and John Surratt, Honora Fitzpatrick, and Lou Weichmann had finished their evening meal and had retired to the parlor to discuss the events of the day. It just happened to be Anna's twenty-second birthday.

John answered the door and ushered John Wilkes Booth into the parlor. Few would disagree that one of the most handsome men to ever set foot on God's green earth strolled into the Surratt home that night. Being a proficient fencer, he was quick and graceful in his movements, yet he bore the physique of an athletic. His perfectly waved hair was jet black. Luminous, melting brown eyes shown from beneath black eyebrows and heavily lashed eyelids. A black, inverted-scimitar mustache reclined beneath a well-formed nose. His skin and teeth were as white and flawless as newly fallen snow.

To perfect his image, Booth wore a wide black silk cravat that was ornamented with a diamond stickpin. His shirt was white. His braided-bound black jacket had a velvet collar. His black twill breeches were perfectly tailored. His ensemble finished with highly polished black boots adorned with shiny silver spurs.[17] His black and white apparel conformed perfectly with the striking contrasts of his moods.

Booth's remarkably handsome face would have shone brightly when he enveloped his admiring audience with an ingratiating smile. No doubt Anna and Honora quickly smoothed their hair and pinched color on their cheeks.

From that night on, the Surratts were mesmerized by John Wilkes Booth, as was most everyone.

To ingratiate himself he would have told them about his family. The Booths had a farm in Bel Air, Maryland, just north of Baltimore in Harford County. He would have added that he was one of ten children.[18] That number of children would have alerted Mary to, no doubt, ask if he was Catholic. Wilkes, as he was often called, would have assured her that he was not.

Perhaps Honora's cat[19] ambled into the room. Nonchalantly she would have glanced at each of the humankind. When her large eyes settled on Booth, perhaps she stopped, sat down in front of the actor, and regarded him silently. Then, without warning, she would have jumped on Booth's lap, and proceeded to purr and groom herself. He had a way with animals, as well as with people.

Wilkes' dark eyes would have sparkled in amusement. It would be a perfect time to tell a true story about his father, Junius Brutus Booth. It seems that the elder Booth had, at one time, invited all the neighbors to his home for a funeral. Dressed in their Sunday finery, they came to where the service for the deceased was to be held. Needless to say, everyone was shocked when they saw that the dearly departed was none other than his father's favorite horse.[20]

Upon hearing Wilkes' story, everyone would have exploded into laughter. When the room had quieted, Booth would have been encouraged to continue.

He probably chuckled, then smiled reflectively before he narrated another story about his father. According to Wilkes, his father did not tarnish his reputation one bit when he asked a clergyman to help give a public burial to a bushel of wild pigeons that someone had shot as pests.[21]

Indeed, Booth would have relaxed them with his humor. Possibly, it was at a time like this when he told them not to be sad, that "life is so short—and the world is so beautiful. Just to breathe is delicious."[22]

An evening of entertainment would not have been complete unless a talented member of the family had been called upon to perform. Mary probably encouraged her daughter to play the piano. Anna would have consented, gotten to her feet, and, with regal grace, crossed the room to the piano. For a moment, her small hands would have lingered on the keys. Then reverently, almost as though she were about to play a hymn, Anna would have begun to fill the room with her sweet voice and the haunting strains of "Hindoo Mother."

> Do not leave me, By my tears thus fal—ling,
> Bit—ter thoughts will grieve me When thou art a——way;
> Dark as night each day will be, Wanting thee! wanting thee!
> All thy vows recal—ling—My life! my love, oh! stay. Fairer
> hands may press thee,
> Richer lips may woo; But none shall e—ver love thee,
> Like thine own Hin-doo, But none shall e-ver love thee,
> Like thine own Hin—doo.[23]

When she had finished, her hands would have fallen to her lap. The room would have been silent. In any case, the first three sentences would prove prophetic. Would they haunt Anna when her mother was no longer with her?

The lovely evening passed too quickly and worry replaced the memory. Mary could never solve her financial problems, no matter how she tried. Money was still owed to the Calverts on the property that her husband had purchased in 1852 to build the Surratt House and Tavern. At that time, Charles Calvert received two notes from her husband, each for $398.50. Apparently, the notes had not been satisfied. Over the years, the interest had mounted until Mary was obliged to mortgage the H Street house in January 1865 to pay $1,000 on the obligation. Three months later, in order to settle the Calvert estate, George Calvert would demand that Mary honor the $764.53 that was still outstanding on the Surratt House and Tavern.[24]

Perhaps it was in connection with the obligation that, on January 13, John asked his employer at the Adams Express Company for leave in order to take his mother to Prince George's County. He said that he wanted to be her protector and accompany her there. John's request was refused. The following day, Mary went to the Adams Express Company office and asked that her son be given leave so he could accompany her to Prince George's County on urgent business. Again, the request was refused. John left the office that day and never returned.[25]

It would have been "urgent business" for Mary to pay George Calvert the $1,000 she owed so she would not lose the Surratt House and Tavern. The long trip to "Riversdale," the Calvert mansion, would have been a dangerous one for a woman alone carrying a large sum of money, especially in war time. However, there are many who have insisted, Lou Weichmann for one, that, at that time, both Mary and her son were confederates of John Wilkes Booth and that the "urgent business" that had to be attended to was Booth's, not Mary's.

That same month, John deeded over all of his shares of the family property to his mother.[26] In John Surratt's letter of February 6, 1865, to Belle Seaman, he mentioned that he was leaving for Europe the following week. He added, "Yes, I am going to leave this detested country . . ." As it turned out, John did not go to Europe.

By mid-January, John Surratt was in league with John Wilkes Booth to abduct President Abraham Lincoln. Of that fact there can be no doubt. But why abduct the president of the United States? Certainly, on the surface, the idea would seem insane. In reality, if the plan worked, it would be no less than a stroke of genius. By holding the president as a hostage, the South would have the trump card. The Confederacy was losing the war. When surrender came, it would have to be unconditional. On the other hand, with Abraham Lincoln held as a hostage in the South, the Confederacy could end the war on its own terms.

Whether the scheme was a Southern plot or not has never been proven. Logically, it would seem that had it been a Southern conspiracy, more experienced men familiar with clandestine operations would have been chosen by the Confederate States government. For one, soldier of fortune George St. Leger Grenfell and his men would have been logical choices. Grenfell directed espionage activities in the Northwestern states and organized guerrilla-type raids against the Union installations below the Canadian border. Furthermore, George Grenfell was already working under the direction of the Confederate government-in-exile, in Canada.

On January 15, and working on behalf of John Wilkes Booth, John Surratt was in Port Tobacco, Maryland. He was in the company of a man by the name of Thomas Harbin. Together, the two men bought a large boat for $250 from William M. Smoot and James A. Brawner. Port Tobacco was a well-known smuggling center. It was an ideal location to keep such a boat sequestered for the purpose of smuggling the biggest prize of all—the president of the United States!

To help in the mammoth smuggling operation was a small, not too bright, German carriage painter by the name of George Andrew Atzerodt. He lived in Port Tobacco and had helped many people to make clandestine nighttime crossings of the Potomac River into Virginia.[27]

No doubt, by now, John Surratt knew what Booth's true mission had been in Southern Maryland for the past three months. Purchasing a farm had been furthermost from Booth's mind.

Meanwhile, back in Washington, Lou Weichmann received a letter on Tuesday, January 17, 1865, under the flag-of-truce ship. The letter was from the Reverend John McGill, Bishop of Richmond. Weichmann had repeatedly written the bishop to obtain permission to continue his studies for the priesthood. Permission was finally granted. Lou would resume his studies at St. Mary's Seminary in Baltimore, Maryland, on September 1, 1865.[28] As it turned out, Louis Weichmann would not keep that appointment.

# CHAPTER TWELVE

# *Strange People*

The remainder of January 1865 was a busy period for John Surratt. On January 22, he and Lou Weichmann were in Baltimore. Lou had gone there to see Father Dubreuil at St. Mary's Seminary.[1] John had gone to meet a Confederate agent by the name of David Preston Parr, who had taken on a new agent. The man's name was Lewis Thornton Powell, alias Lewis Paine. Paine had formerly served as a Confederate Ranger under John S. Mosby.[2] Lewis Paine, the steel-jawed, well-built, twenty-year-old Floridian, would play an important role in the conspiracy to abduct the president and later make an attempt to assassinate a member of the president's cabinet.

Perhaps it was at this time that John Surratt met the two Baltimoreans Samuel Bland Arnold and Michael O'Laughlin. Samuel Arnold and John Wilkes Booth had been school chums at St. Timothy's Hall in Baltimore. Arnold had taken the U.S. Oath of Allegiance after he was discharged from the Confederate Army. He returned to Baltimore in 1862.[3] Arnold was a fine-looking, well-educated young man.

Michael O'Laughlin was another early friend of Booth's. O'Laughlin and his family resided in a home owned by Booth's mother.[4] He too was a good-looking young man who would probably feel at home in any genteel surroundings. Now, all the players had been chosen for the melodrama to come. David Herold, John Surratt, George Atzerodt, Lewis Paine, Michael O'Laughlin, and Samuel Arnold now waited for Booth to call them to serve in their moment in history.

It was about this time that John Surratt went to Bel Air, Maryland, and met the famous Booth family. Perhaps, while he was there, John witnessed the genius and the madness that was part of Junius Brutus Booth, the father of John Wilkes. Junius Brutus had been named Brutus in honor of Caesar's assassin. The elder Booth was a renowned, British-born, Shakespearean tragedian actor. He left England after abandoning his wife and their small son for Mary Anna Holmes, a London Covent Garden Theatre flower girl. For thirty years they lived together in America outside the bonds of matrimony. However, on Wilkes' thirteenth birthday, his parents legalized their union.[5]

Junius Brutus often went far afield in his eccentricities when he was under the influence of alcohol. On one such occasion when he was to appear in Hamlet, Act V, stagehands found Junius high in the rafters, crowing like a rooster.[6]

The Booth children were planted and grew in soil that was rich in the darkness of their father's madness. But, only one would come to an unholy end. Perhaps it was his mother's oft-repeated "vision" that fermented in Wilkes' mind—the "vision" that she had when her son was only six months old. Her "vision" may have convinced him that his fate had been sealed in a malevolent nether world before he was born. Wilkes' sister, Asia, was impressed enough by her mother's "vision" that she composed a poem about it and gave it to her mother for a gift.

It seems that while Mary Anna Holmes sat in front of the fireplace, her baby boy, Wilkes, nursing at her breast, she made a fervent prayer. She asked her God what her little boy would be like when he had grown into manhood. Would he do good or evil? The last two verses of Asia's poem are quite poignant:

> I implore to know on this ghostly night
> Whether 'twill labour for wrong, or right,

For—or against Thee?
    The flame up-leapt
Like a wave of blood, an avenging arm crept
Into shape; and the Country shone out in the flame,
Which fading resolved to her boy's own name!
God had answered Love—
Impatient Love![7]

Wilkes' mother was convinced that her vision had been a bad omen. And for all of her life, Asia, the sister of the son of Brutus, was left to ponder the following thought-provoking lines from another poem:

All of our acts of life are pre-ordained,
And each pre-acted in their several spheres
By ghostly duplicates.
They sway our deeds by their performance.[8]

But the day of that season was yet to come—if preordained it was!

Mary Surratt met the German, George Atzerodt, in early February 1865, when she had returned from a trip to Southern Maryland. He stayed only a few days at the boardinghouse. One day, during Atzerodt's stay, Mary found several bottles of liquor in the man's room. When John returned home she told him that she didn't want "Port Tobacco" (as she called him) to stay there any longer.[9] Before he left, though, Atzerodt and Lou Weichmann had become quite friendly.[10]

During John's stay at home, he wrote a letter to Belle Seaman. He told her that he and Anna were going to a "regular country hoe-down." Then he mentioned that the Smithsonian Institution had suffered a very serious fire.

Finally, in his letter to his cousin, we are treated to another picture of home life with the Surratts that John seemed to enjoy sharing with Belle, "I have just taken a peek in the parlor. Would you like to know what I saw there? Well, Ma was sitting on the sofa, nodding first to one chair, then to another next to piano. Anna sitting in corner, dreaming, I expect, of J. W. Booth. Well, who is J. W. Booth? She can answer the question. Miss Fitzpatrick playing with her favorite cat—a good sign of an old maid—the detested creatures. Miss Dean fixing her hair, which is filled with rats and mice.

"But hark! the doorbell rings, and Mr. J. W. Booth is announced and listen scamperings of the ——————. Such brushing and fixing."[11]

Mary Apollonia Dean, whom John referred to in his letter as Miss Dean, was ten years old when she moved to the boardinghouse. She had come from her home near Alexandria to attend the Visitation School for Girls. The school was affiliated with St. Patrick's Catholic Church,[12] the church that Mary attended.

On February 7, the day after John Surratt had written Belle Seaman, and the day after John Wilkes Booth had visited the Surratts, the Holohan family moved into the boardinghouse.[13] It was a cold, miserable day of twenty-six degrees.[14]

John Holohan was born in Ireland.[15] John and his wife, Eliza Jane Smith, were married in Washington, D.C. He was employed in the business of procuring substitutes for men who were drafted in the Union Army. He was thirty-six years old and his wife was thirty-three. With them were their two children, Mary, age fourteen, and Charles, age twelve. The marriage was, at times, an unhappy one for Eliza Holohan. On one occasion she had her husband arrested for assault. This had happened before they moved to Mrs. Surratt's boardinghouse.[16]

With the coming of the Holohans, and John not moving to Europe, Mary's boardinghouse was finally filled to capacity. With the added work, Mary had to hire a washerwoman. The woman picked up the wash on Mondays and returned it on Wednesdays.[17]

On Sunday, February 19, Augustus ("Gus") Spencer Howell, a twenty-seven-year-old Maryland Confederate agent, appeared at the boardinghouse. He stayed an undetermined length of time.[18]

At the beginning of the war, Gus Howell had enlisted in the Confederate States Army in Fredericksburg, Virginia. Because of a disability, he was discharged in Richmond on July 16, 1862. Whatever his disability, it didn't prevent him from becoming deeply involved in the Confederate underground in Maryland. He was arrested three months after his discharge by Union soldiers patrolling the Potomac River. He was charged with ". . . transporting rebels from Maryland to join the reb army." After Howell was paroled, he was apprehended again on January 29, 1863, in Upper Marlboro, Prince George's County, Maryland. About a month later, Gus was free again and back in Maryland, sowing his wild oats for the Confederacy. In time, he became known as one of the most important Confederate spies and blockade runners along the Potomac River.[19]

Howell's latest mission was particularly interesting, since it included a lovely, twenty-two-year-old, French-speaking courier from North Carolina.[20] Sarah Antoinette ("Nettie") Gilbert Slater had been assigned by the Confederate government to carry important papers and money from Richmond to Montreal, Canada. Five Southerners had been arrested and jailed there. They had admitted having participated in the October 19, 1864, St. Albans, Vermont, raid. They had killed one citizen and had injured several others.[21] In addition, they robbed three banks of more than two hundred thousand dollars!

In Montreal, a Canadian judge recessed the trial of the five men for thirty days so that papers could be obtained from Richmond that would confirm that the raiders were Confederate soldiers, acting under orders of the Confederate government when they raided St. Albans.[22] Mrs. Slater's mission was to obtain the proper papers in Richmond and deliver them to the judge in Montreal.

After she had been given the papers in Richmond, she left for Montreal on January 31, 1865. With an escort guide, she traveled the usual courier and agent's route that ran along the bed of the Richmond, Fredericksburg, and Potomac Railroad (R.F.&P.) to Milford Station and Bowling Green in Virginia. At Port Royal, Virginia, she crossed on the Rappahannock River ferry. On February 2, she met Gus Howell near the mouth of Mattox Creek. Together they left Confederate Virginia, crossed the Potomac River into Maryland and Union territory. Once in Maryland, they traveled through Bryantown, T.B., Surrattsville, and then to Washington, D.C. Gus escorted her as far as the European Hotel in New York City. From there, Sarah Slater continued to Montreal by train with the papers that confirmed that the St. Albans raiders were, indeed, Confederate soldiers. She registered at St. Lawrence Hall in Montreal on February 15, at three o'clock in the morning. Eventually, the Confederate soldiers were released.[23]

Mrs. Slater did not remain in Montreal very long. She had to rush very important dispatches back to Richmond. John Surratt was designated to meet her in New York and take her to Washington and the H Street boardinghouse. Then, Gus Howell would escort her out of Washington and through Maryland. By then, George Atzerodt would be back in Maryland to row the pair across the Potomac River into Virginia.[24]

To prevent the possibly of being recognized, Gus Spencer Howell never ventured from the confines of the boardinghouse while he wait-ed for Sarah Slater's return. During Howell's stay, Lou Weichmann mentioned to the Confederate agent that he would like to return South with Gus, but he was not prepared to go at that time. Weichmann continued by saying that, as soon as he had gotten his business in order, he was going to move to Richmond. Then Weichmann asked Howell if it were possible for Lou to obtain a job in Richmond. Howell said he didn't know since the wounded and invalid soldiers usually got first preference. Then Weichmann said he thought that the South would ultimately win the war.

Then Weichmann "switched to the role of an informant" and told Howell how many Confederate prisoners the United States govern-ment was holding. Weichmann expressed himself as a Southern man, then he added that he had done all that he could for the South. Apparently believing that he could trust John's friend and roommate, Howell showed Weichmann how to make and use a certain code. Weichmann made a copy for himself. In just three months, during the trial of the conspirators, Howell testified that he had gotten the code from a magician's book. However, after Booth was killed, the seem-ingly innocuous code was found among Booth's effects.[25]

It was after the evening meal, in the latter part of February, that the doorbell sounded at the H Street boardinghouse. Lou Weichmann, Honora Fitzpatrick, Anna, and Mary were sitting in the parlor at the time. Lou opened the door to a tall, well-built, young man who asked in a very self-assured voice if Mr. Surratt lived there and, if he did, was he at home. Weichmann told the stranger that John Surratt was not at home. The man introduced himself as Mr. Wood. He asked if he could see Mrs. Surratt.[26]

Weichmann returned to the parlor and told Mary that the person who rang the doorbell was a Mr. Wood. He had come to see John, but since he wasn't at home, he wanted to see her. Mary told Weichmann that she would see the man and to bring him into the parlor.[27] Mr. Wood told her that he knew her son. Then he asked for something to eat and a place to stay. Mary asked Lou if Mr. Wood could eat in Lou's room since the dining room was "in disarray." Lou said that he would have no objection. Weichmann took Mr. Wood to his room and then brought the stranger his dinner on a tray. Lou noticed that Mr. Wood wasn't very communicative. But Mr. Wood did tell Lou that he was from Baltimore and that he was a sales clerk in Mr. Parr's china store.[28] No doubt Mr. Wood was referring to Preston Parr, who was a Confederate government agent in Baltimore and who had introduced John Surratt to Lewis Thornton Powell, alias Lewis Paine—the same man who was now calling himself Mr. Wood. After he ate, he spent the night on a bed in the attic. He left early the following morning.[29]

On March 3, the presidential inaugural crush was on, celebrating Abraham Lincoln's second term in office. The influx of the masses was felt all over Washington. Every available sleeping place had been taken. Even the halls and parlors at Willard's, the National, and the Metropolitan hotels were filled with cots and mattresses.

In the evening, the city rocked with the celebrants. The respectable and not so respectable rubbed shoulders along Pennsylvania Avenue while fireworks exploded overhead. The crowd was in a patriotic delirium that reached near hysteria when red, white, and blue star-bursts lit up the sky. At the same time, gas reflector lights illuminated the Capitol. And from the Capitol dome, Old Glory rippled majestically and unperturbed above it all.

Many of the local citizenry who lived around 7th and H Streets had gathered to watch the festivities. They screamed and yelled with delight when, like falling stars, showers of fireworks drifted down from the sky. In the distance, howitzers boomed like thunder. In the midst of the wild pandemonium, Southern sympathizers looked on in stony silence.

The following day was Inauguration Day. Despite the inclement weather, the celebrants started early with their revelry. It had rained the night before, but weather didn't deter a parade from forming on Pennsylvania Avenue in ankle-deep mud and horse droppings.

By noon, the clouds had cleared. On the east steps of the Capitol, Abraham Lincoln was sworn in for his second term as president of the United States. Nearby, a handsome actor by the name of John Wilkes Booth looked on. Booth had obtained an inauguration ticket from Lucy Hale, his secret fiancée. She was the daughter of Sen. John P. Hale, of New Hampshire.[30] Ironically, before the war, Senator Hale had been a leading adversary against slavery.[31]

While most Washingtonians celebrated the president's inauguration, Columbia, South Carolina, was burning. It was the Lenten season. But prayer and fasting had become a daily way of life in the South.

Southern deprivation was no longer reserved for Lent. The Confederacy had been on its knees for a long time.

For a Catholic, William Tecumseh Sherman did something quite amazing. He celebrated the Lenten season in Columbia by having his men burn a Catholic convent. By the time of the inauguration, Columbia was no more than dust and ashes. Most of the men, women, and children who were left in the city were homeless, and without food. Only the corn that they parched from the leavings of Sherman's horses prevented the people from starving. The clothing on their backs was all that they owned. The soldiers had torn their meager bundles of clothes from the poor wretches who had tried to save them from their burning homes. Then, howling with delight, the soldiers tossed the clothing into the flames.[32]

Back in Washington, on March 7, the vice president was still in a festive mood. Andrew Johnson was so beastly drunk that he was unable to preside over the Senate. Even his conduct on March 4 had been deplorable.[33]

Yet, with the gaiety of President Lincoln's inauguration, the parades and cheering, the carousing and drinking, there was another scene—a scene so pitiful that, in normal times, it would have broken the hearts of the most hardened.

Prisoners were in the process of being exchanged from the middle of February until March 29, 1865. Previously, there had been an equitable North-South exchange until the fall of Vicksburg on July 4, 1863. From that period until the end of the war, the exchange of prisoners was only sporadic. The conditions of most of the Confederate soldiers from Northern prisons defied belief. Booth and his fellow conspirators would have been enraged at the pitiful plight of their fellow Southerners who suffered under the steel hand of "King Lincoln," as Booth referred to the president.

Trains rolled regularly from Northern prisons to Baltimore and Washington packed with their pathetic cargo of suffering and dying men. Upon reaching their destination, the men were often forced to wait in the railroad cars for as long as two days without food or water. Some had died in transit, while others died waiting to be released. Yet, even with the stench of their decaying comrades, the Union guards refused to remove the bodies.[34]

Two sisters in Baltimore did what they could for the suffering Southerners. They told the story of a starving prisoner who begged a guard for a morsel of bread. When the guard harshly refused him food, the young man collapsed and died.[35]

The sisters told another story of a prisoner who was wounded in both legs. When he was released from the train, two Confederate surgeons helped the man to walk. Seeing this, a guard struck the injured man twice with the flat of his bayonet, and told him to move on. Whereupon, the surgeons protested to the guard about his actions toward the injured man. Fortunately, a compassionate United States surgeon saw what had happened. The officer called the guard a brute and ordered him to desist.[36]

There were many women who risked arrest trying to give a little comfort to the suffering men. Some of the prisoners were so pale and emaciated that they could barely stand, much less walk. Whenever the women could, they would slip a little food or even blankets to cover the prisoners' nearly naked bodies.[37]

Such atrocities inflicted on the prisoners no doubt would have reaffirmed Booth's conviction that something had to be done—the sooner the better.

But there was another woman, on a different mission, who was returning to the boardinghouse on H Street. The first week in March 1865, Sarah Slater and Gus Howell had left Richmond for the Confederate States Army signal corps camp near the mouth of Mattox Creek on the Virginia side of the Potomac River. Their final destination was Montreal. But for some reason, Gus Howell did not complete the journey with Mrs. Slater. She was carrying dispatches that quite possibly had to do with the transfer of accountability of clandestine Confederate activities in Canada to Gen. Edwin Lee from Jacob Thompson. (After President Lincoln was killed, authorities in Washington suspected that she had actually carried instructions concerning Booth's scheme to assassinate the president.[38] This was impossible, since Booth's plan, at this time, was to abduct the president.)

It was eight o'clock on the morning of March 10, when Nettie, her face covered with a full veil, arrived at the H Street boardinghouse. This time she had come in a buggy driven by a young man.[39]

Mary asked Lou to carry Mrs. Slater's trunk into the house. Later, Mary told him that Sarah ("Nettie") Slater was a blockade runner and, if the woman got into trouble, there was no danger because she could immediately apply to the French consul for help, speaking French as she did.[40] Actually, Nettie would have had to be a citizen of France in order to obtain help from the French consul.

That night, Weichmann had to give up his bedroom to Nettie and went off to the attic to sleep. The lovely Nettie left the following morning, leaving her dainty slippers in Lou's room. But, the man, still contemplating the priesthood, was not immune to the dainties of womankind. Lou found Nettie's slippers quite beguiling.[41]

# CHAPTER THIRTEEN

# *A Plot Takes Form*

The strange man with many names returned to the H Street board-inghouse on the evening of March 13, 1865.[1] Lou Weichmann answered the front doorbell. When he opened it, a familiar-looking man gazed back at him.[2] He introduced himself as Lewis Paine, a Baptist preacher. Lou showed the young man to the parlor where Mary, Anna, and Honora Fitzpatrick were sitting.[3]

In the course of conversation, one of the young women addressed the visitor as Mr. Wood. The visitor ignored her. He did, however, acknowledge having been in Baltimore recently where he spent near-ly a week in prison. He continued by saying he had taken the Oath of Allegiance "and was going to become a good and loyal citizen."[4] It is not known if the caller justified his frequent identity changes. But, Mary later remarked that she thought that he made a "great looking Baptist preacher."[5] Paine probably was impressive looking, dressed in a fine grey suit.[6]

Actually Lewis Paine's legal name was Lewis Thornton Powell. His father, George Cadar Powell, was a Baptist minister and farmer in Florida.[7] Powell was one of nine children and, at one time, had con-sidered entering the ministry.[8]

Later, at Powell's request, Anna played the piano. The remainder of the evening was spent playing cards and talking.[9] He stayed at the boardinghouse for three days.[10]

John Surratt returned home the following day. After greeting the household, he retired to the bedroom that he shared with Lou Weichmann. While John relaxed on the bed, and Lou wrote at a table, Lewis Powell entered the room. Powell pretended that he didn't know John and asked Weichmann if the man on the bed was Mr. Surratt. When Lou acknowledged that he was, Lou later claimed that Powell asked Weichmann to leave the room so he could talk privately with John.[11]

On Wednesday, March 15, when Lou returned from work and went to his room, he found a false mustache on his table. He decided to play a trick and hide it in a box. Then Lou went to the attic to see if John and Lewis were there. When he opened the door, he saw the pair sitting on a bed surrounded by eight new spurs, two Bowie knives, and two revolvers! Before they realized that it was Lou, they had thrown their hands over the items in an attempt to hide them.[12] Apparently, they would not have attempted to hide them had they known that it was Louis Weichmann.

When Lou saw what they had tried to hide, he left the room, ran down the stairs, and confronted Mary with what he had seen in the attic. "Mrs. Surratt, I do not like this," Weichmann exclaimed. But, Mary, thinking nothing of the matter, told Lou not to be concerned about the guns and knives. After all, both men were in the habit of riding in the country. They needed such items for self-protection, she reasoned.[13]

After Lewis Powell had moved into the boardinghouse, Lou Weichmann probably felt slighted by John's inattention. No doubt he was even more offended when John rudely excluded Lou from an outing to the theater. Booth had given John a ten-dollar ticket for the presidential box at Ford's Theatre to see the play, *Jane Shore,* that night. John invited Apollonia, Honora, and Lewis Powell (Paine) to go with him, but excluded his old friend Louis Weichmann.[14] Possibly, Anna wasn't invited because she was visiting her cousin, Olivia ("Lete") Jenkins, in Surrattsville.

By now, Mary's feelings toward Lou Weichmann had become maternal in nature. After the others had left for the theater, perhaps those feelings surfaced when she noticed how sad and lonely Lou appeared as they sat together in the parlor.

It had been very unkind of John to show Lou the presidential box ticket and then brag that Booth had given it to him. It was heartbreaking to see Lou playfully wrestle the ticket from John and lisp that he was going to the theater too. Good naturedly, John had struck his old friend and told him that Lou couldn't go for private reasons.[15]

On this occasion Lou may have shown Mary the small picture that he had recently purchased. Perhaps he asked her if she thought that Anna would like it. He would have told her the name of the picture was *Morning, Noon, and Night.*[16]

To be kind, Mary would have told him that Anna would love it. With Mary's permission he placed it on the mantel.[17] Then, he would have excused himself and gone to his room.

Sometime later, the young people returned laughing and talking. No doubt it was a memorable evening for Apollonia and Honora, especially in the light of future events.

Yes, they had seen Mr. Booth. He had come to the presidential box where they sat. He spoke to them, then he, John, and Mr. Powell left for a few moments.[18]

After the girls had shared their evening at Ford's Theatre with Mary, John and Lewis Powell left the boardinghouse and joined Booth in an after-theater oyster dinner, in a private room at Gautier's Restaurant.[19]

The after-theater dinner turned out to be a meeting of the conspirators. Arnold and O'Laughlin were there from Baltimore. Atzerodt, Powell, Surratt, and possibly David Herold attended. All of them had gathered with Booth to formulate a scheme to abduct President Lincoln. Booth thought it would be a good idea to seize the president as he watched a play from the presidential box at Ford's Theatre. They would dash into the box, handcuff him, and in the darkness of the theater, lower him to the stage below and hustle him out the back door. Everyone objected loudly to Booth's plan. Booth had no other choice but to return to his first plan.[20]

Booth's earlier plan in the summer of 1864 was to capture President Lincoln when the president went on one of his unescorted trips to the Soldiers' Home located just outside of Washington, D.C. After capturing the president, he planned to rush him over the Navy Yard Bridge across the Eastern Branch of the Potomac, through Southern

Maryland, then by boat on to Virginia. At that time Booth had only two accomplices, Samuel Arnold and Michael O'Laughlin.[21] His abduction motive in the summer of 1864 was to use the president as a bargaining tool to force the release of Confederate soldiers from Union prisons. Booth had said then that his plan was "purely humane and patriotic in its principles, . . . and legitimate as an act of War."[22]

It wasn't long after the conspirators' meeting at Gautier's Restaurant that Booth attempted to activate his original plan to abduct the president. On March 17, the actor dropped in at the Peterson House, across from Ford's Theatre, to see a friend and fellow actor by the name of John Mathews. While Booth was there, two other actors, James W. Wallack and E. L. Davenport, joined the twosome. During the ensuing conversation, one of the actors casually mentioned that his company was giving a play for wounded soldiers at the Campbell General Hospital at the Soldiers' Home that very afternoon and that the president had been invited to attend. "Why don't you come, Booth?" he asked. "You'll see a good performance."[23]

If Booth had listened more carefully, he would have noticed that Davenport had said that the president had been *invited* to attend the performance. And, apparently, no one in the gathering had read the local newspapers or they would have known that the president had been ill for several weeks. He would not be attending the theater at the Campbell General Hospital, after all. As it turned out, the president had improved enough to be able to attend a captured Confederate flag ceremony at the National Hotel[24]—the very hotel where Booth was staying!

Not knowing that the president was not going to the Soldiers' Home that day, Booth went into action. He quickly gathered his men, horses, and a carriage together. Then they raced to the H Street boardinghouse to get John Surratt and Lewis Powell (Paine).[25]

This may have been the time when Mary confronted her son and said, "John, I am afraid there is something going on. Why do those men come here? Now, John, I do not feel easy about this and you must tell me what you are about." According to Weichmann, who was present at the time, John did not tell his mother "why the men were there or what they were about."[26]

After they left the boardinghouse, the men rode to a restaurant near the hospital. There Booth left his accomplices to enjoy a social drink. He rode off to make sure that the president had appeared for the performance at the Campbell General Hospital. He was livid when he learned that the president did not go to the theater, after all. Quickly he returned to the restaurant and his waiting men.[27]

It is interesting to note, in passing, the following events that appeared in Lou Weichmann's book concerning what happened later after John and the others had left the boardinghouse to make an attempt to abduct the president. "On the way to dinner, I met Mrs. Surratt in the hall. She was weeping bitterly. 'Go down,' she said, 'Mr. Weichmann, and make the best of the dinner that you can. John is gone away, John is gone away.'"[28] This would certainly prove that the mother knew nothing of her son's endeavors. She was very upset and she had her suspicions that he was up to no good. That is why she said to him, "Now, John, I cannot allow this, and you must tell me what you are about." Of course, he didn't tell her.

The attempted abduction of the president that day unnerved at least one of the conspirators. Three days later, Samuel Arnold and Michael O'Laughlin returned to Baltimore. There, Arnold decided to have nothing more to do with Booth's wild schemes. Temporarily at least, O'Laughlin remained loyal to the actor.[29]

After the aborted attempt, Powell, Booth, and Surratt hurried back to the Surratt H Street boardinghouse. According to Weichmann, the first person to enter John and Lou's bedroom was Surratt himself. "He held a small four-barreled Sharp's revolver in his hand; . . . I asked him what was the matter. He leveled his pistol at me and exclaimed, 'Weichmann, my prospects are gone; my hopes are blasted; I want something to do; can you get me a clerkship?'" Weichmann told him that he was foolish and to settle down and be sensible.[30]

Again, according to Weichmann, it was about ten minutes later when Powell came into the room. He appeared excited, but said nothing.[31]

Next entered Booth. He had a riding whip in one hand and nervously walked several times around the room. Weichmann claimed that Booth didn't notice him at first, but when he did, Booth signaled the others to follow him to the attic where Powell slept. They remained there for about thirty minutes and then they left the H Street boardinghouse.[32]

On the following morning, Saturday, March 18, John Surratt and George Atzerodt headed for T.B., Maryland, to see David Herold. From there, the three rode to the Surratt House and Tavern. When they arrived, John Surratt asked John Lloyd to hide two carbines, a monkey wrench, and a rope that Davey Herold had brought. When the proprietor finally assented, they hid the items underneath the joists on the second floor.[33]

Back in Washington that evening, Lou Weichmann was finally included in an outing with John. Booth was playing the part of Pescara in *The Apostate* at Ford's Theatre that night. He had given John three tickets. John invited Lou and John Holohan to join him.[34] If anyone happened to notice, John would be seen that night in the company of two men who served the United States government. Before, he had been in the company of a young woman and a little girl. On both occasions, John's guests would have given him the appearance of being a loyal citizen of the Union.

Lou was left badly shaken by the play. Booth, playing the part of the villain, Pescara, dragged a young woman across the stage and proceeded to torture her on a wheel. Later, in his book, Weichmann described Booth as having a "hideous, malevolent expression on his distorted countenance, the fierce glare and ugly roll of his eyes, which seemed ready to burst from the sockets as he seized his victim by the hair, and placing her on the wheel, exclaimed, 'Now behold Pescara's masterpiece!'"[35]

Perhaps it was the following afternoon, March 19, when Lou found Anna alone in the parlor and gave her the picture of *Morning, Noon, and Night.* Expecting a kiss, he received a slap instead. Angry tears welled up in his eyes. He turned and left the parlor.[36]

On March 19, George Atzerodt left his country home and moved into the Pennsylvania House in Washington. The hotel was located at the terminus of the Port Tobacco Stage Line and around the corner from where Booth lived at the National Hotel.[37]

It wasn't long after Anna's unsettling experience with Lou Weichmann that she and Honora went to a daguerreotype gallery to get a likeness that Honora had made of herself. While there, the girls each purchased a photograph of John Wilkes Booth. Anna thought that hers would make a fine addition to her collection of present-day notables. Anna's father had started her collection with pictures of the Southern men: Jefferson Davis, Stonewall Jackson, Pierre G. T. Beauregard, and Alexander Stephens. Her collection also included such Northern heroes as Joseph Hooker, Ulysses S. Grant, and George McClellan.[38]

When Anna showed the photograph of Booth to John, he went into a rage and told Anna to tear up all the photos and throw them into the fire. He said that if she didn't get rid of them, he would take them from her.[39] No doubt John was still livid about the Soldiers' Home fiasco.

As it turned out, Anna didn't do as her brother had demanded. Instead, she tucked her photograph of Booth behind the picture of *Morning, Noon, and Night*.[40] Later, when the boardinghouse was searched by detectives, the Booth picture was found just where Anna had hidden it. The other photographs in Anna's collection were taken as well.

There was another time when John's temper flared. One evening when the family had gathered together, Lewis Powell made a remark from which plans to abduct the president could have been construed. John immediately took Powell aside and told him never to say anything like that again in the presence of his mother or his sister. John continued by saying that they knew nothing about the affair and, furthermore, he didn't want them to know anything.[41]

On the morning of March 25, Nettie Slater came back into the lives of the Surratts. She appeared in Booth's carriage which was drawn by two of his horses. The fair lady was on her way back to Richmond carrying dispatches from Montreal. It had been arranged that John would take her as far as Surrattsville where Gus Howell would be waiting. From there, Howell would escort her to Richmond.[42]

Since there was plenty of room in Booth's carriage for Mary, she accompanied the young couple to the country. When the three arrived at the Surratt House and Tavern, John Lloyd had some distressing news. The night before, Federal cavalrymen from Piscataway had arrested Gus Howell. By now, Howell was probably cooling his heels in Old Capitol Prison.[43]

With Howell out of service, John would have to take Nettie Slater, at least as far as Port Tobacco. At Port Tobacco, John would try to find a reliable person to escort her on to Richmond.[44]

David Barry was at the tavern and offered to help. At the same time, he could help himself. There was a Confederate signal corpsman in Port Tobacco who may have received news about Barry's two sons, who were serving with Gen. Robert E. Lee. One of the sons was Arthur, the young doctor in whom Anna had an interest. After further discussion, Barry agreed to go to Port Tobacco with John and Nettie

Slater. If there was no one to take her to Richmond, John said that he would escort her. Barry, in turn, would return Booth's horses and carriage to Howard's Stable in Washington. As it turned out, that is exactly what happened.[45]

Mary took advantage of the change in plans. After visiting her former servant, Rachel, Mary walked to Zad's where she visited her mother and Zad's family. That afternoon Mary took the stage back to Washington. Zad's daughter, Olivia ("Lete"), returned with Mary to visit over the Easter holidays.[46]

The following morning, Sunday, March 26, John and Nettie left for Richmond. That same day, David Barry returned Booth's horses and carriage to Howard's Stable in Washington.[47] That afternoon, Booth and Atzerodt appeared at the boardinghouse at Mary's request. While they were there, David Barry dropped by to tell Mary that John had taken Miss Slater to Richmond.[48]

Although it is not known why Mary wanted to see Booth, it could be assumed that she would want to tell him that Gus Howell had been arrested. And she would want to tell him that John had to take Sarah Slater to Port Tobacco. So that Booth wouldn't be concerned about his horses and carriage, Mary would assure Wilkes that a friend would be returning them to the stable, since John had to take Miss Slater to Richmond.

Meanwhile, Lewis Powell had been on a trip to New York.[49] He returned to Washington on March 27.[50] He checked into the Herndon House, a hostelry operated by Mrs. Martha Murry. This time, Powell was using the alias of Kincheloe.[51]

That same day, Booth had another plan to abduct the president. A notice appeared in the *Washington Star* that President and Mrs. Lincoln had purchased theater tickets for several performances. Again Booth went into action! He sent a wire to Michael O'Laughlin in Baltimore to "get word to Sam," and "to come with or without him."[52]

Sam Arnold, in turn, wrote Booth a letter. He said that he had told his parents that he had "ceased with you" (meaning Booth). Furthermore, he said that he had applied for employment. Then he advised Booth "to desist" in his plans for the present, and to "go and see how it will be taken in Richmond."[53] Sam Arnold's message to Booth would indicate that the Confederate government was oblivious of Booth's plan. By the end of the month, both Sam Arnold and Michael O'Laughlin had disassociated themselves with Booth and his wild schemes.

Meanwhile, John and Nettie Slater arrived in Richmond on March 29, 1865. Two days later, Confederate secretary of state Judah P. Benjamin had an important mission for both of them. It was obvious that it was only a matter of days before Richmond would have to surrender. After Richmond, so would go the Confederacy. Benjamin gave Surratt ten twenty-dollar gold pieces to pay expenses for their last journey to Montreal.[54] Both John and Nettie would carry dispatches to Gen. Edwin Lee, C.S.A., with specific directions for the disposal of Confederate funds. Benjamin wanted to make sure that the money would be safely deposited in England.[55]

# CHAPTER FOURTEEN

# *The Days of Infamy Begin*

With the surrenders of Petersburg and Richmond, the defeat of the Confederacy was imminent. Just prior to the capture of Richmond, Sarah Slater and John Surratt had managed to escape from the city on April 1, 1865. They were carrying important dispatches to Col. Jacob Thompson, commissioner for the Confederate States government in Montreal, Canada.[1] Two days later, Southern troops retreated from the blazing inferno that had once been the capital of the Confederacy.

At this same time, Mary found the domestic help that she had needed. On April 1, Susan Ann Mahoney arrived to join the Surratt household.[2] Her "fella" was Sam Jackson.[3] He probably helped her move into one of the attic rooms in the boardinghouse.

John returned home from Richmond about eight-thirty that evening.[4] Washington was celebrating the fall of that same city, with a torch-light parade. He had arrived in Washington on the Leonardtown, Maryland, stage. It had arrived at approximately four o'clock that afternoon.[5]

Mary probably wondered where her son had spent the last four and a half hours. When Mary asked John if he had eaten, he said that he had, but added that he had a terrible headache.[6]

Mary asked Honora if she had any cologne. "Perhaps if John sniffed some, it would relieve his headache."[7] When the young woman said that she had none, Mary asked her to ask Susan to make a pot of tea and to slice some bread and ham.[8]

When Honora announced that the food was ready, Mary and John went downstairs to the dining room. Susan poured the tea and Mary introduced her to John. "Don't you think he looks like his sister?" Mary asked.[9]

Susan agreed that he did, but added that a detective had come that afternoon looking for Mr. Surratt while Mrs. Surratt was out.[10] It has never been established who the detective was, or what he had wanted.

When Mary asked John if Sarah Slater had stayed in Richmond, he told his mother that Sarah had returned with him to Washington. He said that she was staying at the Metropolitan Hotel and that she would be leaving for Montreal the following day.[11]

Then Mary asked him if, when he had stopped in Surrattsville on his way back from Richmond, he had paid Mr. Ball the fifty-dollar fee that would exempt John from the draft.[12]

John said he hadn't because he wouldn't have to worry about the draft anymore. Then he picked up the two twenty-dollar gold pieces that he had been aimlessly pushing around on the table. He stood and said he was going upstairs to see if John Holohan could change the pieces for greenbacks.[13]

When Mary asked him where he had gotten the gold pieces, John answered that he had had them for quite some time.[14]

After John left his mother to see John Holohan, she probably wondered why her son was no longer concerned about the draft. John knew that he was in danger of being drafted into the Union army for as long as the war lasted.

Later John called down the stairs to tell his mother that he and Lou were going out.[15] Mary was devastated when Lou returned home that evening and told her that John was going away. John had asked Lou to say goodbye to her for him.[16]

At the grocery store the following morning, Mary learned from Mr. Hinsler, the grocer, that he had seen John the day before.[17] It must have seemed to her that everyone but her knew about her son's activities.

On Wednesday, April 5, Mary received a note from John. It had been mailed from Springfield, Massachusetts. He wrote that he would be laying over a day there. He had overslept and had missed his connection.[18] After she read the note, Mary carelessly tossed it on the window sill.[19] The note was never seen again. Later the authorities asked for it, probably to establish that John had actually left town.

It was raining on Palm Sunday, April 9.[20] General Lee's surrender was imminent. Soon the long war would be over and Isaac would be home. Perhaps, even John would settle down to a normal life.

That night, the stillness was suddenly broken by the booming of cannonading in the distance. From downtown the staccato popping of fireworks and people yelling reached Mary's ears. The news of General Lee's surrender on April 9 had reached Washington! The rain continued through the night. At daybreak, a battery stationed on Massachusetts Avenue behind Lafayette Square opened fire in celebration. The percussions from the guns shook the bed of President Lincoln, and the beds of the inhabitants at 541 H Street, as well. Since the fall of Richmond, the week before, until the news of General Lee's surrender, life in Washington had been a continuous celebration.

That afternoon, Annie Ward, who taught at the Visitation School, paid a surprise visit at the boardinghouse. Annie had received a letter from John. It was actually intended for Mary, but for some reason he had sent it to Annie Ward, instead. Mary invited Annie into the parlor where Mary's daughter, Anna, joined them. Just as they were settled, the doorbell rang. It was John Wilkes Booth. He wanted to know if Mrs. Surratt knew where John was. (It would seem that Booth would have known where he was, if John had still been associated with Booth.) She told him that a young lady had just brought a letter from John and invited Wilkes to join them. When everyone was settled again, Annie Ward handed the letter to Mary to read. Mary waved it aside saying that she couldn't see well enough to read it. She asked Annie to read it out loud, which she did.[21]

Anna Surratt took the letter when Annie Ward had finished. When Lou Weichmann joined the group, Anna handed it to him to read. Weichmann mentioned the letter in his book, but refrained from disclosing its contents.[22]

After Weichmann had read the letter, he turned to Booth and said, "Well, I guess the Confederacy's finished now that Richmond is gone."[23]

Showing his agitation, Booth pulled a map from his pocket and pointed out several routes that Confederate general Joseph E.

Johnston could take through the mountains, where Booth thought he could avoid capture.[24]

According to Weichmann, it was at this time that Booth said he was finished with acting. However, he said that he would like to present the play *Venice Preserved*. Years later, Weichmann said that he read the play. He reported that it was about an attempt to assassinate the officers of the Venetian cabinet in order to save Venice, Italy.[25]

After Booth and Annie Ward left, Mary asked Lou if he would take her to Surrattsville the following day on business.[26]

The next morning, Tuesday, April 11, 1865,[27] Lou and Mary left the city approximately at 9:00 A.M.[28] The purpose of her trip was to try to meet with John Nothey in order to settle the $479.00 debt—plus interest—that he still owed on the property that he had purchased from her husband.[29] If Mary could collect the money, she could pay her long overdue debt to George Calvert.

When Lou and Mary arrived in Uniontown, Washington, D.C. (Anacostia), they happened to see John Lloyd in his buggy in the company of his sister-in-law, Emma Offutt. Mary spoke briefly about Gus Howell being in prison. She said that she wished that Gus would take the Oath of Allegiance. Then she added that she intended to see Judge Turner concerning the matter of Gus's internment.[30]

When Mary arrived at the Surratt House and Tavern, she sent a message to John Nothey, asking him to meet her there at two o'clock that afternoon. From there, Mary and Lou went to Capt. Bennett Gwynn's nearby, where they were invited to stay for dinner. When Mary and Lou, along with Captain Gwynn, returned to the tavern, Nothey was waiting.[31] On Mary's behalf, Captain Gwynn met privately with Nothey. Unfortunately, Gwynn was not successful in getting Nothey to settle the note.[32] Lou drove Mary back to Washington.

On Thursday, April 13, Mary and Honora Fitzpatrick went to confession at St. Patrick's Catholic Church in preparation for Good Friday Communion Mass.[33]

That afternoon, Appollonia's parents came for the little girl to take her back to Virginia for the Easter holidays.[34]

The following morning, April 14, promised a brisk, clear day.[35] Mary and Lou walked to St. Patrick's together to attend Good Friday early Mass. After the service, Lou went to work and Mary returned home. There she found an insistent letter from George Calvert demanding the money that she owed him.[36]

Mary became very annoyed with Nothey after she had managed,

with her poor eyesight, to read Calvert's letter. Calvert stated that on a recent visit to the "lower portion of the county," he had seen Nothey who had told him that he was willing to settle what he owed Mrs. Surratt. Calvert went on to say that it was imperative that she settle the matter with Nothey so she could pay him what she owed.[37] Just a few days before, she had tried to collect the money from the man.

That afternoon, Lou Weichmann came home early. Secretary Stanton had given the rest of the day off to government employees who wished to attend Good Friday religious services.[38]

Again, Lou took Mary to the country.[39] When Lou had gone to hire a horse and buggy for the trip to Surrattsville, Eliza Holohan asked Mary if she would be back in time to attend evening Mass with her. Mary assured her that she would.

Just prior to Weichmann's return, Booth appeared at the door. He asked Mary if she would deliver a package for him to John Lloyd. She said that she would. According to Weichmann, the package was "done up in paper, about six inches in diameter." He said that it looked to him as though it contained "two or three saucers."[40] Lloyd would later testify that the package contained Booth's field glasses.

When Mary saw Lou pull up in the rented buggy out front, she and Booth left the H Street boardinghouse. Mary got into the buggy, Booth mounted his horse, and they parted. That was approximately one-thirty in the afternoon.[41]

Mary and Lou arrived at Surrattsville around four o'clock. Mary's brother, Zad, was there, but Nothey and Lloyd were not present. Mary showed Zad the letter that she had received from Calvert. Since she had two judgments against her, her brother offered to pay the interest on both of them.[42]

Mary turned to Lou and asked him to write Nothey a letter. In the letter she told him that she had received a letter from Calvert that very day. The letter stated that Nothey had represented to Calvert that *she* was not willing to settle with Nothey for the land. Mary reminded him she had been ready and waiting to settle for the last two years. She continued by saying that if he did not pay her within the next ten days, she would settle with Calvert and bring suit against him immediately. Finally, she said that Calvert would give Nothey the deed to the property after receiving his payment. Mary signed the letter as the administratrix of John Surratt's estate. Her letter was dated April 14, 1865.[43]

By the time Weichmann had finished writing the letter, Emma

Offutt entered the parlor. Since Lloyd wasn't there, Mary gave Booth's package to her.[44] Lloyd was attending a trial in Marlboro. In February, he and Edward Perrie had gotten into a fight at the tavern. In the course of the melee, Perrie had stabbed Lloyd.[45] As it turned out, the case wasn't heard on the fourteenth and was continued to the November term of the Prince George's County Circuit Court.[46]

Lloyd would later admit that he didn't return directly home from Marlboro. Instead, he drank and played cards.[47] According to Richard Sweeney, they drank a great deal on the way home and Lloyd became "very excitable."[48] James Lusby, who was with the pair, said that Lloyd was even drunker than Sweeney![49]

Later, Mrs. Offutt would testify that when Lloyd returned home that afternoon, "he was very much in liquor. More so than I have ever seen him in my life."[50]

It was about five-thirty on the evening of the same day when Capt. Bennett Gwynn came down the road toward the Surratt House and Tavern. He, too, had attended a trial in Marlboro. When he reached the house and tavern, Zad called to him. When Gwynn stopped his buggy, Zad told him that Mary wanted to speak to him.[51]

When Mary came out of the house, she met the captain by her buggy. She explained why she had returned to Surrattsville so soon after her last visit. She told him about the letter that she had received from Calvert that morning. Then she handed him the letter Lou had written for her, asking Gwynn to deliver and read it to Nothey.[52] Captain Gwynn took the letter, but explained he couldn't deliver it right away since he wanted to hurry home to his sick wife. When Gwynn helped Mary into the carriage, he noticed that the buggy was broken. He called to Joseph T. Knott, the barkeeper, who was crossing the road, and asked him to get some rope. He explained to Weichmann how the carriage could temporarily be repaired by using the rope that Knott was bringing. Then Gwynn left for home to see his wife.[53]

Lou was working on the buggy when Lloyd finally arrived. After Lou instructed Knott how to complete the repair, Lou and Mary followed Lloyd to the kitchen door. Lloyd had brought oysters and fish back with him from Marlboro and invited Mary and Lou to stay for supper. They declined the invitation.[54] Instead, they started back to Washington through a drizzling rain.

Washington was still celebrating Lee's surrender when they arrived.

A procession of arsenal employees was passing up 7th Street heading toward the White House about the time that Lou and Mary arrived home.[55] It was approximately seven-thirty in the evening when Lou dropped Mary off at the boardinghouse.[56] From there he went to Howard's Stable, where he turned in the horse and buggy.[57]

It was about seven-forty-five by the time Lou returned to the house. Lete, Honora, Anna, and Mary were sitting at the dining room table when the doorbell rang. Anna answered it and returned with some papers. She said a man by the name of Scott had asked her to give the papers to Lete.[58]

During supper, Anna mentioned that Annie Ward had dropped by, leaving another letter for Mary from John. Anna told her mother that the letter was from Montreal and that her brother liked the city very much. He said that he had visited the famous French cathedral. He had purchased a pea jacket for ten dollars in silver. He added that board was $2.50 in gold! Finally, John mentioned that he might go to Toronto. He ended by signing himself John Harrison[59]—the same name as John Surratt, Sr.'s, illegitimate son!

On the way to the parlor, Anna said that she wasn't feeling well and went to bed. Eliza Holohan called down the stairs and asked Mary if she still planned to attend church. Mary answered that she was, pulled on her bonnet, and swirled a woolen shawl around her shoulders against the damp night air.

The two women walked only as far as Dr. Evans' house, on the other side of Sweeney's, when Eliza acknowledged that it was a "heavy disagreeable night." She suggested that they go no farther. Mary agreed and they returned home. For five or ten minutes they stood talking on the stoop before entering the house. Inside, Mary returned to the parlor and Eliza Holohan went upstairs to her room.[60]

By ten o'clock that evening, everyone but Mary had retired to their rooms. The problems with John Nothey and George Calvert probably nagged at her. At least, thanks to Zad, she was able to send Calvert the interest that she owed him on her debt.[61]

Then suddenly, from outside, she heard the sound of loud voices in the distance. They seemed to be getting closer. Mary went to the window and looked out. In the dim illumination of the gas street lights, she could barely see some men walking down the street. At each house they stopped and yelled something. When they arrived in front of the boardinghouse, Mary opened the window and leaned out.

A soldier looked up and shouted that the president had just been shot. Then they turned and continued down the street, bellowing their message into the night.[62]

Much later, after everyone had retired for the night, the persistent ringing of the doorbell shattered the silence of the house. Then Mary heard someone thumping down the stairs and past her door. Mary's heart, no doubt, leaped when she heard the front door fling open and crash against the wall. Then the sound of loud male voices traveled down the hall. Next, someone banged on her bedroom door. By now, Honora was awake. "Who's out there? What do you want?" Mary asked.[63]

Lou Weichmann's voice answered. "Mrs. Surratt, there're some detectives here who say that John Wilkes Booth shot the president at Ford's Theatre. They're demanding to search the house!"[64]

Mary told Weichmann, "Ask them to wait a few minutes and I will open the door."[65] It was 2:30 A.M.[66]

When Mary opened the door, she faced a man who introduced himself as John Clarvoe of the Metropolitan Police Department. Then he asked if she was Mrs. Surratt.[67]

"I am Mrs. Surratt."

"I have come to see your son, John."

"My son isn't even in the city, sir!"[68]

Then, the detective asked when she had last seen John Wilkes Booth. Mary answered that it had been about two o'clock in the afternoon of the day before.[69]

"When did you last see your son?"[70]

"I haven't seen John for two weeks, but I did receive a letter from him today. It came from Canada.[71] What is the meaning of all this? Surely, you know that in these times, there are many mothers who don't know the whereabouts of their sons."[72]

Clarvoe turned to Detective James A. McDevitt who was standing nearby. "Mac, you tell her," and Clarvoe hurried from the hall and started up the stairs to initiate the search.[73]

Probably, McDevitt nervously cleared his throat and stroked his bushy, red beard while he searched for the right words.[74]

He told her that the president had been shot and that Secretary Seward had been attacked. The secretary was in bed, at the time, recovering from a broken jaw that he had sustained in a carriage accident. Seward had been stabbed repeatedly and was near death. His son, Fred, was pistol whipped over the head, and suffered a fractured skull. Then McDevitt told Mary that there was reason to believe that her son had attacked the secretary and the secretary's son.[75]

The next morning, John Holohan and Lou Weichmann left the boardinghouse separately before breakfast. Later they met in front of the post office. There, Holohan bought a newspaper and both of them returned home.[76]

Back at the boardinghouse, Weichmann read aloud from the newspaper, "The man, Surratt, who is believed did the bloody work at Secretary Seward's, has for many years been branded a desperado of the worst kind."[77]

No doubt, Mary flinched when she heard her son being called a desperado and accused of nearly killing Secretary Seward. Weichmann quickly assured her that he believed Atzerodt had been the attacker.[78]

The reaction in Washington to the news of the death of the president at 7:05 that morning bordered on madness. Armed men roamed the streets prepared to shoot anyone known to have been a "Secesh" or who did not advocate the most violent punishment for the conspirators.[79]

According to Judge Campbell of the city, an infuriated mob rushed a man to a lamppost where he was hanged because he was heard to express pleasure at President Lincoln's death.

Although previously controversial and, indeed, hated by many Northerners, Lincoln was suddenly elevated to martyrdom after the assassination. His death became a catalyst to justify bloodshed. People began believing that the assassination was the last act of the dying Confederacy and that Booth and Surratt were the chosen instruments to carry out the Southern plot. President Lincoln's plea of "charity for all and malice toward none" had been forgotten!

Conceivably, it was on this sea of hate that the inhabitants in Mrs. Surratt's H Street boardinghouse found themselves. Angry men and women in buggies or on horseback, no doubt, stopped in front to stare and point their fingers and shake their fists. It would follow that some yelled obscenities while others hollered threats!

To avoid the menacing crowd in the front of the house, Weichmann and Holohan slipped out the back door and hustled to the police station. Weichmann realized that he was in a precarious position. After all, John Surratt was his best friend and he lived in his house and shared his room. Better cooperate, rather than hang, Weichmann probably thought.

As soon as they reached the Metropolitan Police Station, Superintendent Richards placed Weichmann under arrest.[80] Even under arrest, John Surratt's friend served the government well. One of Weichmann's first acts was to take detectives Clarvoe and McDevitt to see John Lloyd in Surrattsville. For some reason, John Holohan went with them. When they arrived at the Surratt House and Tavern, Clarvoe asked Lloyd, many times, if he had seen Booth the night before. John Lloyd lied by saying he hadn't![81]

Back at the boardinghouse, Mary had a caller. Father Bernardine Wiget and a lay brother had come to collect a wheelbarrow that Mary had borrowed. The Catholic school name of "Gonzaga" was painted on it.[82] Hopefully, the priest gave the distraught woman some solace before he left.

About eight o'clock that evening, Mary's friend, Wallace Kirby, visited her. He lived on H Street between 4th and 5th. According to Mary Surratt, he was "employed in the government service. He was married to a family connection."[83]

It wasn't until three o'clock the next morning that John Holohan returned to the boardinghouse. Louis Weichmann was not with him![84]

# CHAPTER FIFTEEN

# *The Curtain Descends*

By Monday, April 17, 1865, three days after the boardinghouse was searched, life had been an ongoing nightmare of events. On Sunday, the day before, Eliza Holohan had left in a frenzy with her children. They had gone to her mother's to stay. She returned Monday morning and stayed just long enough to gather her family's soiled clothes together for the washerwoman to pick up the following day.[1] After she set the clothes out, she bid Mary a hasty goodbye and left.

That same day, on Sunday, some detectives brought John Holohan and Louis Weichmann back to the boardinghouse. They stayed only long enough for Lou to get a change of clothes.[2] On Monday, the following day, John Holohan and Detective Clarvoe returned briefly for Holohan's overcoat.[3]

Now all the men were gone. Only four defenseless women sat in the parlor Monday night. No doubt it passed through their minds that a group of ruffians might burst in and kill them all, to vindicate the president's death.

It was announced in the newspaper that Secretary Stanton was offering a twenty-five-thousand-dollar reward each, for the capture of

David Herold and George Atzerodt. A hundred thousand dollars was offered for the capture of the man who had killed President Lincoln.[4] Strange that John Wilkes Booth wasn't mentioned as the assassin, considering the number of people who had identified him.

The silence was suddenly broken that Monday evening as the women sat in the parlor. Scrape . . . scrape . . . scrape, it was the unmistakable sound of people climbing the outside steps.

Mary dashed across the room, opened a window. "Is that you, Mr. Kirby?"[5]

"No, but open the door at once, if this is Mrs. Surratt's house."[6]

When Mary opened the front door, two army officers, Maj. H. W. Smith and Capt. W. M. Wermerskirch, and two detectives, Eli Devoe and Charles W. Rosch, faced her.

"Are you Mrs. Surratt, the mother of John Surratt Jr.?" Major Smith asked.[7]

Mary acknowledged that she was Mrs. Surratt.[8]

Then the major announced that they had come to arrest Mary and everyone else in the house and take them to General Augur's headquarters for examination.[9]

The major told Devoe and Rosch to go downstairs and guard any Negro servants that they might find.[10]

Major Smith turned to Mary and asked for her keys. Then he informed her that her house would be under guard.[11]

Mary handed him the keys. He, in turn, handed them to Captain Wermerskirch. When they entered the parlor, the major asked, "Who are the ladies?"[12]

Mary introduced Anna first.[13] Anna was sitting on the chair near the sofa.[14]

"That one is my niece and the one next to her is Miss Fitzpatrick who boards in my house,"[15] Mary said, indicating the two girls huddling together on the sofa.[16]

Suddenly, the doorbell rang. Without a word, Captain Wermerskirch left the parlor and returned with two men. "Major, these men are Detectives Sampson and Morgan. They were sent to give us a hand, if we need them."[17]

The major acknowledged the men then asked Detective Sampson to go downstairs to relieve Detective Devoe and tell him to come upstairs.[18]

When Devoe came upstairs, the major instructed him to get the carriage that they had brought and bring it to within one-half block of the boardinghouse. "I don't want to excite suspicion,"[19] he said.

"Let the women walk. It's good enough for them,"[20] Devoe commented before leaving the house.

"Sir, since you are in charge, I expect the ladies to be treated with kindness," Mary said.[21]

"Madam, I will accompany you to get the necessary hats and cloaks for you all to wear to General Augur's headquarters,"[22] Smith instructed, ignoring Mary's comment.

Then he told Captain Wermerskirch, "Please entertain these young ladies while I am gone and do not allow any communication to pass between them."[23]

When the major and Mary had gathered the wraps, they returned to the parlor. Mary had gotten her daughter a warm pair of shoes to protect her against the raw, cold night. Anna began to cry when her mother knelt to put them on for her.[24]

"Do not behave so, Baby. You are already so worn out with anxiety that you will make yourself sick, and the officer who has arrested us is in uniform, and is a gentleman, and will treat us kindly."[25]

"Oh Mother! But to be taken there for such a thing,"[26] Anna whimpered,

"Hush!"[27] Mary scolded, obviously trying to control her daughter so the other girls would not panic.

When Mary had finished putting on Anna's shoes, she asked the major if he would object to her praying before they left. When he said that he had no objection, Mary knelt by the piano and, for about five minutes, prayed.[28]

Meanwhile, Major Smith called Detective Morgan into the parlor. There, the major announced that anyone who came to the boardinghouse that night would be treated as a suspicious character. He said to let everyone in, but no one out.[29]

Then Major Smith turned to Wermerskirch and Morgan and asked what was keeping Devoe. He remarked that he should be back. If he didn't get back soon, someone would have to go and get him.[30]

Subsequently, footsteps were heard coming up the outside steps. Major Smith gave the men a quick glance. "Both of you go out into the hall and stand behind the front door. Wermerskirch, when the doorbell rings, you unlock it and open it. I'll be standing in the parlor doorway to the hall."[31]

When the doorbell rang, Captain Wermerskirch did as he was instructed. A tall man dressed in muddy clothing and carrying a pickaxe strode up to the threshold.[32] Major Smith stepped into the hall.

"I guess I have mistaken the house," the big man said peering inside.[33]

"No, you have not," the major answered.[34]

Detective Morgan walked from behind the door and asked, "Whose house are you looking for?"[35]

"Mrs. Surratt's."[36]

"This is the house. Come in at once." The major loosened his pistol in its holster.[37]

The stranger did as he was told and stepped into a circle of light beneath a flickering gas jet. Captain Wermerskirch shut and locked the door and dropped the key back into his pocket.[38]

Under Major Smith's questioning, the stranger said that he had come to dig a gutter for Mrs. Surratt the next day. The inane reason he gave for coming at such a late hour was so Mrs. Surratt could give him "directions about digging the gutter the next morning." He said that Mrs. Surratt had hired him from the street.[39]

Major Smith returned to the parlor. "Mrs. Surratt, please step here for a moment."[40]

Mary had gotten only as far as the parlor door when Smith asked, "Do you know this man and did you hire him to come and dig a gutter for you?"[41]

From what Mary could see with her poor eyesight, the stranger was a "tremendous hard fellow with a skull cap on with a weapon in his hand."[42] Mary raised her right hand and said, "Before God, sir, I do not know this man, and I have not seen him before, and I did not hire him to come and dig a gutter for me."[43]

Anna joined her mother at the parlor door and probably winced when she saw the frightening-looking man with a pick. She remarked that the stranger had come to kill them all and that "these gentlemen, had come to save their lives, and she hoped that they would arrest him."[44]

"Your story does not hang together. I arrest you as a suspicious person and shall take you to General Augur's headquarters to be examined," Major Smith announced to the stranger.[45]

Mary and Anna returned to the parlor to continue waiting for the carriage. It was eleven-thirty when Devoe arrived and said that he was ready to take the ladies to General Augur. Mary, Anna, Honora, and

Lete put on their bonnets and wraps and went into the hall and left the house.

The last thing that Mary heard on leaving were orders to return with the carriage so the stranger could be taken to headquarters. The other order probably made Mary's skin crawl. The men were to make a thorough search of the boardinghouse. The sanctity of her home would be ravaged. She probably felt violated and embarrassed that soiled clothes were in the house.[46]

At the headquarters of Christopher Augur, commander of all the Union troops in Washington, Mary was ushered immediately into the general's office. He had a thick, walrus mustache which flowed into a wispy side beard that appeared as though it had been starched and ironed. His face was narrow and stern. His graying hair was of medium length that cascaded in front of his sizeable ears.[47]

No doubt, a young lieutenant with a deadpan expression recorded the general's interrogation.

In answer to the many questions that were asked her, Mary said that she had not seen her son John "since two weeks ago today, that is, since the 3rd of April, 1865." Mary continued by saying that, "My son sometime since made the acquaintance of J. Wilkes Booth; I could not say exactly when; Mr. Booth has been coming to our house about two months; sometimes he called twice a day; we found him very much a gentleman. I think my son invited him home the evening he was introduced to him. I did not hear how he came to know him. My son is a country-bred young gentleman. I was not surprised that he should make the acquaintance of such a man as Mr. Booth because I consider him capable of forming acquaintances in the best society." Mary continued by saying that Booth called even when her son wasn't at home. Sometimes he asked for John, sometimes he didn't. She said that everyone was surprised that Booth had killed the president. "We often remarked that Mr. Booth was very clear of politics; he never mentioned anything of the kind, and it was a subject that we never indulged in." When Mary was asked her political sentiments, she said, "I don't pretend to express my feelings at all; I have often said that I thought that the South acted too hastily; that is about the amount of my feelings, and I say so again."[48]

About that time a loud, angry feminine voice came from the outer room where the young women were sitting.

Mary and the two officers rushed into the waiting room. There Anna was standing and yelling and shaking her finger in a soldier's face.

"This man," Anna stormed, "just suggested that this ugly thing [meaning the stranger who turned out to be Lewis Powell] is my brother. I just let him know that he was no gentleman to have said such a thing."[49]

Mary agreed that the man, who had removed his makeshift cap, was not Anna's brother.[50]

Back in Augur's office, the questioning continued. Mary was asked about George Atzerodt, David Herold, the stranger with the pickaxe, the house being searched, the boarders, her trips to the country, and her son leaving home after he had exchanged gold for greenbacks with John Holohan.[51]

She mentioned the note from John that she had received when he had laid over in Springfield, Massachusetts. She said that she had tried to find it, but couldn't. She hadn't seen it since she had placed it on the window sill. She said that she thought that John was going to Canada. She did not mention the two other notes that she had received from John, not even the one from Montreal.[52]

When the questioning was over, Mary and the young women were taken to the infamous Old Capitol Prison.[53]

Soon after Lewis Powell was brought to General Augur's office, he was identified by William H. Bell as the man who had tried to kill the secretary of state. Bell, a Negro servant, had witnessed the attack.[54]

# CHAPTER SIXTEEN

# *Incarceration*

Mary, Honora, Lete, and Anna would have been close to exhaustion as they huddled together in the carriage that was taking them from General Augur's headquarters to Old Capitol Prison. The conveyance rattled down 14th Street, then turned left on Pennsylvania Avenue. The once familiar stores and homes that they passed would have seemed foreign to them now. Ahead, glowing from reflected gas lights, the edifice of the Capitol rode on a cloud of mist. The carriage followed the wrought-iron fence that circled the Capitol grounds. Then the carriage stopped—Old Capitol Prison loomed before them. Two armed guards, with fixed bayonets, marched back and forth in front of the prison. The rhythmic clicking of their heavy boots on the sidewalk echoed in the stillness. Their bodies cast grotesque shadows on the whitewashed brick walls of the three-story building. Strangely, the whitewash ended just below the second-story windows.

Together, Old Capitol Prison and the Carroll Annex occupied an entire block. The two structures and a board fence enclosed a treeless, grassless exercise yard. Hidden in an adjoining yard were the nocuous latrines or "sinks." In the words of one prisoner, "The sinks consisted

*Old Capitol Prison where Mary Surratt was taken on April 17, 1865. She stayed here until April 30, 1865, when she was transferred to the Old Arsenal Penitentiary.* (Author's Collection)

of wide trenches partially covered over, but open in front." Here, the men answered nature's call. Both inside and outside of the prison the thick, nauseating stench of excrement penetrated the clothing and pores of the inmates and those who lived or worked nearby.[1]

When the women were taken inside the prison, they would have been told to wait in the first room that they entered. It was a large, inhospitable, dimly lit place known as the "search room."[2] It had several kitchen chairs on which Mary and the young women would have sat.[3]

Perhaps Zad's former friend, Col. William Wood, would have interviewed Mary, over his monumental stomach,[4] when she was taken to his office. In any case, the women were assigned to Room 41 in Carroll Annex.[5] They had Colonel Wood's permission to walk freely about.[6]

When dawn broke in the eastern sky, Mary and the young women had probably collapsed from exhaustion onto the filthy, straw-filled mattresses. The noxious odor of human waste permeated the air. Then, gradually the sun unveiled their surroundings.

If the room was typical, it was approximately ten by twelve feet in size with a single tall window. The window glass would have been streaked with years of grime. At the foot of the dirt-encrusted iron beds were a couple of broken chairs and a wooden table. The table held a chipped wash bowl and pitcher set. A wooden frame, with jagged pieces of a mirror, dangled from one of the filthy walls.

There was little left of the Carroll building's past glory. It carried the name of the Carroll family of Maryland. Its history went back to colonial times.[7]

The Old Capitol Prison building had housed Congress after the British burned the Capitol in the War of 1812. Later, it became a fine boardinghouse after the Capitol had been repaired. One of the boarders was Southern spokesman John C. Calhoun, who lived and, finally, died there. It was Mrs. Hill's place, then. She was the aunt of Rose O'Neal of Port Tobacco, Maryland. Later, Rose was courted at the boardinghouse by the socially prominent Dr. Robert Greenhow of Williamsburg, Virginia. The couple eventually married. The doctor died while Rose was still quite young, leaving her with a daughter to raise. In 1861, the Widow Greenhow and her nine-year-old daughter returned to the former boardinghouse under entirely different circumstances. By then, the government had purchased the house and had turned it into a Federal prison. Mrs. Greenhow was sent there to serve time as a Confederate spy.[8]

Since the boardinghouse had become a prison, the once elegant rooms had long since lost their opulence. Now roaches paraded up and down the dirty walls. Spider webs festooned the ceiling and corners, while strange stains, drawings, and writings vied for space. Rats and tiny, blood-sucking brown bedbugs ravaged the inmates by night and day.

The women's second-floor prison room overlooked the exercise yard. The yard was surrounded on two sides by a twelve-foot, whitewashed board fence. On top of the fence was a platform sufficiently wide for two sentries to pass and watch the yard below. The fourth side of the yard was occupied by the Old Capitol Prison. Mary later learned that there was a sutler's store in the rear on the first floor of the building. For twenty-five cents, the daily newspaper could be purchased as well as other so-called luxuries.[9]

At approximately nine o'clock their first morning in prison, their door suddenly swung open. An officer and two enlisted men entered and glanced from Mary to the young women. One of the soldiers was holding an open ledger while another held a pen and a bottle of ink. "Four!" bellowed the officer then dipped his pen in the ink and wrote in the ledger.[10] Morning and evening, a head count was conducted at approximately nine o'clock.[11]

Probably it wasn't long before Catherine Virginia Baxley made her-self known to the newcomers. She was a well-educated, outspoken woman.[12] No doubt Mrs. Baxley described Rose O'Neal as an elegant lady who had her way with men! Where spying was concerned, she was the best. Rose O'Neal, her daughter, little Rose, and Mrs. Baxley were among the first females occupants of Old Capitol Prison, the "Yankee rat trap," as Mrs. Baxley christened it.[13] Mrs. Baxley would have described Rose as never having a hair out of place while she was in prison. Even little Rose looked the part of a princess right down to her lace pantalettes.[14] Perhaps it was the guards' respect for Mrs. Greenhow's daring-do that helped win her special treatment. After all, General Beauregard had commended her for the work that she had done to help win the first battle of Manassas.[15]

Catherine Baxley probably would have ended her visit with the new-comers by saying that she had been a Confederate courier. Like John Surratt, she had carried messages to Canada. Mrs. Baxley had been in prison for eighteen months by the time that Mary and the young women arrived.[16]

The prison was much like most prisons of the day. The halls were filthy. Since there were no trash receptacles, probably everything that fell on the floor, remained on the floor. Unabashedly, vermin were free to live, mate, have their young, and die without interference.

The sounds of coughing and spitting echoed everywhere. Most of the prisoners shuffled dull-eyed up and down the halls. The mentally deranged, who hadn't been transferred to the local insane asylum, crouched, excreted, and babbled in dark corners. Then there were the others who terrified everyone with their hideous cackles, screech-es, and screams.

Yet, there were the survivors. Some survived like Catherine Virginia, while others survived quite artfully. The latter were the prostitutes. Arm in arm they promenaded the halls, dressed in risque costumes, splashing color everywhere. They laughed, told ribald jokes, and flirt-ed shamelessly with the guards. The more virtuous women tried to conceal their titillations from the outlandish actions of the Jezebels. The prostitutes' high jinx were a refreshing alternative to the pain and misery of the prison.

Promptly at three o'clock, a small legion of Negro women began to noisily traverse the halls carrying dinner trays to the inmates. Dinner consisted of greasy soup with fatback floating on top. Generally, there was a large bowl of parboiled potatoes. Eating with spoons with broken-off handles would have proved challenging.[17]

On the afternoon of April 18, Mary stood at her window while watching the prisoners in the yard below. Suddenly, she saw *Louis Weichmann!* When the man looked up, Mary gave a little cry and threw him a kiss.[18] He ignored her and looked away. How strange. Why did he ignore her?[19] A guilty conscience, perhaps?

Evening meals generally consisted of four small coffee pots that held about two cups of liquid. A yellow delft bowl, left over from finer times, held four slices of wheat bread with approximately two tablespoons of brown sugar and two pats of butter on top. Yellow delft mugs, streaked with dirty dish water, were set before each of them. The iron knives, forks, and spoons were black with grime and sticky with grease. The sugar bowl crawled with ants, and the coffee looked and smelled like well-aged tobacco juice.[20] The ladies would have eaten by the light of the courtyard gaslights that streamed in their window.[21]

On the night of April 18, the day that Mary saw Lou Weichmann, John Lloyd was arrested in Surrattsville and taken to Bryantown. There, the provost marshal, Col. H. H. Wells, U.S.A., had his head-quarters. Later, Thomas A. Jones, who was arrested by Colonel Wells for helping Booth to escape, described Wells as "a rougher man I have never had to deal with."[22]

Probably none of the witnesses were treated more severely than was John Lloyd. When he refused to say anything against Mrs. Surratt, he was hanged by his thumbs until he could no longer stand the pain. Only then, in order to spare himself any further torture, did Lloyd agree to perjure himself against his landlady.[23]

John T. Ford, the owner of Ford's Theatre, met Lloyd while they were both incarcerated at the Old Capitol Prison. It was then that Lloyd inti-mated to Ford that he had agreed to testify against Mrs. Surratt only after he had suffered extreme duress at the hands of his captors.[24]

The following day, Wednesday, April 19, marked the beginning of a nationwide mourning period for President Lincoln. Reasonably, Mary and the young women did not venture from their room that day. Instead, they would have discussed everything and everybody, and speculated when they would be released.

The following day Honora said goodbye to the others and walked into freedom.[25]

On the day that Honora gained her freedom, George Atzerodt gave up his. He was arrested at the home of his cousin, Hartman Righter, in Montgomery County, Maryland.[26]

By the dark of night, on April 21, John Wilkes Booth and David Herold shoved a boat into the Potomac River and headed for Virginia. Finally, freedom was within their reach with Dixie on the horizon.

Yet, freedom escaped both of the men. On April 26, a few minutes after seven o'clock in the morning, Booth died from a single gunshot fired by Sgt. Thomas H. ("Boston") Corbett, Company L, Sixteenth New York Volunteer Cavalry. The warning "vision" of Booth's mother unfolded at the Garrett's family farm, near Port Royal, Virginia. From there, Union prisoner David Herold and the body of John Wilkes Booth were transported back to Washington, D.C.[27]

Booth's death would, forever, leave many unanswered questions. He had kept a diary during his flight. After his death, it was found in his pocket along with a spur, a pipe, and some tobacco. All but the diary were used in evidence at the trial of the alleged conspirators. In the diary, Booth had made a mysterious entry, "I have . . . almost a mind to return to Washington and in a measure to clear my name, which I feel I can do." At the impeachment trial of President Andrew Johnson, Gen. Benjamin Butler referred to the diary and asked, "How clear himself? By disclosing his accomplices? Who were they?"[28] Who, indeed, beside Booth, could have answered General Butler's questions?

On April 21, Dr. Samuel Mudd kissed his wife and children goodbye when he was arrested at his home in Bryantown, Maryland. More than seven long, hard years would pass before the doctor would see his children again.[29] His wife would visit him in prison.

It was nearly a week after Honora was released that Virginia Baxley was gazing out of one of the front windows to the street below. Perhaps her mind traveled to her son when she saw a young Confederate soldier being brought into the prison. The young man looked up. When he saw Mrs. Baxley, he waved his arm and cried, "Mother! Mother!" Since she didn't recognize him, she thought the lad deranged. Later that day, Colonel Wood went to Mrs. Baxley and told her that her son had been brought to the prison hospital and that the boy wanted to see her. She rushed to his side. He was only seventeen years old. He had joined the Confederate army when he was sixteen.

Mrs. Baxley was allowed to minister to him daily. Since his wounds were not serious, his prognosis was good until he caught typhoid fever. Unfortunately, the prison food did little to help him to recuperate and he began to waste away. The young man became convinced that he would recover if he could just have a small piece of chicken and a cup of coffee. Mrs. Baxley became frantic when so humble a request was denied her son. Because of her behavior, she was no longer allowed to minister to her boy. Mary Surratt took the mother's place. It wasn't long before the young soldier died. He passed away in Mary's arms.[30]

As it turned out, Honora Fitzpatrick would only enjoy freedom for three days. When she was brought back to the prison, she was assigned to share a room with Virginia Lomax.[31]

Out of desperation, on April 23, Mary wrote a note to Fr. Jacob A. Walter and asked him to please come and visit them at the prison.[32]

The priest went to the prison on April 25. When he arrived, he was told that Mrs. Surratt had been transferred to the Old Penitentiary.[33] The priest had been misled. Mary was still at the Carroll Annex of Old Capitol Prison. It is not known why Father Walter had been told otherwise. Perhaps because Superintendent Wood had been a Roman Catholic before he had converted to atheism.[34]

Yet on Sundays, Wood's loud voice jarred the prisoners to piety: "All ye who want to hear the Lord God preached according to Jeff Davis, go down to the yard; and ye who want to hear the Lord God preached according to Abe Lincoln, go down to Number 16."[35]

On April 28, Mary was taken to Colonel Wood's office. There, she was interrogated by Col. Henry Steele Olcott, special commissioner of the War Department. Colonel Olcott had been sent by Secretary Stanton to specifically question Mrs. Surratt. In appearance, the colonel looked more like a Shakespearean actor than a military man.

At first the questions were the usual, primarily concerning her son, and her April 14 visit to Surrattsville. Since John Lloyd had been arrested and questioned, Olcott's questions to Mary took a different turn. For the first time, the subject of "shooting irons" was mentioned. Lloyd had freely admitted to John T. Ford that he had experienced "a great deal of duress at the hands of his captors." Was it then that Lloyd possibly lied when he claimed that Mrs. Surratt had told him, when she visited Surrattsville concerning her business with John Nothey, to have "shooting irons" and "whiskey" ready for whoever came that night—the night of April 14—the night that the president was shot? Here are Colonel Olcott's questions and Mrs. Surratt's answers concerning the shooting irons:

Q. What did you say about any shooting irons or carbines? [Referring to the April 14 meeting Mary had with
Lloyd.]


A. I said nothing.


Q. Any conversation of that kind? Did you not tell him
[Lloyd] to have shooting irons ready, that there would be
some people there that night?


A. To my knowledge, no conversation of that kind
passed.


Q. Did you know any shooting irons were there?


A. No, Sir, I did not.[36]


Unfortunately, for Mary Surratt, John Lloyd would testify at the trial
of the alleged conspirators that Mrs. Surratt had told him to have
shooting irons ready. His testimony did much to "prove" that Mary
Surratt was, indeed, deeply involved in the plot to assassinate
President Lincoln.[37]

After Mary was interrogated, Colonel Olcott reported to Col. H. L.
Burnett that Mrs. Surratt "repeats substantially the story that she told
on her first examination." The colonel finalized his report by saying,
"She denies in toto having had any conference with Lloyd about
firearms, or any conversation with Booth, Herold, or others about the
projected assassination or of having known that her son was implicated in it, or of having done anything prejudicial to the public interest.
Her manner throughout was cool and collected."[38]

That same day, Anna and Honora were questioned. Their statements coincided with Mary's.

Beyond the prison walls, spring and love were alive and well. On
April 28, Samuel Jackson and Susan Ann Mahoney, Mary's maid at the
H Street boardinghouse, were married.[39]

In contrast, love and spring were far from the thoughts of seven men. From the time that they were arrested until April 28, they had been held captive on the *Saugus,* a U.S. gunboat, in the Potomac River. On April 28, Powell, Atzerodt, Herold, Edward "Ted" Spangler, O'Laughlin, Arnold, and Dr. Mudd were transferred from the boat to the Old Penitentiary, a military prison at the U.S. Arsenal, in Washington, D.C.[40]

It has been maintained that Mary Surratt was offered an unconditional pardon for herself and for John if she would accompany an officer in a buggy and point out the road that her son had taken when he left home. She said that she had no idea what road he had taken. Since she could be of no help, she refused to accompany the officer. The offer of clemency was maintained to have taken place at the Old Capitol Prison.[41]

During Mary's stay at the prison, she nursed the sick and consoled the sorrowful. In her book, Virginia Lomax referred to Mary Surratt as an "angel of mercy."[42]

As an example of Mrs. Surratt's kindness, Virginia Lomax related the following:

One morning during Mrs. Lomax's frequent visits to her cousins' cell room, whom she referred to as the Windsors, a guard took Mr. Windsor away.

He had been summoned by "the Board." No one knew whether the gentleman would be returned to his room or be sent to another prison.

When her husband left, Mrs. Windsor became desperate and cried without restraint. Then a lady, who was approximately forty years old, entered the room. "She had a commanding figure, rather stout, with brown hair, thin nose, and a small well-shaped mouth, denoting great firmness."

Mrs. Lomax continued by saying: "The woman took a seat beside my weeping cousin, put her arm around her shoulders: then she talked to her in a most consoling manner, and though my cousin had never seen her before the imprisonment, she was as tender and kind as if she had been an old friend. There was a calm, quiet dignity about the woman, which impressed me before I even knew who she was. After that day, I saw her often, she would come in and read the daily paper."[43]

Mrs. Lomax recounted another instance: ". . . one of the papers contained an outrageous account of herself [Mrs. Surratt] and household, aspersing both her character and reputation. We endeavored to withhold the papers from her, but she insisted on reading it. I watched her closely while doing so, and for an instant a flush of womanly indignation over-spread her pale countenance at the insults. After she had read it all, she laid the paper down and clasping her hands, raised her eyes to Heaven and said, 'I suppose I shall *have* to bear it.'"[44]

Mrs. Lomax said that this was "the only illusion to her suffering" that she ever saw Mrs. Surratt exhibit.[45]

Mrs. Lomax said that Mary Surratt "avoided conversation, and never uttered one word of reproach or virulence against those by whose authority she was imprisoned."[46]

Again, from Mrs. Lomax's book, we learn that the superintendent of the prison, whom Mrs. Lomax referred to as "H,"[47] was actually Colonel Wood. She said that he "frequently spent hours talking with Mrs. Surratt. He hoped to entrap some incautious expression, which would enable him to discover where her son, John Surratt, was concealed."[48] This seems to agree with the assertion that Mrs. Surratt had been offered an unconditional pardon for both her and John, if she would help to find her son. It was during her stay at Old Capitol Prison that Colonel Wood became convinced that Mary Surratt did not, in any way, conspire to assassinate President Lincoln.

In her book, Virginia Lomax narrated another story concerning Mary Surratt. A woman prisoner was brought in who circulated freely among the inmates. She was very talkative, and generally selected the assassination as her topic of conversation. When the woman became ill, ". . . kind Mrs. Surratt, as usual, took charge of her, and ministered to her necessities." One day, after the woman had recovered, she impulsively threw herself on her knees in front of Mary and said, "Oh, Mrs. Surratt, when they offered me the twenty five hundred dollars, to find out, I did not know what to do. I was penniless and . . ."

"'Never mind now,' said Mrs. Surratt, interrupting and raising the woman from her knees. 'We will talk of something else.' Soon after, the woman left the prison."[49]

After enjoying a short freedom, on Sunday, April 30, under the orders of Edwin Stanton, Louis Weichmann was brought back to Old Capitol Prison. In his report, Colonel Wood mentioned that Weichmann had been a former employee "of the Government in the Office of the Commissary General of Prisons." Wood continued by saying: "I am satisfied he has frequently purloined important papers which have been forwarded to Richmond by or through John Surratt."[50]

Like Lloyd, Weichmann came in contact with John T. Ford while they were in prison. They frequently conversed about Mrs. Surratt, of whom Weichmann said: "She was an exemplary Christian woman, to him she had fully filled the place of mother, and in every relation of life she was eminently a consistent, pious lady." This occurred, according to Ford, before Edwin Stanton, Col. H. L. Burnett, and their detectives had gotten to Weichmann. Weichmann recounted to John Ford that when he was brought before Secretary of War Stanton, in an intimidating manner the secretary expressed the opinion that Weichmann's hands had as much of the president's blood on them as Booth's. It has been said that Stanton, in order to impress Weichmann even further, placed a rope around Weichmann's neck. According to Weichmann, he claimed that Stanton told him that if he *didn't* testify *as the government wished,* he (Weichmann) would be hanged.[51]

On the same Sunday, April 30, that Louis Weichmann was returned to Old Capitol Prison, Mary Surratt was transferred, nearby, to the Old Penitentiary at the U.S. Arsenal.

According to Virginia Lomax's account, Mary was transferred on a

*The Old Arsenal Penitentiary where Mary Surratt was imprisoned, stood trial, and was hanged.* (Author's Collection)

gloomy Sunday evening. Mary, Anna, Virginia Lomax, and some others were visiting together when two soldiers appeared. (One of the soldiers Mrs. Lomax referred to as Nelson.) Mrs. Surratt was told that she was wanted and to "put on your bonnet and cloak, if you please, and follow me."

Again according to Mrs Lomax, when Mary arrived at her room, Anna was "clinging to her, and begged to be allowed to accompany her, which request was unheeded. Mrs. Surratt kissed each one of us, and when she came to me, she threw her arms around my neck, and said in an agitated voice, 'Pray for me, pray for me.'"

Nelson stepped forward, and gently disengaged Anna who was still weeping and clinging to her mother. Then he took Mary by the arm and led her down the stairs, out the door, and into a waiting carriage.

Mrs. Lomax's account continued: "For a while, all but Anna were silent, shocked by the suddenness of the whole proceeding. She, poor girl, knelt by her iron bedstead, wringing her hand and crying, 'Oh, mother, mother!' None of us thought that Mrs. Surratt had been taken away to remain, and we sat up all night watching and waiting for her to return."[52]

From the penitentiary ledger of the special provost marshal general, Brig. Gen. John F. Hartranft, it was noted that Mrs. Surratt was brought by Col. Lafayette C. Baker, under the order of the secretary of war, to the U.S. Arsenal Prison (the Old Penitentiary), on April 30. She arrived at seven o'clock in the evening. After she was searched, she was taken to cell number 157. The contents of her pockets contained: "a $10.00 bill, a note drawn in her favor for $216.67; an order about horses; a gold watch ring; three keys; two pocket knives; a thimble; and a piece of red velvet and needles."[53]

Meanwhile, back at the Old Capitol Prison, we return to Virginia Lomax's book. In it she said that, night after night, she and Honora heard the patter of Anna's "little slippered feet, as she restlessly paced the room above. I fancy that I can see her now, her light hair brushed back from her fair face, her blue eyes turned towards heaven, her lips compressed as if in pain, and her delicate little white hands clasped tightly, as she walked up and down that room, hour after hour, seeming insensible to fatigue, and speaking to no one. Sometimes she would be quite hysterical, then again perfectly calm, except for the constant walking. We all thought she would lose her mind if the strain were not relieved." (Olivia "Lete" Jenkins must have been released from prison by this time.)

"We could ascertain nothing in regard to Mrs. Surratt. If Nelson knew, he would not tell us, and 'H' [meaning Wood] was absent. After a week had elapsed, he returned, and we immediately beset him with questions. He told us that Mrs. Surratt had been taken on board a gunboat, lying in front of the arsenal, in the hold of which she, and the other prisoners implicated in the assassination, were confined in perfect darkness and solitude. Around the neck of each prisoner was an iron collar, from which was suspended a short chain terminated by an iron ball, which rested on the floor, so that the head was bowed down and retained in that position, and in *that* position the prisoners sat day and night, with a soldier guarding each.

"'What are they going to do with Mrs. Surratt?' asked a Miss Lewis.

"'It is not decided yet,' he replied; 'but there is some talk of taking the gunboat further into the stream and scuttling her, with the prisoners on board.' [Of course, by now, all of the prisoners had been removed to the Old Penitentiary.]

"That was the first intimation we had, that Mrs. Surratt's life was endangered. We had supposed that she might be sentenced to the penitentiary for life, or something similar, but we did not realize that she was doomed to a violent death. She had endeared herself to all by her kindness and consideration, and she was the last person we would suspect of cold-blooded murder. Conscious of her innocence, she never apprehended the awful fate awaiting her. That her position sorely tried her, was apparent to all; but there was never the least appearance of guilt, and not for one moment did her faith in an All-merciful Providence waver. There was no pretence about it—you felt that the woman was deeply and sincerely religious, yet without any ostentation. It is impossible to describe the state of wretchedness, into which this news threw Anna Surratt. 'H' told her himself—none of us having the nerve to do so. She was frantic for a time, her constant cry being, 'Mother, Mother!' I believe 'H' would have withheld this from her, had she not insisted on hearing the truth. He told us she had begged the officer in charge to allow him an interview with Mrs. Surratt, but was refused, as she was not permitted to see or hold communication with any one, not even the guard.

"We asked Anna Surratt what she intended doing. She said she thought of entering a convent, as she had no longer a home."[54]

*The alleged conspirators.* (Library of Congress)

# CHAPTER SEVENTEEN

# *The Trial Commences*

Carroll Annex had been luxurious compared to Mary Surratt's new surroundings at the Old Penitentiary. Her cell, number 153, measured only seven by three-one-half feet. A pallet to lie on and a bucket for excrement were the only furnishings.[1]

*A typical cell block at the Old Arsenal Penitentiary. Mary Surratt was confined in such a cell. It measured 2½ x 8 ft. Later she was removed to better accommodations.* (Author's Collection)·

No doubt, thoughts of Anna and how they had been suddenly wrenched apart sent arrows through Mary's heart. How would her daughter survive with only wild imaginings and anxieties to keep her company? Anna had always been a fragile, high-strung, sensitive child.

On May 6, the adjutant-general's office of the War Department issued Special Orders No. 211 in compliance with President Andrew Johnson's executive order of May 1.

> Special Orders, No. 211
>         Extract.
> * * * * * * * * * * * * * * * * * * * * * * * * *
> 4. A Military Commission is hereby appointed to meet at Washington, District of Columbia, on Monday, the 8th day of May, 1865, at 9 o'clock A.M. or as soon thereafter as practicable, for the trial of David E. Herold, George A. Atzerodt, Lewis Payne [sic], Michael O'Laughlin, Edward Spangler, Samuel Arnold, Mary E. Surratt, Samuel A. Mudd and such other persons as may be brought before it, implicated in the murder of the late President Abraham Lincoln and the attempted assassination of the Honorable William H. Seward, Secretary of State, and in an alleged conspiracy to assassinate other officers of the Federal Government in Washington City, and their aiders and abettors.[2]
>
> Brigadier-General Joseph Holt, Judge Advocate General, U.S. Army, is appointed the Judge Advocate and Recorder of the Commission, to be aided by such Assistant for Special Judge Advocates as he may designate.
>
> The Commission will sit without regard to hours. By order of the President of the United States
> (Signed)                    W.A. Nichols
>                              Assistant Adjutant-General[3]

The Hon. John A. Bingham and Bvt. Col. Henry L. Burnett were appointed by Judge Holt to serve as his two assistants or special judge advocates.[4]

The following nine officers were appointed as judges on the Military Commission:

*Major General David Hunter*—U.S. Volunteer, president of the Military Commission. He had been a friend of President Lincoln and was one of the officers who had accompanied the late president's body to Springfield, Illinois. After the trial, General Hunter signed the clemency paper on behalf of Mrs. Surratt.[5]

*Major General Lewis Wallace*—U.S. Volunteer. General Hunter was a lawyer, soldier, diplomat, and author. He would later author the book *Ben Hur*. He did not sign Mrs. Surratt's clemency plea.[6]

*Brevet Major General August V. Kautz*—U.S. Volunteer. His division of the XXV Corps was among the first to reach Richmond in April 1865. He signed Mrs. Surratt's plea for clemency.[7]

*Brigadier General Albion P. Howe*—U.S. Volunteer. General Howe was a member of the guard of honor that escorted the late president's body to Springfield. He did not sign Mrs. Surratt's plea for clemency.[8]

*Brigadier General Robert S. Foster*—U.S. Volunteer. General Foster participated in the siege of Charleston, South Carolina. He served gallantly on the Petersburg front. He signed Mrs. Surratt's plea for clemency.[9]

*Brigadier General Thomas M. Harris*—U.S. Volunteer. General Harris took part in the final operations against the Army of Northern Virginia at Petersburg. He did not sign Mrs. Surratt's plea for clemency.[10]

*Lieutenant Colonel David R. Clendenin*—Eighth Illinois Cavalry. Colonel Clendenin served with the Army of the Potomac throughout the war. He did not sign Mrs. Surratt's plea for clemency.[11]

*Colonel B. Comstock*—U.S. Volunteer, General Grant's staff. Colonel Comstock believed that the prisoners should be tried in civil court. It disturbed him that the prisoners were ironed. He was eventually replaced.[12]

*Brevet Colonel Horace Porter*—Aide-de-camp, General Grant's staff. General Porter was later relieved from serving on the Military Commission.[13]

The replacements for Comstock and Porter were:

*Brevet Brigadier General James A. Ekin*—General Ekin signed Mrs. Surratt's plea for clemency.

*Brevet Colonel Charles H. Tompkins*—Colonel Tompkins signed Mrs. Surratt's plea for clemency.

By May 5, according to the *New York Times,* the conspiracy cases had been prepared under the direction of Colonel Burnett. The trial was expected to start no later than Saturday, May 7. The hearing would be *open* to the public.

On May 5, Mary Surratt was transferred from cell number 157 to cell number 200. On the same day, she requested that Fr. Francis E. Boyle of St. Peter's Church pay her a visit. She had eaten very little since her internment at the penitentiary on April 30.[14]

By now, Mary knew why she had been transferred to the Old Penitentiary. She was there to stand trial as one of the accomplices in the assassination of President Abraham Lincoln. As unbelievable, no doubt, as the accusations seemed, it still did not negate the fact that she needed legal counsel. She requested, through Colonel Burnett, that Richard T. Merrick and H. F. Zimmerman act in her defense. Both men were prestigious Catholic attorneys.[15]

In a letter to Colonel Burnett, Zimmerman refused the request, "I desire to say that my acquaintance with Mrs. Surratt is but a store acquaintance; our families never visited each other; and I therefore decline having anything to do with the matter."[16]

On the other hand, Richard Merrick wanted to defend Mrs. Surratt. According to one of Merrick's abbreviated biographies, we learn ". . . that he desired to be counsel for Mrs. Surratt, but was prevented by his father-in-law." Merrick's father-in-law was J.C. McGuire, one of the wealthiest men in Washington. He had high aspirations for his son-in-law to succeed in politics. Evidently, he felt that defending Mrs. Surratt would be detrimental to his son-in-law's future.[17]

On May 9, the prisoners were finally allowed to read the charges and specifications against them.[18] It was charged that Mary Surratt did ". . . on or before the 6th day of March, A.D. 1865, and on divers other days and times between that day and the 20th day of April, A.D.1865, receive, entertain, harbor, and conceal, aid and assist the said John Wilkes Booth, David E. Herold, Lewis Payne [sic], John H. Surratt, Michael O'Laughlin, George A. Atzerodt, Samuel Arnold, and their confederates, with the knowledge of the murderous and traitorous conspiracy aforesaid, and with intent to aid, abet, and assist them in the execution thereof, and in escaping from justice after the murder of the said Abraham Lincoln, as aforesaid."[19]

When Zimmerman and Merrick refused to defend Mary Surratt, she was able to enlist the help of Sen. Reverdy Johnson. He had been a member of the Maryland state senate and had served as attorney general under President Tyler. Reverdy Johnson was a Democrat and was presently serving as a U.S. senator. He had been influential in keeping Maryland in the Union. Senator Johnson had never met Mary Surratt, but he had read about her plight and "deemed it right" that she should not go without defense.[20] Associated with the senator in his law firm were Frederick Aiken and John W. Clampitt.

It was about this time that the stress and the insufferable living conditions caused Mary to have painful, menstrual problems. No doubt her anxiety over Anna, John, Isaac, and her mother, Bessie Jenkins, filled every waking hour. Where was Isaac? Certainly he had heard what had happened to his family. What must he think? She would have prayed that he was alive and well and would stay away from Washington. Certainly, John must do the same.

Until the trial began, her days and nights would have been spent either sitting or lying on a thin, straw-filled pallet that was spread on the cold floor of her cell. There was no relief from the agony that she felt in her back or in her churning uterus. It would have been dehumanizing for her to live without privacy, in plain view of the guards. When she began to spot and then hemorrhage, Mary probably wished that a gentle woman would be sent to sustain her.[21] It was humiliating that young men had to empty the blood-filled bucket and supply her with thick bandages. As if in answer to Mary's prayer, relief came in the name of Priscilla ("Kate") Dodd. Mrs. Dodd was the wife of Brig. Gen. Levi Axtell Dodd, a member of General Hartranft's prison staff. She would eventually become a good friend to both Mary and Anna.[22]

The penitentiary, including the grounds, covered nearly two acres. There were four tiers of cells, forty cells to a tier, totaling 160 cells in all.[23]

While Mary and the other prisoners waited to be tried, preparations were being made for the trial. The third floor, northeast corner of the penitentiary was selected for the courtroom. The room was fifty-five feet long by twenty feet wide. The eleven-foot ceiling was supported by three wooden posts standing along the center line of the room. There were four iron-barred windows on the north side of the room. Near the southwest corner was an iron-barred door that led to the prisoners' cells.[24]

The employees at the penitentiary had whitewashed and painted the courtroom. Even gas lighting had been installed. The prisoners' dock was constructed along the west wall. It was four feet wide and elevated a foot from the floor. A railing separated the prisoners from the rest of the courtroom. There was a door in the dock that allowed entry from the prison cell block. Mrs. Surratt would sit apart from the other prisoners.[25]

New tables and chairs were placed in the courtroom for the use of the Military Commission, recorders, reporters, and the counselors for the accused.[26]

On May 11, Anna Surratt and Honora Fitzpatrick were released from Old Capitol Prison, Carroll Annex.[27]

By ten o'clock in the morning of that same day, the courtroom was filled with spectators. The room grew quiet when the door behind the dock swung open. The prisoners shambled in and appeared dazed as they squinted around the courtroom. Their wrists were bound with heavy iron cuffs that were connected by a ten-inch-long bar. Their legs were weighted down with shackles joined by short chains that clanged and limited walking to a shuffle.[28]

All of the prisoners, with the exception of Mrs. Surratt and Dr. Mudd, were required to wear heavy, cotton-padded, helmet-like hoods while in their cells. The hoods were removed before the prisoners appeared in court.[29]

Six well-armed soldiers were interspersed among the seven male prisoners. Samuel Arnold, the young Baltimorean, appeared first and sat at the extreme right of the spectators. Following close behind with his guard was Dr. Samuel Mudd, followed by Edward ("Ned")

*The conspiracy trial. Mary Surratt is seated in front of the back wall, left corner. The male defendants and their guards are seated on the right. In front of the railing the military commission is on the right, reporters in the center, and spectators on the far left.* (Author's Collection)

Spangler (former employee of Ford's Theatre who allegedly had held Booth's horse when the actor dashed into the theater to shoot the president), then, a soldier; Michael O'Laughlin and a soldier; George Atzerodt and a soldier; and then, Lewis Powell sauntered in with his guard. Finally, David Herold, who looked like a frightened boy, entered the courtroom followed by his guard.[30]

The woman was the main attraction. When Mary appeared at the door, she swayed, straightened herself, then glanced fearfully around the room. With the help of a soldier, she shuffled a short distance then collapsed heavily in a chair near the door. Behind her densely veiled face and lowered eyes, she found sanctuary from the hateful looks and whispers of the onlookers.[31]

As it turned out, the trial was *not* open to the general public, as had been previously announced.[32] Brigadier General William E. Doster, defense attorney for George Atzerodt and Lewis Powell, said years later, that "the trial had been a contest on which a few lawyers were on one side and the whole United States on the other—a case in which the verdict was known beforehand."[33]

Mary Surratt's junior defense attorneys were an interesting pair. In time she would despair over their apparent inability to represent her.

*Frederick A. Aiken* was born in Boston, Massachusetts, in 1837. His loyalty to the United States during the war had only been sporadic.[34]

On April 5, 1861, Mr. Aiken had written a lengthy letter to Jefferson Davis offering his service to the "Southern Confederacy." He said that he wished to offer his pen to the cause rather than his blood. It is not known whether Aiken received the speedy reply to his letter that he had requested.[35]

Perhaps the Confederacy rebuffed Aiken's offer. In any case, he later became a volunteer aide, with the rank of captain, on Union general Winfield S. Hancock's staff. Aiken participated gallantly in several engagements. During one, he had two horses shot out from under him.

When he served as counsel to Mary Surratt, Aiken was an unseasoned attorney in his late twenties. Mrs. Surratt's trial was his first major case.[36] After the trial of the conspirators, Aiken would eventually serve on the Supreme Court of the United States. In 1877, he became city editor of the *Washington Post*.[37]

*John Wesley Clampitt* was in his mid-twenties when he assisted in the defense of Mary Surratt. As with Aiken, Mary Surratt's trial was Clampitt's first major case.[38] Clampitt was born in Washington, D.C., in 1839. During the war he served in the Union Company C, Washington Light Infantry.[39]

On May 12, Gen. T. M. Harris, a member of the commission, stunned everyone when he objected to Mary Surratt being represented by Sen. Reverdy Johnson. The general accused the senator of not recognizing the moral obligation of an oath as being used as a test for loyalty. Harris was referring to a previous letter that Senator Johnson had written in October 1864. In the letter, the senator had questioned the binding effect of the loyalty oath as a prerequisite to being allowed to vote in the state of Maryland, during the late war. When Senator Johnson became indignant that *his* loyalty had been questioned, General Harris withdrew his objection.[40]

As it turned out, Reverdy Johnson would only appear twice more during the course of the trial. Unfortunately, this turn of events left Mrs. Surratt to be defended by two unseasoned junior attorneys from Reverdy Johnson's law firm.

On May 12, under advisement of their counselors, the accused requested that they be allowed to withdraw their pleas of *not guilty* that had been previously filed. This was done so the defendants could plead to the jurisdiction of the commission. In other words, they were questioning the legality of civilians being tried by a military commission.[41]

According to the Constitution, civilians could be tried by a military court only when civil courts were not in session. Civil courts had been functioning in the District of Columbia, without interruption, during and since the end of the war.[42]

The U.S. attorney general, James Speed, answered the prisoners' request to be tried in civil court by saying the assassins had acted as "public enemies" of the United States and "ought to be tried before a military tribunal." He closed by saying that they might have disobeyed the laws of war—the accepted rules of conduct for belligerents—and therefore could not be tried before a civil court.[43] Speed's conclusion should have been challenged on the grounds that the Civil War, or the War Between the States, had never been declared formally by either side.

The attorney general's decision was an unfortunate one for the prisoners, since defendants in civil courts are considered innocent until proven guilty. Being tried by a military court placed the accused in the position of being presumed guilty and therefore called upon to prove their own innocence.[44]

Many years later, retired brigadier general William E. Doster, former provost marshal of the District of Columbia, and George Atzerodt's counsel at the trial, made the point, in 1915, that most of the evidence that had been acquired by the Bureau of Military Justice had been published prior to the trial. Consequently, Doster believed that the judges would have felt that the country expected the tribunal to find the prisoners guilty. It was merely left to the judges to determine the degrees of guilt and to impose the sentences.[45]

Being tried by a military court presented other serious obstacles for the accused. The prosecution had nearly a month to prepare its case. Naturally, the prosecutors used every investigative means at their disposal to make an impregnable case. On the other hand, the defendants did not receive their charges until the opening day of the trial! At that time Mary Surratt was the only prisoner who had counsel. When counselors were finally found for the other defendants, none of the attorneys had enough time to prepare their clients' cases. Furthermore, it was seldom allowed that the defendants and their attorneys could confer beyond the confines of the courtroom.[46]

Again, according to General Doster, ". . . the court not knowing anything about the rules of evidence, ruled out practically everything the Judge Advocate objected to and admitted everything the counsels opposed. Additionally, many of the witnesses for the Prosecution were detectives on government pay."[47]

After the assassination, statements, rumors, and reports flooded the War Department accusing the Southern government of having masterminded the conspiracy to kill President Lincoln and other high-ranking officials. By the second of May, President Andrew Johnson had issued a statement that "it appears from evidence in the Bureau of Military Justice that the atrocious murder of . . . Abraham Lincoln and the attempted assassination of William H. Seward . . . were incited, concerted, and procured by and between Jefferson Davis, late of Richmond, and Jacob Thompson, Clement C. Clay."[48]

At the trial on May 12, the first witness to be called for the prosecution was Henry Von Steinacker.

Von Steinacker had served as a Confederate engineer-officer in the Topographical Department on the staff of Gen. Edward Johnson.

Even though Von Steinacker did not witness the incident, he testified that Booth had attended a meeting of Confederate officers and members of the Second Virginia Infantry Regiment. Von Steinacker testified that a certain Lieutenant Cockrell had told him that the purpose of the meeting was to plan the assassination of President Lincoln.[49]

During the next couple of weeks, attorneys Clampitt and Aiken did some investigating on their own. When they had completed their investigation, Clampitt asked that Von Steinacker be recalled. With Von Steinacker on the stand, Clampitt informed the court that he had found proof that the witness had, at one time, served as a Union soldier and had been arrested when he attempted to desert. For this malfeasance Von Steinacker had been given the death sentence, but managed to escape before he was executed. After his escape, Von Steinacker joined the Confederate Army, serving under Gen. Edward Johnson. Again, Von Steinacker managed to get into trouble. He was convicted for theft and the abuse of Union prisoners. Once again, he escaped before he was punished.[50]

When Clampitt completed his denouncement of Von Steinacker, Gen. Lew Wallace announced before the court that he held the defense attorney's efforts "in supreme contempt."[51]

Later Gen. Joseph Holt, the judge advocate, stated that he would be happy to return Von Steinacker to the witness stand, if the man *could be found.* As it turned out, the man could *not* be found! Von Steinacker had disappeared! It appears that a deal had been struck with the malfeasant. Von Steinacker had been serving a three-year sentence in Federal prison up until the time that he testified, indicting the South in the assassination of President Lincoln. After he had rendered his testimony, he was immediately released from serving the remainder of his sentence![52]

Richard Montgomery, a professed double agent for the Confederacy in Canada and the United States, testified on May 12. He said that Confederate agent Jacob Thompson had told him that there were plans afoot "to rid the world of such tyrants as Lincoln, Stanton, Grant, and others." Montgomery was told that John Wilkes Booth and Lewis Powell were both parties in the scheme. Thompson added that he had been offered an opportunity to collaborate in the undertaking, but claimed to have delayed his answer until he could confer with the government in Richmond.[53] After the conspiracy trial had ended, it was found that Richard Montgomery and Jacob Thompson were one and the same man! Montgomery was discredited even further when it was learned that he had a long criminal record in New York. He was no more than a common thief![54]

The following day, May 13, Judge Holt announced that, henceforth, the court would be *open* to the press. *The New York World* of May 15 applauded the decision, but deplored the overall judgment that refused to try the defendants in civil court.

On that same day, May 13, James B. Merritt, a Canadian physician, testified that he knew of a similar plot to kill President Lincoln. He named Booth, Surratt, and Atzerodt as being parties in the scheme. It wasn't until after the trial and after the executions that it was learned that *the United States Government had paid Merritt six thousand dollars to lie at the conspiracy trial!*[55]

On May 20, Sanford Conover testified for the prosecution. He attested that he had been conscripted into the Rebel service and claimed to have run the blockade from Richmond to Canada. While in Canada, he had become intimately acquainted with several important Confederates. He claimed that when John Surratt brought certain dispatches from Richmond, James Thompson had laid his hands on them and exclaimed, "This makes the thing all right," referring to the assent of the Confederate government to assassinate President Lincoln, Vice President Johnson, the secretary of war, the secretary of state, Judge Samuel Chase, and General Grant. Then Thompson added, according to Conover, that the United States government would be left entirely without a head.[56]

As it turned out, Sanford Conover's actual name was Charles A. Dunham. His testimony had been a complete fabrication! Oddly, he was convicted for perjury and sentenced to ten years in a Federal prison. Yet, James Merritt had received six thousand dollars from the United States government for the same offense.[57]

Nevertheless, it was chiefly the testimony of these unscrupulous men (one of whom was in the pay of an equally unscrupulous government) that the Bureau of Military Justice had built its case against the Confederacy.

Meanwhile, in Montreal, John Surratt was beside himself worrying about his mother. A friend and emissary of John's arrived in Washington from Canada and clandestinely met with Mary Surratt's counsels. Surratt wanted Clampitt and Aiken to know that he was ready to give himself up, provided that his mother would be released. The counsels advised that John Surratt remain in Canada. They were sure that Mrs. Surratt would never be convicted.[58]

Louis Weichmann was called to the witness stand to testify for the prosecution on May 13.[59] Mary probably welcomed his familiar face in the hostile atmosphere that surrounded her. Perhaps she closed her eyes when she listened to Lou's familiar lisp as he talked about happier times. He narrated how he had met John Surratt at St. Charles College. Then, Lou spoke about living at the boardinghouse. As he talked, events of the past probably flashed through Mary's mind like pages in a book. Yet, Weichmann testified to some events that seemed inconsequential, while other events, Mary knew nothing about. For example, she didn't know that Booth had paid for the horse and carriage that she and Lou had used to go to Surrattsville on April 11.

Weichmann testified that Mrs. Slater and John carried messages back and forth between Richmond and Canada. Unlawful, yes, but both sides were guilty of having a quasi-citizen mail service. What other choice was there after Lincoln had discontinued the United States mail service to the South? Besides, carrying the mail was a far cry from assassinating a president.

Weichmann rambled on about Powell's many names and disguises. Lou mentioned the mustache that he had found in his room that had belonged to the one-time boarder. While she listened, Mary probably wondered what the mustache had to do with Powell's attack on Secretary Seward.

Then Weichmann told about Booth's visits to the boardinghouse. If Mary believed that John was helping Booth with the actor's cotton and oil holdings, she would have seen nothing unusual with Booth's visits to the boardinghouse. Yes, it was true that Wilkes had called when John wasn't there. It was no secret that the young actor liked to visit. He probably preferred the warmth of a real home to the impersonal hotel surroundings where he stayed. Then Lou testified that she and Wilkes had had private conversations. Yes, there were a few innocent conversations between them. Why not? Was he suggesting that she was in league with Booth to kill the president? Mary possibly thought these things as she listened to her former friend testify against her.

At times, the noise in the courtroom made hearing difficult. When she leaned forward to listen, she probably cringed when Lou testified about finding John and Lewis Powell "playing" in the attic with two Bowie knives, some guns, and spurs. Hadn't she allayed Lou's suspicions when he had come to her and complained about what they were doing? He had seemed satisfied, at the time, with her explanation that John needed the protection when he traveled in the country. Why was Lou putting a different connotation on such innocent activity, she may have wondered.

Undoubtedly, Mary was appalled when Lou claimed that "Port Tobacco" (Atzerodt) had visited John ten or twelve times. On the contrary, it was Lou and Port Tobacco who had become close. They often left the house together.

Mary may have noticed an inconsistency in Weichmann's testimony concerning their trip to the country on April 14. She had told him that she had received a letter from George Calvert demanding the money that she owed him. Yet, Lou denied at first that she had told him about the letter. Then when he was reasked two questions later, he admitted she had told him about the Calvert letter, after all.

At least, Lou's next statement would probably have been more gratifying to Mary. He testified that she was exemplary and ladylike in every particular and that she attended church regularly.

When the prosecution had concluded questioning Lou Weichmann, handsome Gen. Thomas Ewing, defense attorney for Dr. Mudd, confronted the young man. Ewing was respected for being the brother-in-law of Gen. William Tecumseh Sherman.[60] Ewing's questions related to the evening that Dr. Mudd introduced John Surratt to John Wilkes Booth. He was particularly interested in their meeting in Booth's room at the National Hotel and their later meeting that same night, at the Pennsylvania House, where Dr. Mudd was staying. Weichmann testified that Booth had drawn lines on an envelope while John Surratt and Dr. Mudd looked on. He didn't bother to mention that Booth had claimed to have gotten lost while in Prince George's County. It seems reasonable, then, that Booth used the envelope in order to draw the roads so John could show the actor how he had gotten lost. Weichmann's testimony made the mere act of drawing some lines on an envelope seem very sinister. No question that Booth ended up with a better map, albeit innocently improved by John Surratt. With Dr.

Mudd's warning in mind, John probably thought that he was helping a government man. Then Weichmann testified that Booth and Mudd had a private conversation in the hall outside of Booth's room. When they returned to the room, John Surratt followed them back to the hall. When the four men left the National Hotel, they went to the Pennsylvania House. There, according to Weichmann, John Surratt and John Wilkes Booth talked privately, while he (Weichmann) and Dr. Mudd sat in innocent conversation.[61]

Louis Weichmann testified that the date that Dr. Mudd introduced John Surratt to John Wilkes Booth was January 15, 1865. That date appears both in the Pitman and Poore transcripts of the trial.[62]

Weichmann's testimony under John Clampitt's cross examination was uneventful. However, under Frederick Aiken's examination, Weichmann admitted that, while in Surrattsville on April 14, he had written the note for Mrs. Surratt to have delivered to John Nothey. It was in that note that she demanded payment of the money that Nothey owed her or she would bring suit against him. She needed the money in order to satisfy her indebtedness to George Calvert.[63] This was *the* only purpose of Mary Surratt's visit to Surrattsville on the day of the night that John Wilkes Booth shot the president. It was not to take a message to Lloyd from Booth to have shooting irons and whiskey ready, or to deliver Booth's field glasses. Earlier, in his testimony, Weichmann failed to mention that he had written the note to Nothey.

Retired brigadier general William E. Doster, former provost marshal of the District of Columbia, was the defense attorney for George Atzerodt. Consequently, he was only interested in asking Weichmann questions relative to his client's case.

Weichmann's lengthy testimony, for the prosecution, ended with questions from Judge Advocate Holt. Nothing new was brought to light.

The next witness, on May 13, who had a direct bearing on Mary Surratt's case, was John Lloyd. When he was called to the witness stand, Frederick Aiken applied to the commission for a postponement of Lloyd's examination until Monday, May 15. At that time, Reverdy Johnson, the senior counselor, would be present. Aiken pointed out that "the testimony of the witness now called would be of the gravest importance affecting Mary E. Surratt." The commission overruled the application since two of Mrs. Surratt's counselors were present.[64]

John Lloyd appeared on the witness stand that afternoon. Assistant Judge Advocate John Bingham interrogated for the prosecution. He gave no quarter. Under the grueling interrogation, Lloyd testified that John Surratt and David Herold had gone to the Surratt House and Tavern to hide two carbines, ammunition, rope, and a monkey wrench. Lloyd admitted that under his protestations he had hidden the articles between the floor joists above the dining room. This was the place where John Surratt had directed that they be hidden.

Lloyd testified about meeting Mrs. Surratt in Uniontown on April 11. He said that he was positive that she had told him to have shooting irons ready, that someone would be calling for them in a few days. Then, in almost the next breath, he added that he was "not altogether positive" whether she had mentioned the shooting irons, or not.[65]

The questions that followed dealt with Mary's visit to Surrattsville on April 14. Again, Lloyd implicated her concerning firearms. He said that she had told him to have "those shooting irons ready that night— there would be some parties call for them." Then Lloyd proceeded with his testimony by saying that she had handed him something wrapped in a piece of paper and that he later found out the package contained field glasses. (That was the package that Booth had asked Mary Surratt to deliver to John Lloyd.) Again, according to Lloyd's testimony, he claimed that Mrs. Surratt also instructed him to have two bottles of whiskey ready for the parties who came for them that night. When Lloyd was asked if the items Mrs. Surratt referred to were called for that night by Booth and Herold. He said that they were.[66] Bingham had asked the right question. The trap had been sprung, and Mrs. Surratt was well within.

Lou Weichmann had been with Mrs. Surratt the entire time that she was in Surrattsville on April 14. He had even written the note to Nothey for her, demanding that the man settle what he owed her. Certainly her real mission to Surrattsville would have been obvious to Weichmann and should have been obvious to the court. According to Mrs. Surratt, when she was questioned by Colonel Olcott at Old Capitol Prison on April 28, she had said nothing to Lloyd about shooting irons. When Lloyd had returned from Marlboro on April 14, she and Lou had met him behind the wood pile, in back of the house. They had left Joseph T. Knott to repair the buggy. Lloyd, in a drunken condition, was unloading fish and oysters and asked them to stay for dinner. After declining, they returned to Washington.[67]

She did not wait for Lloyd's return to give him Booth's package or to tell him to have whiskey and shooting irons ready for men who would call for them that night. Had she been intrusted with such an important message, she would have wanted to deliver it to Lloyd herself. It was the broken buggy that detained her. She was sitting in it and ready to go when Bennett Gwynn noticed that the buggy was broken and needed repair.

Lloyd concluded his testimony for the prosecution when he admitted that, when Booth and Herold were about to leave the Surratt House and Tavern after the president had been shot, Booth had said to Lloyd, "Well, I am pretty certain that we have assassinated the President and Secretary Seward."[68]

At the very time that John Lloyd was being examined, Judge Holt was holding, in his possession, a letter dated May 9, from Maj. A. C. Richards, superintendent of the Metropolitan Police. In the letter Richards stated ". . . that when detective Clarvoe, of my force, called at the tavern kept by Lloyd on Saturday morning after the murder, and interrogated him as to whether Booth or any other party had passed that way the night before, he denied all knowledge of their having passed, and called God to witness the truth of the assertion." It was later learned that Judge Holt had kept the information in the letter secret from the Military Commission![69]

# CHAPTER EIGHTEEN

# *The Trial Continues*

Every day, except Sundays, the Military Commission met at ten o'clock in the morning, adjourned around noon for lunch, then returned, and sat until six o'clock in the evening, when it was adjourned for the day.[1]

According to Brig. Gen. John F. Hartranft's ledger, twice a day, usually at seven o'clock in the morning and again at noon, either the general or Dr. George L. Porter, the prison physician, visited the inmates. Both men were kind to Mary and appeared concerned over her health. Each day, General Hartranft sent a report in the form of a letter to his superior, Maj. Gen. W. S. Hancock.

General William Harrison McCall was another who was concerned about Mary Surratt's well-being. The general was only in his twenties when he was placed in charge of the prisoners.[2] In time, Mary and the fine-looking young general became very fond of each other.

However, it was Kate Dodd who, being a woman, was in the position to do the most for Mary Surratt. Being, obviously, a kind and sensitive woman, she took care of Mary's most intimate needs. It wasn't until Wednesday, May 17, that the next witness was called to the stand who

*General William H. H. McCall befriended Mary Surratt at the Old Arsenal Penitentiary.* (Author's Collection)

had a direct bearing on Mary Surratt's case. For two days Mary had sat in the courtroom and listened to the constant drone of the witnesses. Conceivably, her mind snapped to attention when the name of Emma Offutt, John Lloyd's sister-in-law, was called. Perhaps, for Mary, a ray of hope came when the woman took the stand. Mrs. Offutt would tell the court that Mary had given Booth's package to her and not to John Lloyd. Furthermore, Mrs. Offutt would testify to the real nature of Mary's visit to Surrattsville on April 14.

If Mary had entertained such hopes, they were soon dashed when Mrs. Offutt denied knowing what Mary's business was in Surrattsville. She denied that Mary had given her the package from Booth. When Frederick Aiken asked if Mrs. Offutt had heard any reference made to "shooting irons," Judge Bingham objected.[3]

At one time, Emma Offutt had been deeply involved in a prior scheme to abduct President Lincoln. Whether this was the same abduction plot that Booth was involved in is not known. The objective of that abduction was to hold the president for ransom in order to bring the war to an end. It had been rumored that John Lloyd had served as Emma Offutt's replacement in that same conspiracy.[4]

The following day, May 18, Louis Weichmann was recalled to the stand by the prosecution. He described the March 4 episode when John Surratt had dashed into the bedroom the two men shared at the boardinghouse. John was very upset and waved a Sharps revolver around and yelled that he would shoot anyone who came into the room. Then John added that his prospects were gone. He asked Lou to find him a clerkship. Then Powell, seemingly undaunted, entered the bedroom. Ten minutes later, Booth dashed in with a whip in his hand and began to pace the floor. According to Weichmann, when Booth noticed that Weichmann was present, the three men adjourned to the attic to talk.[5] This had happened on March 17, when Booth and his men planned to abduct President Lincoln at the Campbell Hospital. At that time, the president was supposed to attend the play, *Still Waters Run Deep*. Booth went into a rage when he learned that the president did not attend the production.

Under Reverdy Johnson's cross-examination, Lou Weichmann's testimony concerned the day of April 11. This is when Weichmann first took Mary Surratt to Surrattsville for the purpose of seeing John Nothey about the money that he owed her. Near Uniontown, Mary and Lou inadvertently met John Lloyd and Mrs. Offutt. Weichmann testified that there was nothing mentioned about shooting irons at that meeting. He said that Mrs. Surratt spoke to Mrs. Offutt about Gus Howell. Mrs. Surratt said that she was going to go and see him and ask him to take the Oath of Allegiance so he could be released. Furthermore, she said that she was going to see General Augur and Judge Turner "for that purpose." Judge Advocate Holt questioned Weichmann next. The judge reminded Weichmann that he had previously testified that he did not hear the conversation between Lloyd and Mrs. Surratt. Weichmann agreed that he had not heard the conversation between Lloyd and Mrs. Surratt, after all.[6]

Then Aiken returned and questioned Weichmann about Mrs. Slater. What Weichmann related about the woman was basically correct.[7]

On the other hand, Weichmann's testimony concerning Augustus Spencer Howell was sinister by insinuation. He said that Howell used the name of Spencer while he was at the boardinghouse. He said that "they" refused to tell him Spencer's correct name. Later, John Surratt told Weichmann that Spencer's name was Augustus Howell. But in the house, Howell was to be referred to by his nickname, Spencer.[8] In reality, Augustus Howell's legal name was Augustus Spencer Howell. Years later, when Weichmann wrote his book, he referred to this incident and made the point that Howell was using the name of *Mr. Spencer*.[9] In his testimony Weichmann minimized his relationship with Augustus Howell. He did, however, admit that he had mentioned to Howell that he wanted to go to Richmond to continue his studies for the priesthood.[10] This was a curious remark for Weichmann to make, in light of the fact that he had been accepted to continue his studies on September 1, 1865, at St. Mary's Seminary in Baltimore, Maryland.[11] But, of course, Weichmann failed to testify that he had told Gus Howell that he (Weichmann) was a Southern man. Nor, did he testify that he had given Gus Howell United States government classified information on the number of Southern soldiers held in U.S. prisons! Naturally, Weichmann did not testify that he had told Howell that he wanted to go to Richmond with him.

When Frederick Aiken had temporarily finished his cross-examination of Lewis Weichmann, John Wesley Clampitt cross-examined the man. He wanted to know from Weichmann why he had a "greater desire to continue your studies in Richmond than the North?" Judge

Advocate Bingham objected to the question. He declared that Clampitt "was attempting to get to the interior motive of the witness, which you can not do, unless you can obtain the power of omnipotence." Needless to say, the question was waived.[12] Too bad!

However, no one objected to Weichmann testifying that he had considered telling Captain Gleason, a clerk in Weichmann's office: "There is a blockade-runner at Mrs. Surratt's; shall I have him delivered up?" Then, Weichmann said that he doubted that Howell would return to the boardinghouse and wished him to go in "God's name."

Here we will deviate from sequential testimonies and advance to May 27. On that day, Augustus Spencer Howell testified for the defense. He established that he had known Mrs. Surratt and her son for about a year and a half. He said that he had first become acquainted with them in Surrattsville. After that fact had been established, the defense moved to the time when Howell stayed at the boardinghouse while he waited for the courier, Sarah Slater, to return from Canada. He claimed that he stayed at the boardinghouse because it was cheaper than staying at a hotel. He said that he met Louis Weichmann during that stay. When Howell was shown the cipher that had been found among Booth's effects, Howell said that it was the one that he had shown (given?) to Weichmann. The following questions and answers are interesting, even though they do not relate to the cipher:

> Q. Did Mr. Weichmann at that time give you any information in regard to the number of prisoners that we had on hand?

> *Assistant Judge Advocate Bingham objected to the question* [author's emphasis] inasmuch as Mr. Weichman [*sic*] had not previously been questioned in relation to that matter in cross examination. The question was waived.

> I had some conversation with Mr. Weichman [*sic*] with respect to his going South; he said he would like to go South, or intended to go South.

> Q. Did he say any thing in connection with his wishes to go South, of his sympathies?

*Assistant Judge Advocate Bingham objected to the question,*[author's emphasis] inasmuch as Mr. Weichman [*sic*] had not been asked, in cross examination, whether he had stated any thing to Mr. Howell about his sympathies at that time and place. [Author's note follows. As a matter of fact, on May 18, John Wesley Clampitt asked Louis Weichmann, "Why had you a greater desire to continue your studies in Richmond than in the North?" Judge Bingham, himself, objected to the question, by saying the question was an attempt "to get at the interior motive of the witness."] The question was waived.

Mr. Weichmann said he would like to go South with me [Howell], but he was not ready, he said, to go at that time: but as soon as he got his business arranged he was going. He asked me if I thought he could get a position in Richmond; I told him I did not know whether he could or not, as the wounded and invalid soldiers generally had the preference in the offices there by an order of the War Department. *He told me that his sympathies were with the South, and that he thought it would ultimately succeed* [author's emphasis]. I believe he said he had done all he could for that Government—referring to the South. *We had some conversation in regard to the number of prisoners on hand, and he stated to me the number of Confederate prisoners the United States Government* [author's emphasis], had and the number they had over that of the Confederate Government. I doubted it at the time, but he said it would not admit of doubt; that he had the books in his own office to look at.[13]

Certainly, the veracity of Louis Weichmann as a witness for the prosecution, once again, had to be questioned.

On May 19, several witnesses for the prosecution were called to the witness stand. One of these was former captain Richard C. Morgan. Morgan was employed by the War Department under the command of Col. H. S. Olcott. It was Colonel Olcott who had questioned Mary Surratt on April 28 at Old Capitol Prison. Captain Richard Morgan was second in command of the search party and the arrest of Mrs. Surratt and the others on April 17. However, both men claimed to be in charge of the operation.

Morgan testified that he arrived at the boardinghouse at half-past-eleven that night. He said that when he arrived he found Major Smith and Captain Wermerskirch, and some other officers who had preceded him by ten minutes. Mrs. Surratt and the others were in the parlor. He said that after he had sent for a carriage to take the women to headquarters and while they waited for the carriage, someone knocked then rang the doorbell. Morgan said that he and Wermerskirch opened the door. Before them stood the prisoner Powell. He came in the house with a pickaxe over his shoulder, dressed in a gray coat, gray vest, black pants, and a hat made from a sleeve of a shirt. When Morgan closed the door. Powell said, "I guess I am mistaken." When Powell was asked who he wanted to see, he said Mrs. Surratt. Morgan told him he had the right place. Then Morgan asked why he had come. He said that he had come to dig a gutter, that Mrs. Surratt had sent for him. He told them that he was supposed to dig the gutter in the morning. Then Morgan asked him where he last worked and where he boarded. Powell answered that he had no boardinghouse, and that he was a poor man who lived by the pick. When Morgan asked Powell why he had come at that hour of the night, Powell answered that he had come to find out what time he should start work in the morning. He said that he had had no previous acquaintance with Mrs. Surratt. Morgan told Powell that he would have to go to the provost marshal's office.[14]

Morgan continued his testimony by saying that the following morning when he had returned to the boardinghouse, he had found the carte-de-visite pictures of Jefferson Davis, Pierre G. T. Beauregard, and Alexander H. Stephens. Morgan added that Lieutenant Dempsey, the officer in charge, had found the picture of John Wilkes Booth behind another picture (Anna's picture titled *Morning, Noon, and Night*). A card with the "arms of the State of Virginia" was also found. Two Confederate flags were emblazoned on the card with the inscription, "Thus will it ever be with tyrants, Virginia the Mighty. Sic Semper Tyrannis."[15] The last three words were the very words that Booth had shouted immediately after shooting President Lincoln. It would have been negligent of Morgan not to have mentioned finding the card as an attempt to prove that Booth's ideology was the same as that of the Surratts. Of course, Morgan didn't mention that Anna's photographs of Union generals Grant, Hooker, and McClellan were also found in the Surratt H Street boardinghouse.

Next Maj. H. W. Smith was called for the prosecution. He had been in charge of the party that took possession of Mrs. Surratt's home and had arrested Mrs. Surratt, Miss Surratt, Miss Fitzpatrick, and Miss Jenkins. He testified that when he arrived at the house, he rang the bell. Mrs. Surratt came to the window and asked if he was Mr. Kirby. He told her that he wasn't Mr. Kirby, and told her to open the door. After she admitted being John Surratt's mother, Smith said that he announced that he had come to arrest her and all in the house in order to take them to General Augur's headquarters for examination. After Lewis Powell arrived at the door, Major Smith went to the parlor and asked Mrs. Surratt to follow him into the hall. There he asked her if she knew the man who had just arrived and if she had hired him to come and dig a gutter. She raised her right hand and declared that "before God" she did not know the man, neither had she seen him before, nor had she hired him to dig a gutter. At that point, Powell was taken from the court and dressed in similar clothing that he had worn on the night of April 17. When he was brought back into the courtroom, Major Smith was asked if he would have recognized Powell that night, if the last time he had seen him, Powell was dressed as a preacher. By the benefit of daylight, and, no doubt, possessing much better eyesight than Mrs. Surratt, Major Smith said that he would have recognized Lewis Powell.[16]

Captain W. M. Wermerskirch, another officer who was at the boardinghouse on April 17, was called to the stand. He substantiated what Major Smith had testified. Mrs. Surratt had sworn that she did not know the man who had come to the boardinghouse to dig a gutter. Then Captain Wermerskirch was asked to look at Powell and indicate whether he would have recognized him the night of the seventeenth if the last time he had seen him, Powell had been dressed as minister. Wermerskirch answered that he *thought* that he would have recognized Powell. The rest of the testimony concerned the photographs that had been found at Mary Surratt's boardinghouse.[17]

On May 22, Honora Fitzpatrick appeared as a surprise witness for the prosecution. Honora's testimony was very short. She merely said that she had seen John Wilkes Booth, John Surratt, Mr. Wood (Lewis Powell), and George Atzerodt at the boardinghouse in March. She added that she had never seen David Herold there. Concerning her visit to Ford's Theatre with John Surratt, Lewis Powell, and Miss Dean, she said that she did not know what box they had sat in that night. Yes, John Wilkes Booth did come into the box while they were there.[18]

After court was adjourned on May 22, it recessed until Thursday,

May 25, so members of the court could attend the Grand Review of the Armies of the Republic.

The *Washington Chronicle,* May 23, described the following scene of the preceding day:

> Weary indifference and listless, dreamy drowsiness continue to characterize the male prisoners from Herold to Atzerodt, but a great change has come over Mrs. Surratt. For the first time we read unmistakable letters upon her still features, the record of an ineffable woe. It is not fear, it is not excitement of a mighty doubt, but withering, blasting woe. She occupies her old corner, her right cheek resting upon her right hand, her eyes closed, but now and then she raises her hand to smooth back the parting hair on her forehead, her full face meets the eye.
>
> On that face, whatever apocalyptic sign may have evoked it, certain it is that [the past] thirty-odd hours had been sufficient to paint upon that face a haunting revelation of some horrifying scene. Either from within or without, during the murky hours of the past Sabbath, there has flashed upon that woman some awful vision, either of future woes or some new-lighted memory of past testimony.[19]

When the Military Commission reconvened on May 25, the trial of the conspirators suddenly changed tone to a war crimes court indicting the Southern government for the treatment of Northern soldiers interned in Southern prisons. Such stratagem would not have been allowed in a civil court. If this chicanery was meant to enrage the court, it was successful. The incendiary effect was unmistakable in the hate and rage visible in the smoldering eyes of the spectators. From time to time they swore aloud as they listened to the accusations from the prosecution. The drama that took place in the arena of the courtroom did not go unnoticed by the members of the press. They, in turn, ignited the pages of their newspapers and nurtured the public's hatred for the South in general and the alleged conspirators in particular.

As the prisoners listened to the tirades of the prosecution and witnessed the dangerously hostile atmosphere around them, they undoubtedly grasped the hopelessness of their situation.

*Mary Surratt's rosary. It has been alleged that this is the rosary that Mary Surratt had while in prison. It has since disappeared.* (Courtesy of John Brennan)

As the testimonies continued concerning the maltreatment of the Union soldiers in Southern prisons, Mary Surratt may have relived the dreadful scene when Catherine Virginia Baxley's son had died in Mary's arms. For the want of a bit of decent food, in the land of comparative plenty, a mother's son had died.

The Confederate government had pleaded for a prisoner exchange, since they could no longer feed themselves much less their prisoners.

In August 1864, when the Confederacy offered a man-for-man prisoner of war exchange, General Grant was against it. He said that an exchange of prisoners would be of more benefit to the Confederacy than to the Union. "It is hard," he wrote, "on our men held in Southern prisons not to exchange them, but it is humanity to those left in the ranks to fight our battles. Because every Confederate who is exchanged becomes an active soldier against us at once."[20] General Grant by his own admission knew how hard the Southern prisons were on his men. Yet, he refused a prisoner exchange. He certainly should have known that most of the Confederate soldiers in Northern prisons were physically unable to return to battle.

It could have been on this day that Mrs. Jane Swisshelm, special correspondent of *The Pittsburgh Daily Commercial*, attended the trial of the alleged conspirators. As an eyewitness, she described the following graphic scene of Mary Surratt:

Her face, and indeed her whole figure, while on trial, was soft, rounded, tender and motherly. Her large gray eyes alone gave indication of reserved strength. Her behavior, during that long and terrible ordeal, was full of delicacy and dignity. She made no scenes, as a weak or vain woman would have done. All the long, hot days, she sat with her heavy mourning veil down, and a large palm-leaf fan held between her face and the crowds who gathered and crushed and struggled to gaze at her, as if she had been an alligator—hundreds of persons in these crowds making the most insulting remarks in her hearing.

You readers are no doubt familiar with the form of the courtroom, and know that her position was in the southwest corner facing the east, and that a door leads in from the anti-room on the south, about four feet from the railing behind which she sat. On my one visit I had a chair close to the wall behind this door and the railing, so that I was within less than two feet of the rail, with orders to keep that space clear but the press at the door for entrance was so great that I gradually moved my chair until it was close to the rail and I stayed there an hour before being discovered. During all that time she leaned her head wearily, against the wall by changing hands kept her hands steadily before her face and every few minutes a low, stifled moan escaped her. Men and women stood tiptoe, and stretched and strained, or having gained entrance, stood coolly and made such remarks as, "Where's Mrs. Surratt?" "I want to see her." "Oh, goodness, just look if she isn't pretending to be modest!" "I wish I could see her better!" "Isn't she a devil?" "She looks like a devil!" "Hasn't she a horrid face?" "I hope they'll hang her—tee, hee, hee!" All these remarks and more such, some of them again and again, and often accompanied by course [*sic*] laughter, I heard during the two hours and a half I sat near her, and she must have heard them as distinctly as I did. They were evidently meant for her.

It appeared to me so cruel and cowardly thus to insult a prisoner in chains that I could not refrain from answering, and several times say: "She has not a bad face. She has a good face, and if she had not, it is cowardly to insult her."

She dropped her fan and looked at me with such an expression of gratitude as I shall never forget. I looked full into her eyes; mine were not dry, while her's [sic] filled with heavy tears. Several asked me if "I was a friend of Mrs. Surratt," so strange did any pity for her appear.

Once she arose in an effort to touch her counsel with her fan as he passed out of the door. I asked her if she wished to speak to him, and on the offering to have him called, she thanked me in a low, sad, sweet, tone. I became a suspicious character and an officer came and planted himself between us to see that there was no communication. I afterwards applied to the authorities for leave to visit her but it could not be granted. Perhaps it was best she should be thus isolated from human sympathy, but I thought and still think it a grave mistake.[21]

On May 20, Mrs. Swisshelm wrote Maj. Gen. David Hunter of the Military Commission. Below is an excerpt from that letter:

Will you pardon me for saying that there might be a velvet glove drawn over that iron hand. Nothing should be done to lesson [sic] the public horror of the crime, and everything like vindictiveness will, in time, awaken sympathy. It is common to allow women, on trial for murder to be accompanied in the dock by one of her own sex. Would this gentleness to Mrs. Surratt defeat the ends of Justice? Of course you could not let any of her personal friends have an opportunity of carrying to her the means of self destruction; but could you not trust me to go with her when sentence is to be passed and to visit her in prison and carry her a few blades of grass to recall the green fields in the days of innocence and childhood?[22]

# CHAPTER NINETEEN

# *A Ray of Hope*

Thursday, May 25, 1865, was a dreary day with intermittent showers. The temperature was a comfortable seventy-six degrees.[1] The court had reassembled after its brief recess for the celebration of the Grand Army of the Republic. May 25 marked the day that the witnesses for the defense began their testimonies.

Frederick Aiken called Honora Fitzpatrick to the stand.

When she was asked, Honora testified that she and Anna had each purchased a picture of John Wilkes Booth. She said that she didn't know until the trial that Anna had concealed her photograph behind the picture of *Morning, Noon, and Night.*

Honora continued by saying that the last time she had seen John Wilkes Booth was on Monday, April 10. John Surratt had left a fortnight before.

Honora verified that Mrs. Surratt's eyesight was very bad. She declared that Mrs. Surratt had actually passed her friend, Mrs. Kirby, on the street without recognizing her.

When Defense Counsel Aiken completed his questions, Judge Advocate Henry L. Burnett strode to the stand. When he asked her, Honora assured him that the pictures of Stephens, Beauregard, and

171

Davis did not belong to her. He seemed satisfied with her answer and returned to his seat.

Then, Frederick Aiken returned to question Honora. She testified that she did not recognize Powell when he came to the boardinghouse on April 17. She said that she didn't recognize the man until his skull cap was removed at General Auger's headquarters. She reiterated that Mrs. Surratt's eyesight was defective and that she had often threaded a needle for her when she was sewing during the day. She added that Mrs. Surratt never sewed or read by gaslight. Then Honora acknowledged that Anna Surratt had "given away to her feelings" when a soldier suggested that Powell was her brother. Honora added that, on the night of the arrest, at the boardinghouse, she did not remember if Mrs. Surratt had been asked to identify Lewis Powell or not.

When Aiken finished questioning Honora, Assistant Judge Advocate Burnett cross-examined the witness, but revealed nothing new.[2]

Eliza Holohan was called the same day to testify for the defense. Once again Frederick Aiken did the questioning.

Mrs. Holohan said that she had only seen Powell at the boardinghouse twice. The first time she saw him was in February when he had spent the night. The second time, perhaps the middle of March, he had spent two or three days there. Mrs. Holohan testified that Anna Surratt had told her that his name was Mr. Wood and that he was a Baptist minister. This was incorrect. Powell was using the name Paine when he posed as a Baptist minister.

Concerning George Atzerodt, Mrs. Holohan said that he was known as "Port Tobacco" at the house. She said that she had seen the man come at different times and that he had dined once or twice. She said that Mrs. Surratt had objected to the man boarding there.

Mrs. Holohan added that she had never heard Mrs. Surratt say anything in reference to a conspiracy to assassinate the president.

Assistant Judge Advocate Bingham severely objected to the last question after the answer above had been given. He said, "The law hedges about this matter of crime that those who are charged with it are never permitted to prove their own declaration in their own favor," adding that, "an abundant amount of testimony out of the mouth of the most truthful, could be made in behalf of the accused."

After Aiken's unsuccessful rejoinder, the court waived Aiken's question.

Mrs. Holohan confirmed that Mrs. Surratt's eyesight was "defective." She added that she had accompanied Mrs. Surratt to church during the Lenten season and that "she [Mrs. Surratt] was very constant in her religious duties."

Lastly, Mrs. Holohan testified that she had not seen John Surratt since early March. There was no cross-examination.[3]

The Reverend Father Bernardine Wiget was called to the stand. Again Frederick Aiken did the questioning.

The priest testified that he had known Mrs. Surratt for ten or eleven years. He said that he knew her well and had heard everyone speak highly of her character as a Christian lady. He could not testify as to her loyalty since they had never discussed political matters.[4]

The Reverend Father Francis E. Boyle took the witness stand and testified that Mrs. Surratt was a fine Christian. He had never heard her utter a disloyal sentiment.[5]

Then the Reverend Father Charles Stonestreet testified. He said that he had known Mrs. Surratt for twenty years. He remembered her as being "a proper Christian matron." He had scarcely seen her in the last year or two. He concluded by saying that, at the time of his acquaintance with her, there was no question as to the woman's loyalty.[6]

Probably, by the time Reverend Stonestreet had finished his testimony, Mrs. Surratt no longer felt deserted by her Church. Even though she had requested spiritual support, to date she had received none.

Possibly past memories surfaced when she saw Father Stonestreet. Had it been twenty years since he had gone to Mrs. Neale's bedside and baptized the dying woman? The priest had even baptized two of Zadoc's daughters.

On May 25, George Calvert took the stand for the defense on behalf of Mary Surratt. He verified sending her the letter that he had written on April 12, concerning the money that she owed him. As it turned out the "Government" had the letter, consequently, the remainder of George Calvert's testimony had to be postponed until the letter was produced.[7]

When the letter was brought to court the following day, May 26, George Calvert identified it as the letter that he had written to Mrs. Surratt. In it he had stated that John Nothey was willing to settle what he owed Mrs. Surratt. Calvert had written: "However unpleasant, I must insist upon closing up this matter, as it is imperative, in an early settlement of the estate, which is necessary. You will, therefore, please inform me, at your earliest convenience, as to how and when you will be able to pay the balance remaining due on the land purchased by your late husband."[8]

Calvert's testimony, at least, in part, substantiated Weichmann's testimony that Mrs. Surratt had returned to Surrattsville on April 14 in order to conclude her business with John Nothey so she could settle her debt with George Calvert. However, when Mary Surratt arrived at the tavern (the Surratt House and Tavern), Nothey was not there. This is why Lou Weichmann had written the note, for Mrs. Surratt, to Nothey demanding that he pay her in ten days what he owed her or she would bring suit against him.

Captain Bennett Gwynn was the next witness. He testified that he had known Mrs. Surratt for seven or eight years. He said that he stopped at the tavern on his return trip from Marlboro (April 14). When he saw Mrs. Surratt, she asked him to deliver and read the note that Louis Weichmann had written for her to John Nothey. The Surratt-Nothey letter was entered into evidence on the following day, May 26.[9] So far, everything agreed with the two statements Mary Surratt had made at Old Capitol Prison.

In continuing with Captain Gwynn's testimony of May 25, the captain testified that he saw John Lloyd on the road (April 14) coming from Marlboro and he had noticed that the man, as Gwynn put it, "had been drinking right smartly."[10]

The next witness to testify for the defense was George Cottingham. He was the officer in charge of John Lloyd after Lloyd's arrest. Cottingham had obviously been called in error for the defense. As his testimony progressed, he would have better served the prosecution.

According to Cottingham, for two days Lloyd had denied knowing anything about the assassination. Cottingham testified that he told Lloyd that he was sure that he (Lloyd) knew all about the assassination. Then he said to Lloyd that he realized that Lloyd had a heavy burden on his mind and that the sooner that he got rid of it, the better. According to Cottingham, Lloyd said, "O, my God, if I was to make a confession, they would murder me!" When Cottingham asked who would murder him, Lloyd said the parties that had part in the conspiracy. Then Cottingham testified that he told Lloyd, "Well, if you are afraid of being murdered, and let these fellows get out of it, that is your business, not mine."[11]

According to Cottingham, Lloyd had said that while Mrs. Surratt was at Surratt's Tavern on April 14, she had told him to have firearms ready, that two men would call for them at twelve o'clock that night.[12]

Two men *did* call for the firearms at twelve o'clock that night. As it turned out, David Herold took one of the firearms while John Wilkes Booth refused the other. Cottingham quoted Lloyd as saying, concerning Booth, ". . . it was as much as he could do to carry himself, as his leg was broken." Then Cottingham testified that Lloyd had known all along that President Lincoln had been killed, that Booth had told Lloyd, and that Herold had taken credit for having "fixed Seward." According to Cottingham, Lloyd had revealed all of this on their way from Bryantown to Washington, D.C., in the company of a squad of cavalry. They stopped at the Surratt House and Tavern and there Lloyd began to cry, "hollooing out, 'O, Mrs. Surratt, that vile woman, she has ruined me! I am to be shot! I am to be shot!'"[13]

According to Cottingham, before they left the Surratt House and Tavern, he asked Lloyd where the carbine was. (The one Booth refused.) He said that it was upstairs in a little room where Mrs. Surratt kept some bags. When Cottingham looked for the carbine, it wasn't there. Eventually, he found it in a bag behind a plastered wall in the family dining room. It had been suspended by a string tied to the muzzle of the gun. When the string had broken, the carbine had fallen.[14]

Again, according to Cottingham, before they left for Washington, Lloyd cried bitterly and "threw his hands over his wife's neck, and hallooed for his prayer-book." Mrs. Offutt had been present and witnessed Lloyd's hysteria.[15]

The rest of Cottingham's testimony was enlightening. It seems that Cottingham related to Aiken, at a private meeting, that Lloyd had said *nothing* to him about Mrs. Surratt telling Lloyd to have firearms ready! When Aiken asked Cottingham to testify for the defense to that effect, Cottinham refused. However, he added that if Aiken were to ask questions that he (Cottingham) would answer them. This is assuming that at the.time, Cottingham was expecting to be a witness for the prosecution. It is not clear why Cottingham still became a witness for the defense. In any case, Cottingham testified that Mrs. Surratt *did tell* Lloyd to have firearms ready that night. Cottingham either had lied under oath for fear of losing his position, or, for some other reason, had lied privately to Aiken when he said that John Lloyd had *said nothing* to him about Mrs. Surratt concerning firearms.

For the sake of clarity, let us advance from May 25 to June 13, when Mrs. Offutt returned to the stand. This time she appeared for the defense. The last time that she had appeared before the court, she had appeared for the prosecution. Mrs. Offutt's testimony concerned the day of April 14. She said that on that day, John Lloyd was "very much in liquor, more so than I have ever seen him in my life." She testified that she was at the Surratt House and Tavern on the Sunday that John Lloyd was taken under guard from Bryantown to Washington by way of Surrattsville. She said that she was there all the time and she did not hear Lloyd say, referring to Mrs. Surratt, "That vile woman has ruined me."[16]

Then, Frederick Aiken made a surprising announcement. He informed the court that when Mrs. Offutt had previously testified (May 17) that she hadn't been well. At that time, she had been in pain and was under the influence of "considerable laudanum" that had confused her mind, consequently, now she wished to correct her testimony.[17]

Mrs. Offutt was allowed to correct her previous testimony. This time she testified that she had been mistaken when she had earlier testified that Mrs. Surratt had *not* handed her the package. In fact, Mrs. Surratt *did* hand her a package and said that she had been requested to leave it there. Mrs. Offutt was referring to the package that John Wilkes Booth had asked Mrs. Surratt to deliver. Mrs. Offutt said that, later on, she saw the package lying on the sofa in the parlor. Shortly after that, John Lloyd returned from his trip to Marlboro.[18] She said that she saw Lloyd and Mrs. Surratt "talking together at the buggy in the yard, I was in and out all the time. I did not see Mr. Lloyd go into the parlor, but I saw him on the piazza [porch], and I think from that that he must have gone into the parlor. He had a package in his hand, but I did not see Mrs. Surratt give it to him. After the package was handed to me, it might have been taken by Mrs. Surratt and handed to Lloyd, but I did not see her give it to him." Mrs. Offutt's testimony did not prove or disprove whether Mrs. Surratt was in league with John Wilkes Booth. Nor did it disprove that she had simply delivered the package as a favor to Booth. It did prove that Lloyd was a fellow conspirator as the package from Booth was meant for Lloyd. Then, Mrs. Offutt told the court that Mrs. Surratt had said "that she would not have come down to Surrattsville that day, had it not been for the letter she received; and I saw business transacted while she was there." Mrs. Offutt continued her testimony by saying that Mrs. Surratt's eyesight was defective. Mrs. Offutt testified that she had seen Mrs. Surratt several times since January. One day Mrs.

Surratt had come to see her mother, who was very sick. "On being told by a servant that Mrs. Surratt was coming toward the door, I went there to her, and said, 'Why, Mrs. Surratt!' When she said, 'O, Mrs. Offutt, is that you?' and then she added, 'I can scarcely see.' I led her to the parlor and she told me that her eyes were failing very fast."[19]

The numerous testimonies to Mrs. Surratt's poor eyesight would explain why Lou Weichmann had written the note for Mary Surratt to John Nothey. Furthermore, it certainly explains that Mrs. Surratt *did not* lie when she said that she did not recognize Lewis Powell, on the night of April 17, when he appeared at her boardinghouse, claiming to be a ditch digger.

Now to continue with the testimonies given in May. The following day, May 26, John Nothey was questioned briefly by Frederick Aiken. Nothey testified that Mrs. Surratt had been in Surrattsville on Tuesday, April 11, and, again on Friday, April 14, concerning the money that he owed her. On April 14, she sent him a note by Captain Gwynn concerning the same matter.[20]

The preceding testimonies and written communications prove that Mrs. Surratt's *primary* business on both April 11 and April 14, concerned her financial problems. And, furthermore, to reiterate, had Mrs. Surratt left Surrattsville a little earlier or had John Lloyd returned a little later, possibly things would have turned out differently for Mary Surratt.

The Reverend Peter Lanihan took the stand for the defense. He testified that in the thirteen years that he had known Mrs. Surratt she had always been, in his estimation, a highly honorable Christian woman.[21]

Under Bingham's cross-examination the Reverend Lanihan testified that he had conversed with Mrs. Surratt on current events and he did not remember her ever expressing a disloyal sentiment.[22]

The Reverend N. D. Young's testimony followed. He appeared on behalf of Mary Surratt's character. He said that she was a good Christian woman and "a lady in every sense of the word." He said that he had visited her about once a month and had known her for eight or ten years. In that time he had not heard her speak upon current events loyally or disloyally. He had always heard her spoken of with praise and had never heard anything that wasn't highly favorable to her character.[23]

Five men of the cloth had sworn under oath supporting Mrs. Surratt's unblemished character. Would they have lied? If so, why?

Before court convened on Tuesday, May 30, the tension in the courtroom was unusually high. There were whispered conversations, where
normally boisterous rancor filled the air. There was sure to be a good
show as only the upper strata of society had been admitted *that* day.

Even though the other prisoners had been in frequent consulta-
tions with their attorneys, Mary Surratt had not conferred with hers
since May 15.[24] Therefore, it was unlikely that she had known that
Anna and Zad were scheduled to testify that day, unless she had been
forewarned.

The spectators were probably disappointed when Joseph T. Knott,
bartender at the Surratt House and Tavern, was the first to be called
to the stand.

He testified to John Lloyd's drunken condition, when Lloyd
returned to the tavern from Marlboro on April 14. He added that his
employer had, for several weeks, been drinking excessively. Knott
even went so far as to say: "At times, he [meaning Lloyd] had the
appearance of an insane man from drink."[25]

After Knott finished his short testimony, Mary's stomach, no doubt,
twisted and tears filled her eyes when her brother, Zad, was brought in.

Under Frederick Aiken's questions, Zad responded. Once again,
the reason for Mary's visit to Surrattsville on April 14 was recounted.
But Zad added something new. He said that Mary had told him that
she *did not* want to see Lloyd while she was at Surrattsville. He said
that, to his knowledge, his sister had never breathed a disloyal word
against the government. Nor did she ever indicate that she was aware
of any plans to capture or to assassinate the president or any other
government official. He added that he knew her to "frequently give
milk, tea, or such refreshments as she had in the house to Union
troops when they were passing." Then Zad added, "I recollect when a
large number of horses escaped from Giesboro, many of them were
taken up and put on her premises. These horses were carefully kept
and fed by her, and afterward all were given up. She received a receipt
for giving them up, but never got any pay, to my knowledge."[26]

Zad mentioned Mary's poor eyesight. Then he said that he knew
that a man by the name of G. S. Howell (Gus Howell) had stopped at
"Mrs. Surratt's hotel." He had stopped there as other travelers had.[27]

Next Assistant Judge Advocate Bingham approached the witness
stand to cross-examine for the prosecution. Zad acknowledged that
he had been in prison for the last ten days.[28]

It seems that a neighbor, by the name of Andrew Kallenbach, and some others had been threatened by Zad if they testified against Mary. Zad said that he did not tell Kallenbach or anyone else that he (Zad) would send Kallenbach or anyone else to hell or see that they were put out of the way if they testified against his sister.[29]

When Zad was asked about his loyalty to the government, he said that he considered himself a loyal man during the war and claimed that he had spent three thousand dollars in his district to hold it in the Union. Then he testified that during the struggle, he had taken no part against the government.[30]

When Bingham finished, Frederick Aiken reexamined Zad. Zad said that he was under arrest, but that he did not know the charges. Then he was asked to narrate what happened right after the first Battle of Bull Run in 1861. As a show of patriotism, Zad explained that he had raised the United States flag and then had to have it guarded from being torn down by "Secesh sympathizers." He said that at the election for Congress, in 1862, he had not been allowed to vote and that he had been arrested on the morning of the election. Undoubtedly that was the time when he and his son had gotten into a fracas with the pro-Union neighbors, the Robeys. He said that he had suffered from the war in the loss of his Negroes. He added that when the state had made its new constitution, he was willing to let his Negroes go.[31] In the days that followed, every possible witness both for and against Zad was brought forward to testify. It was as if he were on trial, as well.

After Zad was taken from the courtroom, Anna was brought in. She stopped, her eyes darting from prisoner to prisoner, as she viewed those who were seated to her left. At first she did not see her mother, who was seated to her right. Then Anna cried out in terror! "Where is my mother? Where is my mother?"[32] Then with streaming eyes, her lips quivering, Anna turned her head and saw Mary. For an instant Anna's blue eyes held a desperate light as she looked at Mary. Then from the depth of Anna's small frame, she rent the courtroom asunder with hysterical screams. Mary summoned her strength and with a gesture of command and entreaty, she was able to compose her daughter.[33]

Anna was dressed in a black silk dress and a white straw hat with a black veil.[34] Trembling, Anna turned and was led to the witness stand. She stood unsteadily, raised a diminutive hand and was sworn in. Nervously, she answered Frederick Aiken's questions.

She testified that she had been arrested on April 17 and had been held at Old Capitol Prison, Carroll Annex.[35]

After the date of Anna's arrest was established, she answered questions about George Atzerodt. She said that he called often at the boardinghouse, asking "for that man Weichmann."[36] (This would substantiate John Holohan's testimony at John Surratt's trial two years later.[37]) Anna continued by saying that, he (Atzerodt) "was given to understand that he was not wanted at the house; Ma said she did not care about having strangers there." Anna said that the last time Atzerodt was there, Weichmann had asked her mother to allow him (Atzerodt) to stay there all night. Her mother gave her permission. Then Anna identified Weichmann as having been a boarder and that he had been ". . . too kindly treated there. It was my mother's habit to sit up for him at night, when he was out of the house; she would sit up and wait for him the same as for my brother."[38]

Then the questions turned to the subject of the other prisoner, Lewis Powell. Anna acknowledged that the first time he had come to the boardinghouse was one night after dark. He left early the following morning. Then he came again some weeks later. At that time, everyone, except her mother, was seated in the parlor when the young man arrived. Anna said that she recognized him as the man who had been there before when he was using the name of Wood. Then she said that when she went down to the dining room and told her mother that the young man was there, her mother remarked that she did not understand why strange people came, but she supposed that they had come to see John. When her mother went upstairs, the young man asked if he could spend the night, stating that he would leave the following morning. Anna said that she believed he did leave the following morning. She said that Powell called two or three times after that.[39]

Aiken's following questions centered on John Wilkes Booth. Anna said that she thought that the last time that Booth was at the house was on Friday, April 14. She said that she did not see him, but that she had heard he was there.

Subsequent questions centered on Mary Surratt's visit to Surrattsville on April 14. Anna testified that she thought that her mother's carriage was at the front door when John Wilkes Booth called. She said that she heard someone come up the (outside) steps when the buggy was at the door and her mother was ready to leave.

She said that her mother had spoken about going to Surrattsville before Booth had stopped by the house. Perhaps, she had even spoken about going the day before. In any case, her mother was going to Surrattsville concerning some land. When Booth arrived, he only stayed a few minutes.[40]

Then Aiken showed Anna the picture of *Morning, Noon, and Night.* She stated that "that man Weichmann" had given it to her. She admitted to having hidden Booth's photograph behind the picture, because, when she showed it to her brother, he had told her to tear it up and throw it into the fire, adding that, if she didn't, he would take the picture from her. Anna admitted to possessing photographs of Southerners: Davis, Stephens, Beauregard, Stonewall Jackson, and perhaps some other leaders of the rebellion. She said that her father had given them to her. She added that she had photographs of Northern generals Hooker, Grant, and McClellan, as well.[41]

Anna testified that she hadn't seen her brother since Monday, April 3. Then she acknowledged that John Wilkes Booth had called on John, from time to time. She said that she had never asked her brother what his friendship was with the actor. Then Anna attested to the fact that one day when Booth was coming up the steps, John had said that he believed that the man was crazy. He said that he wished that Booth would take care of his own business and let him stay at home. Then John asked Anna not to leave the parlor while Booth was present, but she said that she left anyway.[42]

Then Anna was asked about her brother's early days at St. Charles College. Whether Anna misunderstand the question or not will never be known, but she testified that her brother had not been a divinity student there.[43] Of course, the statement may have been an error of one of the trial transcribers.

Subsequently, Anna testified to her mother's poor eyesight. She said that for a long time her mother hadn't been able to either read or sew by gaslight. Anna remarked: "I have often plagued her about getting spectacles, and told her she was not too young-looking to wear spectacles just yet; and she has replied that she could not read or see without them."[44]

General Thomas Ewing, counselor for Samuel Arnold and Edward Spangler, merely asked when her brother, John, had left St. Charles College. She said that her brother had left college the year of her father's death in 1861 or 1862. She attended school in Bryantown from 1854 until 1861. In conclusion, she testified that she had never seen Dr. Samuel Mudd at her mother's house in Washington.[45]

At the time of the trial, Col. Henry Kyde Douglas, C.S.A., was incarcerated in the Old Penitentiary. His offense was disobeying a military order. Colonel Douglas had had a picture taken of himself in his Confederate uniform, after General Lee's surrender. For that infraction, he was sentenced to two months imprisonment at Fort Delaware. On the way to the fort, Douglas was detoured to the penitentiary to give testimony for the defense. During the war, Colonel Douglas had been a member of Stonewall Jackson's staff. He was called upon to substantiate that Von Steinacker, the witness for the prosecution, had perjured himself when he had sworn that Booth had visited the Confederate camp where Douglas had been stationed.

After the war, Colonel Douglas wrote a book describing his wartime adventures. The following is a quotation from that publication. The narrative describes Anna Surratt on May 30, the day that she testified.

> It was a pitiable scene. She [Anna] was tall, slender, fair, handsome, for her to stand the stare of the cruel, stony eyes riveted upon her, was a trying ordeal. She must have known that her testimony made no impression on that tribunal, and toward the close of it she began to show signs of a collapse. The veins and muscles of her neck seemed swollen and she gave evidence of great suffering. General Hartranft was about to go to her, but knowing her horror of him as her Mother's jailor, he, with delicate consideration, asked me to bring her from the stand. I brought her out, passing just in front of her mother, and as she reached my room [she] fell forward and fainted. The door was shut quickly, and a doctor called, and at his insistence General Hartranft and I carried her below to his room. There she had a spasm and began to tear out her beautiful hair and to rend her dress. Women arriving, she was left with them and the Doctor, who succeeded in a while in quieting and putting her to sleep.[46]

On Thursday, June 1, Anna was allowed to be in court. She was seated in the section reserved for the press. A reporter for the *Philadelphia Inquirer* wrote, "The presence of the daughter and the affectionate

*Dr. Mary Edwards Walker, M.D. Dr. Walker attended both the trial and the execution of the alleged conspirators.* (National Portrait Gallery)

glances, mutually exchanged between the two seemed to have achieved an effect upon the mother, for she seemed more hopeful and in better spirits."[47]

Another eyewitness account was made on June 2, by a reporter with the *New York Times*. "Miss Surratt has been released from custody and sat during the entire session today within a few feet of, but separated from, her mother by the prisoners' railing. They were not permitted to converse, but were occasionally observed looking wistfully at each other and making significant signs. The daughter seems to be suffering from poignant grief.

"The attendance of the visitors to the trial is undiminished, and today the courtroom was packed to its utmost capacity, not withstanding, the very sultry weather, which made the atmosphere in the room almost unendurable."[48]

Perhaps it was this same day that the court was treated to another curiosity. A reporter for the *Washington Evening Star* wrote the following: "Among the visitors in the courtroom this afternoon was The

Bloomer, Doctor (or Doctress) Walker, who took a position near the prisoners' dock. The prisoners appeared considerably interested and amused by the appearance of The Bloomer. Payne [*sic*] grinned, Atzerodt grinned, Spangler grinned, and Herold snickered right out loud."[49]

The woman who inspired the levity was Miss Major Mary Edwards Walker. She was a petite, black-haired, dark-eyed, attractive woman who dressed in a self-styled uniform of a Union officer. She was a physician and surgeon.[50] Dr. Walker was probably used to the taunting of healthy males. However, when they were injured, their male buffoonery was abandoned. Then, like little boys, they looked to her for her delicate touch, her soft words, and her healing gifts.

# CHAPTER TWENTY

# *The Trial Ends*

Brigadier General John F. Hartranft wrote the following to Gen. W. S. Hancock on Monday, June 5, 1865: "At 11:30 A.M., Miss Annie Surratt presented a pass to see her mother. Mrs. Surratt was brought into the courtroom and her daughter admitted to see her under the usual restrictions."

The first meeting between mother and daughter is best described by Capt. Christian Rath, provost marshal under General Hartranft.

Some time after Annie had been released she appeared at the prison gate with an order from the Judge [possibly Judge Advocate Holt] giving her permission to visit her mother with an officer present. I was that officer. When the mother met her daughter she welcomed her warmly, but not as you would have expected. Mrs. Surratt was rather good-looking, well-dressed and of attractive figure. The daughter was comely. The poor girl threw herself into her mother's arms, and of course, burst into tears. They stayed

185

in this position for fully ten minutes. Not a word spoken. I could not witness such a scene longer, and I walked away. Mrs. Surratt and her daughter then talked over an hour and a half. When they had been in the courtroom nearly two hours Mrs. Surratt called to me and asked me to take Annie from the prison, saying that she was tired. The poor girl was almost worn out. The mother bore a determined look on her face. She had not shed a tear.

I took Miss Surratt to her home and then returned to the arsenal. I told Major Akaryote [an aide to Secretary of War Stanton] of the stoicism displayed by Mrs. Surratt. He informed me that her daughter had no sooner left the jail than the mother fell into a dead faint. She bore up remarkably well before her child, but the strain was too much for her. After that Annie came to the prison almost daily. Every time she came in I hoped that she carried with her something which she could administer to her mother so that, the dreadful hangman's noose would not have to be placed about her neck.[1]

One month later, Capt. Christian Rath would serve as that hangman!

On June 7, Anna was recalled to the witness stand. After Frederick Aiken showed her a card with the state of Virginia coat of arms that included the motto "Sic semper tyrannis," Anna identified it, saying it had been hers. She said that a lady had given it to her about two and a half years earlier.[2]

Then the counselor for Dr. Samuel Mudd, Gen. Thomas Ewing, questioned Anna. He asked if she had ever seen his client at her home. Anna answered that she hadn't.[3]

When Anna was dismissed, Col. William P. Wood, superintendent of Old Capitol Prison, was called to the stand for the *defense!*

The colonel testified to John Zadoc Jenkins' loyalty to the Union at the beginning of the war, but, he said that, like most of the people in Southern Maryland, Zad's loyalty had changed to the South.[4]

Under Judge Advocate Holt's probing, Wood testified that he didn't consider that his former friend was very sound on the subject of the war.[5]

After Colonel's Wood's testimony, two men were called separately to testify for the defense. Both J. H. Blanford and J. C. Thompson testified that Zad had been loyal to the Union.[6]

When Thompson and Blanford had finished their testimonies, John Holohan (Mrs. Surratt's boarder) was called. He appeared as a witness for the prosecution, giving testimony in rebuttal.

John Holohan said that he was not aware of Mrs. Surratt's poor eyesight. He said that the last time that he had seen John Surratt was on the night of April 3. He testified that it was at that time that he had exchanged John Surratt's gold for greenbacks.[7] This is the gold that John was given in Richmond to pay for his and Sarah Slater's trip to Canada.

Then Holohan testified that George Atzerodt had gone to the house several times to see John Surratt.[8] (Two years later, John Holohan testified at John Surratt's trial that Atzerodt had gone to the house to visit Lou Weichmann.[9] At that time he testified on behalf of the defendant, John Surratt.)

In answer to a question by the prosecution concerning Dr. Samuel Mudd, Holohan said that he had never seen the doctor nor heard him mentioned at the boardinghouse. Holohan added that during the time that he had lived at Mrs. Surratt's he had never heard of a plot either to abduct or to assassinate the president.[10]

When the prosecution finished, Gen. Thomas Ewing questioned Holohan for the defense. It was his intent to prove to the court that Louis Weichmann had been a co-conspirator in the assassination, ". . . he [Weichmann] comes here clearing himself by being a swift witness against others."[11]

Unfortunately, when General Ewing asked John Holohan if Lou Weichmann had turned himself in to the authorities after the assassination, Judge Advocate Burnett objected. Immediately, Judge Advocate Bingham interjected that Lou Weichmann had previously admitted to having been taken into custody.[12]

Nevertheless, Ewing was tenacious. He wanted the word *arrested* used rather than *custody*. Again, he asked John Holohan if Weichmann had been *arrested* at the time that Weichmann and he had gone to Superintendent Richard's office at the Metropolitan Police.[13]

The question was waived after the court was treated to one of Judge Bingham's familiar theatrics.[14]

Ironically, what General Ewing was unable to accomplish where Weichmann was concerned was about to be accomplished by the prosecution itself! When James McDevitt of the Metropolitan Police was questioned, McDevitt testified that Louis Weichmann had, indeed, been *arrested* "when he came to our office."[15]

The next testimony for the prosecution in rebuttal was that of Andrew Kallenbach. According to Kallenbach, on April 17, Zad Jenkins had threatened him for spreading lies. According to Kallenbach, Zad had said that if Kallenbach testified against him or anyone connected with him (Zad), he would give Kallenbach a "damned whipping." Apparently, Kallenbach took Zad's threat seriously because he said that he had known Jenkins about ten years: "He has always said in my presence that he was a Union man; and I have never heard him express any disloyal sentiments. I can not say what his reputation for loyalty is in the neighborhood."[16]

Under Frederick Aiken's cross-examination, Kallenbach said that he didn't know what had induced Zad Jenkins to call him a liar. Then he testified that he had a son who served in the Rebel army. He stated that his son had gone into the Confederate service without the elder Kallenbach's consent. He told the court that he had lived as a neighbor of Mrs. Surratt's for many years. He said that she hadn't done more for his family than any other. He testified that he had been a Democrat all of his life. However, he had never expressed any disloyal opinions and he never said that he wished that the South would win the war.[17]

After court that day, June 7, Anna visited her mother in cell number 200.[18]

Two newspapers gave accounts of that day. Both stories appeared the following day on June 8, 1865.

The *Philadelphia Inquirer.*

> Mrs. Surratt appeared very feeble today, so much so that she almost [had] to be lifted into her chair. The lady visitors show very little consideration for her feelings, crowding around her closely, and making many impudent remarks in her hearing, which by no means add to her serenity of mind; then, too, she is so thickly veiled as to threaten herself with asphyxia; and being seated in a corner where scarcely a breeze can reach her, her situation is by no means pleasant.
>
> It was rumored today that she intended making a confession soon as to her participation in the plot, but on her

counsel being asked if such was the fact, he replied that there was no truth in it; that she would make no confession, as she had none to make.

The *Boston Journal*:

Washington, June 7—Mrs. Surratt appeared quite overcome by the heat, and somewhat annoyed by the remarks made about her by the lady visitors.

Payne [*sic*] declares his desire to be hung at once, and says that he is ready to make a clean breast of it, but Mrs. Surratt is innocent, and Arnold had no knowledge of the murder.

Six, long, hot days would pass before another witness appeared for Mrs. Surratt. It was Monday, June 13. Now and then an occasional raindrop dashed against the windows and trickled down the window glass.[19]

On June 13, Henry Hawkins, Mary's former slave from Surrattsville, was sworn in. He testified of Mrs. Surratt: "She always treated me kindly, and she was very good to all her servants." Then he spoke of the government horses that had broken away from Giesboro. After the horses were caught, they were brought to Mrs. Surratt's stables. They were treated well during the fortnight that they were there. He said that he did not know if she had received a receipt for the horses or not, but he knew that she bought them hay and grain.[20]

Hawkins further testified that he had "never heard Mrs. Surratt talk in favor of the South; never heard any expressions, loyal or disloyal, while I was there. She often fed Union soldiers that passed her house, and always gave them the best she had; and I do not think she took any pay for it." He concluded by saying that he had heard that "she could not see some time back."[21]

When Henry Hawkins was dismissed, Aunt Rachel Semus was brought into the courtroom. No doubt, she had followed the court proceedings. Rachel would have known that Mrs. Surratt was very ill. She would have known about the abuse that her former mistress and friend had suffered daily from the constant parade of spectators who filled the courtroom.

Rachel's answers to Frederick Aiken's questions disclosed a great deal about Mary Surratt. The following is her testimony:

"I have lived at Mrs. Surratt's house for six years; was hired to her by Mr. Wildman. She treated her servants very well all the time I was with her; I never had reason to complain. I remember Mrs. Surratt had Union soldiers at her house, sometimes a good many of them; and I know that she always tried to do the best for them that she could, because I always cooked for them.

"She always gave them the best she had, and very often she would give them all she had in the house, because so many of them came. I recollect her cutting up the last ham she had in the house, and she had not any more until she sent to the city. I never knew her taking any pay for it. I never heard her express herself in favor of the South; if she used such expressions, I did not hear them. Her eyesight has been failing for a long time, very often I have had to go upstairs and thread her needle for her because she could not see to do it; I have had to stop washing to go up and thread it for her in the daytime. I remember one day telling her that Father Lanihan was at the front gate, coming to the house, and she said, 'No, it was not him, it was little Johnny [meaning her son].'"[22] If Mary could not recognize her own son, how could she have recognized Lewis Powell in his disheveled condition while standing in poor light on April 17, the night that he, Mrs. Surratt, and the others were arrested? The answer is obvious, she couldn't. Yet, her denial was very damning to her.

For reasons of their own, the prosecutors did not cross-examine Rachel. Perhaps, Mary was able to manage a weak smile of recognition when Rachel, her former servant, was led past her and out of the courtroom. Possibly, as Rachel passed she had time to whisper to Mary, "I reckon I told 'em!"

That same day, June 13, Dr. John T. Hoxton and William W. Hoxton testified for the defense. Both men lived about a mile from Surrattsville. They had known Mrs. Surratt for about twelve years. Both testified to her flawless reputation. William Hoxton added that Mrs. Surratt was especially kind to the sick. However, the men agreed that Zadoc had secession proclivities after 1862.[23]

This concluded the testimonies for the defense. Next, the counselors for the defense were scheduled to present arguments on behalf of their clients. Court was adjourned until Friday, June 16, so the counselors could prepare their arguments.

When the court reconvened, the first argument by the defense was for Mary Surratt. The reasoning had been prepared by Sen. Reverdy Johnson. It was read by the round-bellied, richly bearded attorney,

John Wesley Clampitt. The senator's long and able argument questioned the jurisdiction of the Military Commission. The crimes, as charged, were not offenses against military rule or law. Consequently, these crimes could only be judiciously heard and determined by common and statute law and, therefore, were not triable by a military tribunal, according to Reverdy Johnson.[24] Furthermore, none of the prisoners had served in the United States military, therefore, they should be tried in civil court before a jury of twelve men.[25] In addition, the senator, through Clampitt, argued that the war had ended by the time the trial had commenced. He explained the Constitution where applicable to the trial, then deftly proved the unconstitutionality of the Military Commission.[26]

On behalf of Mrs. Surratt, Reverdy Johnson continued by saying: "That a woman well educated and, as far as we can judge, from all her past life, as we have it in evidence, devout Christian, even kind, affectionate and charitable, with no motive disclosed to us that could have caused a total change in her very nature, could have participated in the crimes in question, it is almost impossible to believe. Such a belief can only be forced upon a reasonable, unprejudiced mind, by direct and uncontradicted evidence, coming from pure and perfectly unsuspected sources. Have we these? Is the evidence uncontradicted? Are the two witnesses, Weichmann and Lloyd, pure and unsuspected? Of the particulars of their evidence I say nothing. They will be brought before you by my associates. But this conclusion in regard to these witnesses must be in the minds of the Court, and is strongly impressed upon my own, that, if the facts which they themselves state as to their connection and intimacy with Booth and Payne [sic] are true, their knowledge of the purpose to commit the crimes, and their participation in them, is much more satisfactorily established than the alleged knowledge and participation of Mrs. Surratt. As far, gentlemen, as I am concerned, her case is now in your hands."[27]

Frederick Aiken, also, gave an impassioned argument on behalf of Mrs. Surratt. His statements were convincing. He said that both Louis Weichmann and John Lloyd had more intimate knowledge of a conspiracy than his client had. Moreover, Lloyd, in his advanced state of inebriation on April 14, could hardly be considered a credible witness as to what anyone was doing or saying on that day. In fact, Lloyd testified that he wasn't *exactly* sure if Mrs. Surratt had told him to have the shooting arms ready or not.[28]

Then Frederick Aiken reminded the court that the primary purpose of Mrs. Surratt's going to Surrattsville on the day of the assassination was to transact private business. Next, Aiken made an important point that, at the time that Booth had asked Mrs. Surratt to deliver his package, Booth did not know that President Lincoln was going to attend Ford's Theatre that night! Furthermore, had she left the boarding-house a little earlier for Surrattsville, she would have missed Booth all together.[29]

In regard to Mrs. Surratt's not recognizing Lewis Powell, Aiken reminded the court of her defective eyesight. The last time she had seen the man, he had been impeccably dressed as a Baptist minister. When he appeared at the boardinghouse on the night of her arrest, he was in the guise of a dirty, uncouthly dressed, ditch digger.[30]

Then Aiken reiterated Reverdy Johnson's statement to the fact that neighbors, friends, and clergy, all agreed to Mrs. Surratt's fine reputation. On the other hand, the prosecution could find not one person to testify to the contrary. It was inconceivable that such a woman could conspire in the murder of President Lincoln.[31]

This concluded Frederick Aiken's argument on behalf of Mrs. Surratt. The following day was used by the other counselors to prepare arguments for their clients.

On Saturday, June 17, Lewis Powell was questioned in private for three hours and forty minutes by Maj. Thomas T. Akaryote and by Dr. John T. Gray, a noted insanity expert.[32] Powell's only defense would be guilty by reason of insanity. It seems that, for a long time after his arrest, Powell could not remember what state or even what country he had been born in or how old he was. For weeks he wouldn't even speak to William Doster, his counselor. In court he would stare without expression at the spectators.[33] On June 1, Powell had tried to commit suicide in his cell.[34] At that time, three doctors were called, all of whom had serious doubts about Powell's sanity.[35] As it turned out, the plea for insanity was not accepted by the court.[36]

On Sunday, June 18, it was decided that the prisoners should be taken "for awhile" to the yard each day. Reading material and "a chew" of tobacco would be furnished after each meal. That same day, Dr. Gray recommended that each prisoner, except Mrs. Surratt, be given a box to sit on. An arm chair was recommended for her. Heretofore, the prisoners had only their straw pallets on which to sit.[37]

That same day, Jane and Kate Herold visited their brother, David. Also, "Miss Surratt presented a pass from the Secretary of War to see her mother. She was admitted to see her from eleven o'clock in the morning until 5:30 that afternoon."[38]

On Monday, June 19, at twelve o'clock, Mrs. Surratt became so ill that it was necessary to remove her from the courtroom. An adjournment was called until two o'clock that afternoon. At that time, Mrs. Surratt was placed on a chair in the doorway between a former witness room and the courtroom. She was still in the presence of the court and "where the air was much more cool and pure."[39]

The outside temperature on that day was ninety degrees and it was very humid.[40] It would have been considerably hotter and more humid in the crowded courtroom.

General Hartranft wrote in his report to General Hancock on June 20 that "Mrs. Surratt had been removed [from her cell] to a side room, and as her illness seems to be growing more severe, I would suggest that her daughter be allowed to remain and wait on her as her illness is evidently such as to require a female attendant."

The "side room" to which General Hartranft referred was one of the two former witness rooms that were adjacent to the courtroom. It was in the doorway of her newly assigned prison room where Mary Surratt sat that afternoon.

Mary Surratt's prison room was bright and cheerful. The walls had been whitewashed in preparation for the trial. There was even a white marble fireplace. The only window faced the south. It looked down on the penitentiary yard. Beyond, but out of sight, was the Potomac River, Alexandria, and Southern Maryland, the places she loved so much.

Another world of its own existed within the confines of the twenty-foot-high, brick, penitentiary wall. Marching soldiers and vehicles of every description shared space with grazing cattle, pigs, and mangy dogs. Off-duty soldiers lounged, played cards, pitched quoits, or conversed beneath the shade of oak and maple trees.[41]

On hot, humid days, when the breeze came from nearby James Creek, the area was blanketed with a sickening stench. The creek served as a reservoir for nearly all the filth from Washington. The waste from both private and public facilities drained into the stinking caldron. Here, clouds of flies and malaria-carrying mosquitoes bred and fed before returning to their human hosts.[42]

The eastern windows of the courtroom faced the befouled James Creek, a short distance away.[43] Consequently, the torrid heat was not the only thing that bedeviled the occupants of the courtroom. Any easterly flow of air filled the room not only with the vile foulness from the James Creek, but disease-carrying flies and mosquitoes as well. Perhaps, on the day that Mrs. Surratt became ill, the courtroom was plagued with the filthy air from the creek. This would account for General Hartranft's comment in his letter to General Hancock that he had Mrs. Surratt placed in the doorway of the courtroom where the air was "cool and pure." The words to describe the air as "cool and pure" are, to say the least, questionable.

By Tuesday, June 20, every possible comfort, even her pillow[44] from home, had been provided Mrs. Surratt. So that Anna could assist her mother, she was now sharing Mary's prison room.[45] To help in any way that he could, General Hartranft daily sent Mary delicacies from his own dining table.[46]

On Wednesday, June 21, the arguments for the defense resumed. General Thomas Ewing, who represented Dr. Samuel Mudd and Ned Spangler, and Walter S. Cox, who represented Michael O'Laughlin and Samuel Arnold, both made very able arguments by analyzing and discussing the evidence so far as it applied to their clients.

General Ewing was very emphatic, almost abrasive, when he said "that the findings and the sentences of the Commission could not be justified under the color of lawful authority."[47]

William E. Doster, who represented Lewis Powell, made an impassioned plea for the life of his client. He endeavored to persuade the commission that his client, even though guilty of attempting to assassinate Secretary Seward, was a young man who was only a product of his "misguided Southern environment." Doster informed the court that alias Paine's real name was Lewis Thornton Powell, and that he was the son of a Florida Baptist minister. Furthermore, when the war broke out, four years earlier, the lad was only sixteen years old.[48] According to the Powell family Bible, Powell was seventeen years old at the outbreak of the war.

Doster argued that slavery was the custom to which the prisoner had been born. Politicians had told him that slavery was constitutional. Preachers had taught him that slavery was accepted in the Bible. Doster argued that "in the eyes of the lad, the war meant—his inheritance would be dissipated—his laws invaded, his religion confounded, his politics a heresy and his habit criminal."[49]

"What then has he done," Doster asserted, "that every Rebel soldier has not tried to do? Only this: he has ventured more; showed higher courage, a bitterer hate, and a more ready sacrifice; he aimed at the head of a department, instead at the head of a corps; he struck at the head of a nation, instead of its limb." Doster continued, "This boy was ready to offer his life for what he believed to be good for his Country."[50]

If Doster's argument thus far had been masterful, certainly what followed was at least militarily persuasive: "If, then, you praise men because they kill such as they believe oppressors, you must praise him; if you praise men who are ready to die for their country, you will praise him; and if you applaud those who show any courage superior to the rest of mankind, you will applaud him."[51]

Doster pleaded for mercy for a young man, whom Doster claimed, "differed from the Southern Army simply because he surpassed it in courage; that he differed from a patriot and a martyr, simply because he was mistaken in his duty."[52]

Doster failed to save his client, but he inspired respect for the impassioned, steel-jawed young patriot—a man who happened not to be a Union supporter, but a brave patriot nonetheless, something that all military men appreciate. Besides, Lewis Thornton Powell (alias Lewis Paine), had, at one time, been a member of Mosby's Partisan Rangers. Colonel John S. Mosby, the "Gray Ghost," had become a legend in his own time. Powell would have been respected for his association with that great leader.

When Doster had finished his argument for Lewis Powell, he argued for the life of George Atzerodt. Unlike Powell, the faint-hearted little German could not harm anyone. Nevertheless, Atzerodt had been charged with "lying in wait" with the intent to kill Vice President Andrew Johnson. Atzerodt had refused to kill the vice president, even though John Wilkes Booth had ordered him to do so. As Doster maintained, "Assassination and murder were things for which he was not by nature intended, and he had nothing to do with it." As to Atzerodt's "lying in wait" to kill the vice president, Doster asserted that his client did not "lie in wait" to kill anyone. Atzerodt was neither principal nor accessory to the "lying in wait" for the vice president. Neither was he an accomplice or an accessory to Powell's assault on Secretary Seward, or to Booth's killing the president. Doster contended that Atzerodt was neither an accessory before or after the fact. To be an accessory before the fact, Atzerodt would have had to procure, counsel, or command another to commit the crime. Of that charge, Atzerodt was innocent. To be an accessory after the fact, Atzerodt would have known that a felony had been committed and would have had to "receive, relieve, comfort, or assist the felon." Of that charge, Atzerodt was also innocent. He never saw Booth after the eight o'clock meeting on the night of the assassination. He didn't see Powell again until he met him as a fellow prisoner on the *Monitor.*

Doster concluded by saying that George Atzerodt was guilty of only one act and that was conspiring to abduct the president and of that offense he could only be found guilty under a new indictment.[53]

When William Doster completed his argument in behalf of his client, he read a statement that George Atzerodt had made. In the statement, Atzerodt admitted that he was one of a party who agreed to abduct President Lincoln, but he was not one of those who had agreed to kill the president, the vice president, General Grant, or any member of the cabinet. Then in his statement, Atzerodt described the meeting at the Herndon House at eight o'clock on the evening of the assassination, April 14. John Wilkes Booth said then that he would kill President Lincoln and General Grant, Powell would "take" Secretary of State Seward, and Atzerodt would "take" Vice President Johnson. Atzerodt told Booth that he would not do it, that he had agreed to help capture the president, but not to kill him. Booth told Atzerodt that he was a fool, that he would be hung anyway, and that it was death for every man who backed out; after which, Atzerodt, Booth, and the others parted company.[54]

Since David Herold was guilty as an accessory after the fact by giving aid and comfort to John Wilkes Booth, attorney Frederick Stone spent much of his argument in behalf of his client by questioning the jurisdiction of the Military Court and questioning the actual meaning of the charges that had been set forth.

Stone argued that it was bad reasoning to conclude that because Herold had helped Booth to escape that he was guilty in the murder or helped to assassinate President Lincoln. Even Booth had found the boy unfit for "deeds of blood and violence; he was too cowardly." However, Booth with his persuasive powers was able to enlist Herold to act as a guide, since Herold knew that part of Maryland that Booth would be traveling through.

Booth declared before his Maker, at the time of his capture, "that this man [Herold] is innocent." Stone argued: "In natures the most depraved there seems to be left some spark of a better humanity, and this little remnant of a better nature urged Booth to make that declaration while it was yet time to do so." According to Stone, Booth tried to convey that Herold did help him to escape, but Herold's hands were free from the stain of blood.[55] After court adjourned on Wednesday, June 21, it did not reconvene until Friday, June 23.

An item appeared in the newspapers that raised a few eyebrows. John T. Ford sold his theater and the adjoining building on Tenth Street to the Young Men's Christian Association (Y.M.C.A.) for $100,000.[56]

When court assembled on June 23, Gen. Thomas Ewing tried once more to convince the tribunal that it was unconstitutional. The Constitution had been written to protect citizens from unrestrained executive power. General Ewing continued by saying that Judge Advocate Holt had controlled the admission and rejection of all the evidence and that the detailed horrors of Libby Prison had been used to excite the commission against the prisoners who had had nothing to do with the conditions in Southern prisons.[57]

General Ewing argued that the counselors were in court to represent the accused without knowing explicitly what the crimes were, as *defined* by law. Consequently, the counselors had been in court not knowing specifically against what charges they were to defend their clients. In other words, according to General Ewing: "The Judge Advocate puts these parties on trial, and refuses to advise their counsel on what law or authority he rests his claim to jurisdiction; or what crime he intends to convict each or any of the defendants."[58]

Then the general quoted the third section of the third article of the Constitution: "The trial of all crimes, except in cases of impeachment, shall be by jury. The Constitution does not permit the military to try, or has Congress attempted to deliver over to the military for trial, judgement, and execution, American citizens, not in the land or naval forces or in the militia in actual service, when accused of crime."[59]

Ewing pronounced the Military Commission as being "no Court at all under the Constitution," and claimed that it had "no jurisdiction in these cases, unless you obtain it from some other source which overrules the constitutional provision."[60]

Certainly, the defendants had cause for hope when court adjourned on Friday, June 23. As it turned out, their confidence would be short lived.

For two grueling, torrid days, beginning on Tuesday, June 27, Special Judge Advocate Bingham tore asunder any hopes that the prisoners may have had. According to William Doster, Bingham's mind "seemed to be frenzied and his conduct violent."[61]

Lieutenant Colonel Richard A. Watts, acting assistant adjutant general, described John Bingham as being "small of statue, spare but most expressive of face, and when excited his eyes fairly glowed. During his address he wore a long black frock coat. It reached almost to his shoe tops. When referring to the Rebellion or any of its leaders, especially Mr. [Jefferson] Davis, his invectiveness [sic] burned and seared like hot irons, but when he touched upon the great and lovable qualities of the martyred Lincoln, his lips would quiver with emotion, and his voice become as tender and reverent as if he were repeating the Lord's Prayer."[62]

Half of John Bingham's argument was confined to the question of the jurisdiction of the court. The trial, according to the special judge advocate, military commissions, had been legally sanctioned when a state of martial law was declared throughout the United States by President Abraham Lincoln's proclamation of September 24, 1862.[63]

Then Bingham reminded the court that the Congressional Act of March 3, 1863, section 38, basically said that all persons who, in time of war or rebellion against the United States, were in the pursuance of a conspiracy to commit assassination upon the commander-in-chief would be tried by a military commission. (*Stat. at Large* 12, 736—'7, Ch. 8.)[64]

Judge Bingham reminded the court that, by the Congressional Act of March 3, 1863, President Lincoln was empowered to suspend the writ of habeas corpus which ordered that "all rebels, insurgents, their aiders and abetters, and persons guilty of any disloyal practice affording aid and comfort to rebels—should be subject to martial law and liable to trial and punishment by a military court."[65] In other words, the accused were found guilty before they were tried!

After hours of quoting and reciting statuary laws to justify the Military Commission, Bingham turned to Mary Surratt and sneered. "That Mary E. Surratt," he thundered, pointing a bony finger at her, "is as guilty as her son of having thus conspired, combined and confederated to do this murder, in aid of this rebellion, is clear!"[66] (Judge Bingham's actual words taken from the trial transcript.)

Conceivably, Bingham's well-known histrionics would have come into play. With clenched fists, his chin raised high, Bingham would have whirled around and faced the commission to confirm that his attack had hit its mark. It had! He would have been pleased. Then he would turn from the commission and slam his fist on the table beside him and point again at Mary Surratt: "First her house was the headquarters of Booth, John H. Surratt, Atzerodt, Payne [*sic*], and Herold. She is inquired for by Atzerodt; she is inquired for by Payne [*sic*], and she is visited by Booth, and holds private conversations with him. His picture, together with the chief conspirator, Jefferson Davis, is found in her house. She sends to Booth for a carriage to take her to Surrattsville on April 11 in order to perfect necessary arrangements of conspiracy and to especially facilitate and protect the conspirators in their escape."[67]

Bingham treated Louis Weichmann's and John Lloyd's testimonies as sacrosanct. By the time the judge had finished, he had expunged any hope that the prisoners may have held. He had cleverly turned day to night and white to black. Lloyd and Weichmann, actors in Mrs. Surratt's prosecution, had adeptly played their roles.

On June 28, after seven weeks, the trial for the alleged conspirators came to an end. The future of seven men and one woman was now in the hands of the Military Commission.

A total of four hundred sixty-three (463) witnesses had been subpoenaed. Three hundred sixty-one (361) were examined, including recalls. For the prosecution, four hundred twenty-two (422) were subpoenaed, two hundred forty-seven (247) were examined. For the defense, one hundred ninety-eight (198) were subpoenaed, two hundred thirty-six (236) were examined. There were forty-three hundred (4,300) pages of testimony, making a solid stack of twenty-six (26) inches high. The arguments made an additional seven hundred (700) pages.[68] Yet, with the exception of Dr. Samuel Mudd's case, the Military Commission was able to complete their deliberation in only one day!

# CHAPTER TWENTY-ONE

# *Verdict and Sentencing*

On Friday, June 30, the Military Commission met to decide the fate of the accused.

The power of the Military Commission, unlike civil courts, with a single judge and a jury of twelve, was unlimited. Military courts created their own procedural rules. They were sole judge of law and facts! They passed on the admissibility of all the evidence offered during the trial. Any exceptions made to their rulings were neither entertained nor recorded! Military courts not only decided the question of guilt, but they fixed the penalties, as well.[1]

The president of the United States was the only person, not part of the commission, who could review, change, modify, approve, or disapprove the findings and the sentencing of the tribunal.[2]

The deliberations of the commission were held in secret. The president of the court, the Military Commission, and the judge advocate and his assistants were the only ones allowed to be present.[3] The verdicts and sentences were required only by two-thirds of the nine-member Military Commission.[4]

When the commission convened, it was first proposed to acquit Mrs. Surratt or, at least, to spare her life. This, however, turned out to be unacceptable. Instead, another proposal was made that the commission render the same judgment on Mrs. Surratt that would be rendered on the other conspirators with a recommendation to the president of mercy for the woman. This was done. The judgment was rendered and a petition for clemency was drawn up and signed by the majority of the commission.[5]

According to John Clampitt, Gen. David Hunter, one of the judges on the Military Commission, had told him that the first vote cast by the commission in the case of Mrs. Surratt had not been for capital punishment. General Hunter continued by saying that Judge Holt and Assistant Judge Advocate Bingham demanded, in the absence of counsels for the defense, that the testimony be reread, "and such interpretation placed upon it as they thought best." Since there were no counsels for the defense to object, or at least be present to oversee the veracity of the commission, the testimony was reread and reinterpreted! According to General Hunter, this was done in violation of all principles of law and equity.[6]

General Hunter continued by saying, "Judge Advocate General Holt then moved that the same judgement of the court martial administered upon the others be visited on Mrs. Surratt and that a recommendation for mercy signed by each member of the Commission to the President of the United States should be attached to the findings of the court martial, which was done."[7]

Unfortunately for Mrs. Surratt, President Andrew Johnson later claimed that he never saw the petition for clemency! Judge Holt was in charge of taking the findings of the court and the recommendation of mercy for Mrs. Surratt to the president. The recommendation did not come to light until two years later at the trial of John Surratt, in 1867! It was then that John Surratt's counsel, R. T. Merrick, asked what had happened to Mrs. Surratt's clemency plea. It had been rumored that such a plea existed. The instrument, that could have saved Mrs. Surratt's life, was brought to court and thrown on a desk. Before anyone could examine the petition, Judge Holt retrieved it and returned it to the War Department![8]

For as long as President Johnson and Judge Holt lived, a feud existed between them concerning Mrs. Surratt's clemency petition. Judge Holt would, forever, declare that he had shown the petition to the president. On the other hand, the president would deny ever having seen it. He said that the petition was not with the papers that Judge Holt had brought from the Military Commission, on July 5, for his signature. The package of papers, in question, consisted of a letter dated July 5, 1865, from Judge Holt to the president.[9] The five-and-a-half page letter summarized the trial of the conspirators. In addition, there were eighteen pages of documents containing the formal findings and sentences.[10] It would seem that on Mary Surratt's sentencing pages there would have been a note stating that a plea for clemency was attached! However, no such notification existed!

After examining the papers that Judge Holt brought from the commission, President Johnson issued the following order:

Executive Mansion
July 5, 1865

It is ordered that the sentence of David E. Herold, G. A. Atzerodt, Lewis Paine [*sic*], Mary E. Surratt be carried into execution by the proper military authority, under the direction of the Secretary of War, on the 7th of July 1865, between the hours of 10 o'clock A.M. and 2 o'clock P.M. of that day.

It is further ordered that the prisoners Samuel Arnold, Samuel A. Mudd, Edward Spangler and Michael O'Laughlin be confined at hard labor at the Penitentiary of Albany, New York, during the period designated in their representative sentences.

Andrew Johnson
President[11]

Prior to the president's order, Mrs. Surratt and her daughter were almost constantly together in the prison room. The days and nights of waiting for the verdict from the commission must have seemed interminable, but the moments together were very precious. Anna may have read to her mother from Mary's prayer book and the book of devotions that Fr. Joseph Finotti had given her so many years before. Perhaps they discussed the meaning of life and death, of the triumph of good over evil, and of the saints who had found their rewards in heaven. Conceivably they reminisced about the past and dreamed of the future. On insufferably hot nights, they probably stood at the barred window and watched heat lightning flash across the sky.

On the afternoon of July 5, Maj. Thomas Eckert, aide to Secretary of War Edwin Stanton, received orders to have a gallows built. The major ordered Capt. Christian Rath to build a scaffold that would accommodate four people. But Eckert confided that, probably, only three would be hanged.[12]

This would not be the first scaffold that Christian Rath had constructed. Once before, he had built one to hang a deserter from the Forty-Sixth New York Infantry. As it turned out, the soldier was never hanged.[13]

So Rath did as he was ordered and drew the plans and handed them to the arsenal carpenter. He would need good stout rope that would not break during the hanging.[14] His supervisors would certainly take a dim view of such a mishap.

It wasn't until July 5 that Fr. Jacob A. Walter heard that the trial was over.[15]

Early on July 6, the sound of construction, which had started the day before, stirred the prison inmates. The window in Mary Surratt's cell room remained open for the night air. Below, no doubt, she heard men talking, sawing, and hammering. Possibly from her vantage point, she saw the scaffold being built.

That same morning, Captain Rath gathered some soldiers together from the Invalid Corps. "I want four able-bodied men to volunteer for special duty!" Rath announced loudly.

Being bored from an overdose of monotony, most of the men stepped forward. Rath looked them over as he strode in front of them. Abruptly, he stopped in front of William Coxhill. "What ails you?"

The young soldier held up a hand with a missing finger.

"Anything else?" Rath asked, perhaps with a tinge of sarcasm in his voice.

"Not a thing."

"All right, your [*sic*] elected," Rath exclaimed and continued his inspection while choosing likely soldiers for the job that he had in mind.[16]

When Rath had finished, all but seven soldiers remained. The others had been dismissed. When they followed the captain, they were unprepared for the sight of the gallows that was being built.

The soldiers were ordered to pick up the debris that was scattered around the yard from building the scaffold.[17] When they finished, the soldiers were given additional orders. D. F. Shoupe, William Coxhill, G. F. Taylor, and H. C. Haslett were to knock the gallows props from under the drops of the condemned. Three other soldiers were selected to escort three of the prisoners to the scaffold. General William H. H. McCall was requested to lead Mrs. Surratt, if her sentence was not commuted.[18]

The platform of the gallows was thirteen steps above the ground. It was hinged at the front to two leaves or drops. The front of each drop was held up by a beam at the front. Halfway back were two parallel upright beams through which ran another beam that was horizontally suspended by a rope from the gallows. Two of the four men were in charge of each drop. Coxhill and Shoupe were in charge of Lewis Powell's and Mrs. Surratt's drop. Taylor and Haslett were in charge of George Atzerodt's and David Herold's drop. The condemned would stand on the drop with nooses in place. At a given signal, the suspended beam would be pulled back and thrust through the parallel uprights which would knock out the front props. At that moment, the drops would fall and the prisoners would be hanged.[19]

Captain Rath had served in the U.S. Navy and knew about ropes. He decided on three-fourths-inch, thirty-two-strand Boston hemp halyard rope that he had gotten at the Navy Yard on the afternoon of July 4. That night, alone in his room, Rath made the nooses. The regulation hangman's knot had seven turns. But, according to the captain, by the time he had gotten to the last noose, he was tired and only made five turns. That noose would be Mrs. Surratt's. She wouldn't be using it anyway, he reasoned.[20]

On July 6, Coxhill, Shoupe, Taylor, and Haslett were ordered to attach four 140-pound shells with chains to the hanging ropes. For two, long, hot hours the soldiers rehearsed their parts in the execution for the following day.[21]

After the exhaustive session, the men were ordered to dig four graves beside the gallows.[22] They would be three and one-half feet deep by seven feet long by three feet wide.[23]

When the graves had been finally dug in the hard clay soil, Rath announced, "I want you boys to do a good job tomorrow. Don't make any mistakes and, when it's over, I'll give you each a canteen of whiskey." According to Coxhill, they "never got that drink."[24]

It was around ten o'clock in the morning of July 6 when Father Walter went to the War Department to ask Col. James A. Hardie for a pass to visit Mrs. Surratt.[25] The colonel asked him if he needed the pass immediately. If he did, Secretary Stanton was not available to issue it. Father Walter answered that there was no hurry and he returned home. Apparently, the priest had not heard that there was a distinct possibility that Mrs. Surratt would be executed the following day.[26]

Soon after the priest had returned to his home, John Holohan and a Mr. Callan called on Father Walter to tell him that Mrs. Surratt was in danger of being hanged the following day.[27]

Soon after the men left, Father Walter was called to dinner. While the priest was eating, an orderly came with the pass that he had requested. It was signed by Colonel Hardie instead of Secretary Stanton. When Father Walter took the pass, he remarked to the orderly that he had read the evidence of the trial, "and, as regards to Mrs. Surratt, there was not enough evidence to hang a cat. Besides, you cannot make me believe that a Catholic woman would go to Communion on Holy Thursday and be guilty of murder on Good Friday."[28]

Soon after the orderly left, Colonel Hardie paid the priest a visit. "Father," he said to the priest, "the remarks that you made to that young man [the orderly], have made a deep impression on him; I was afraid that the pass that I sent you would not answer, so I have brought you one from Secretary Stanton, but I want you to promise me that you will not say anything about the innocence of Mrs. Surratt."[29] It sounds as though there was some doubt as to Mrs. Surratt's guilt.

The priest replied coolly and deliberately, "You wish me to promise that I shall say nothing in regard to the innocence of Mrs. Surratt? Do you know the relation existing between a pastor and his flock?" The priest continued by saying that he had no fear and would defend the poorest woman in the parish. Then, Father Walter added that he knew from whom the order had come. Father Walter said that the order had come from "your Secretary of War." Then the priest informed Hardie that he knew a congressman who had said that the secretary was a brute! The priest was referring to Secretary Stanton. Then suddenly it occurred to Father Walter that he would have to agree to say nothing about Mrs. Surratt's innocence, or he might not be allowed to give the Sacraments to her. It was two o'clock in the afternoon when Colonel Hardie finally handed the pass to the priest, signed by Secretary of War Edwin Stanton.[30]

It had been around noon of that same day when the verdicts and sentences, sent by the Military Commission and signed by the president, were read to the prisoners.[31] Yet, part of the day before and all morning, Mary and Anna had heard the gallows being built and the drops being tested!

Anna was not with her mother when Generals Hancock and Hartranft read the verdict and the sentence to Mary. Anna was in town on an errand. We have to depend on the July 7, 1865, edition of the *Washington Evening Star* newspaper for the description of the following scenes. When the two generals made their rounds and read the sentences to the prisoners, Paine (Powell) showed no surprise. Atzerodt tried to appear indifferent, but the "pallor upon his face and his trembling extremities gave him away." The sentence came as a "thunderbolt" to Herold. He was sure that he would be sent to prison for a short time, but surely not hanged! It was reported that Mrs. Surratt grew pale. She faintly uttered a few words saying, "I had no hand in the murder of the president." Then she burst into a "violent paroxysm of grief" and asked for Father Walter, Father Wiget, Anna, and John Brophy, a friend of Weichmann's who had interested himself in her case.[32]

Undoubtedly, General McCall rushed to Mary as soon as he heard the news. It may have been at this meeting, as a show of appreciation for his kindness that Mary gave him her carved mother-of-pearl fish that hung from her rosary.[33] It, too, may have been at this time that she extracted a promise from the general that would require all the strength that he possessed in order to comply. It is commonly believed that it was General McCall who placed the noose around Mrs. Surratt's neck. Perhaps she would have preferred a friend, rather than a stranger, to perform the act.

General McCall probably assured Mary that there was still time. An article had appeared, that day, in the *New York Times* that had conveyed the belief that a reprieve for Mrs. Surratt was forthcoming.[34]

Colonel William P. Wood, the superintendent of Old Capitol Prison, had never believed that Mrs. Surratt was guilty. As soon as he learned that she was to be executed, Wood rushed to the White House in an attempt to save her life. Strangely, he was denied admittance through either the front or the rear entrance of the executive mansion! Colonel Lafayette C. Baker showed Colonel Wood a written order that "particularly" excluded Colonel Wood from seeing President Johnson![35]

Anna had returned to the prison by the time that Father Walter arrived. It is reasonable to believe that Mrs. Dodd had dashed to the prison when she heard the news of Mrs. Surratt's plight.

Conceivably, Mrs. Dodd took Anna from her mother's room while Father Walter heard Mary's confession in preparation for Communion the following morning. The priest could not divulge what she had told him regarding her guilt or innocence. However, after Father Walter heard her confession, he and Anna both rushed to the White House to see President Johnson in an attempt to save Mary Surratt from the gallows. The priest was obviously sure of her innocence. No Catholic would ever lie to a priest, particularly when facing death. To do so, in the eyes of the Church, would have meant everlasting damnation.

They met former Pennsylvania congressman, Thomas Florence, at the gate to the White House. When the priest told Florence his mission, the former congressman remarked, "Father Walter, you and I are on the same errand of mercy. The President must not allow this woman to be hanged."[36]

On the second floor, in a room adjacent to President Johnson's office, the threesome encountered General Mussey, the president's private secretary, as well as former New York senator Preston King, and others. When Mussey told the president who had come, Johnson refused to see Mary's supporters. The priest asked Mussey to try again, emphasizing that he would only detain the president for five minutes. Again, the president refused. The priest changed his tactics and asked Mussey to tell the president that he had not come for a pardon or commutation of the sentence. All he wanted was a ten-day reprieve to prepare Mrs. Surratt for eternity. Probably he thought that such a request from a priest could not be denied, not that it would take ten days to prepare Mary's soul for eternity. Then Anna begged to speak to the president. She was denied permission, as well. Instead, Johnson directed them to Judge Holt.[37]

Holt was of no help. According to Father Walter, the judge showed no more feeling toward Anna than he would "a piece of stone." Holt referred them back to the president. The priest recalled later that "the poor child with eyes streaming with tears, was left without any sympathy from this cold, heartless man."[38]

Father Wiget and John Brophy were with Mary when Anna and Father Walter returned at four-forty that afternoon.[39] At that time, John Brophy told Father Walter that Lewis Powell had declared Mrs. Surratt's innocence, "all through the trial." Brophy urged the priest to get permission to see Powell and to ask him if he still believed in Mrs. Surratt's innocence. The priests obtained permission, whereupon they spoke to Powell. According to the prisoner, Mrs. Surratt was innocent![40]

While the priests were visiting Lewis Powell, Mrs. Samuel Mudd was coming from visiting her husband. She had just said her final good-bye before the doctor would commence to serve his life sentence for setting Booth's leg. They had met in the room next to Mrs. Surratt's and adjacent to the courtroom.

On the way down the circular, narrow stairway, Mrs. Mudd met "a poor girl who was weeping bitterly." She was told later that it was Anna Surratt.[41]

It wasn't until nearly five o'clock that afternoon, while working at their office, that Clampitt and Aiken heard a paper boy heralding the news that Mrs. Surratt would be executed the following day![42]

Stunned by the news, the two attorneys made a hasty trip to the White House to see President Johnson in hope of securing an executive clemency for a few days. Senator Preston King denied the attorneys entry beyond the main floor of the White House.[43]

The two men left and hurried to the prison. There, they got Anna and sped to Judge Advocate General Holt's office. Clampitt described the following scene with Anna at the judge's office: "Upon her bended knees, bathed in tears, the forlorn girl besought him to go to the President and beg a respite for three days—three days more of life for her mother about to be murdered by the strong arm of the Government." The judge advocate general agreed to meet them at the executive mansion.[44]

Judge Holt had already met with the president by the time that Clampitt, Aiken, and Anna had arrived at the White House. Holt told them, "The President is immovable . . . and has no reason to change the date of the execution."[45]

Meanwhile, since early evening, hundreds of people had been milling around the outside of Mary Surratt's H Street boardinghouse. Neighbors sat quietly at their doors and windows, watching for anyone going in or coming out of the house.[46]

According to the *Evening Star,* about eight o'clock that evening, "Miss Anna Surratt, who has been in constant attendance upon her mother, drove up to the door in a hack accompanied by a gentleman. She appeared to be perfectly crushed with grief and as she alighted from the carriage, ladies who were standing near were moved to tears in sympathy with the unfortunate girl, who's [*sic*] every look and action betrayed her anguish."[47]

Back at the prison, Lewis Powell was not thinking about himself the night before his execution. He wanted to talk about Mrs. Surratt and called Christian Rath to his cell. He admitted to the hangman that he was largely to blame for Mrs. Surratt's troubles. He said that he would gladly suffer two deaths if they would save her from the noose.[48]

After leaving Powell, Rath went immediately to see Major Eckert. Soon after he saw the major, Rath received a message from Secretary of State William H. Seward. The secretary said that he wanted to see him. At the meeting with Seward, Rath repeated what Powell had told him. Whereupon, the secretary said that "the officials were considering the advisability of withdrawing Mrs. Surratt's death sentence."[49]

That evening, July 6, back in his room, Christian Rath made the three hanging hoods from a shelter tent. When the hoods were finished, he tore strips of material from the tent that would be used to bind the legs of the doomed, just prior to their hanging.[50] According to the *West Virginia Follansbee Review,* Priscilla Catherine Dodd made Mary's hood.[51]

Mrs. Dodd and Captain Rath were not the only busy ones that night. Acting Assistant Adjutant General R. A. Watts was writing the names of each of the condemned on slips of paper then sealing each name in a bottle. The next day, a bottle, with the name of the deceased, would be placed in each coffin. This was done to identify the remains in case of exhumation at a later date.[52]

In Baltimore, Maryland, that same night, John T. Ford was in his room laboring over a letter to the president. In the morning, he would catch the early train and take the letter to Washington. In his letter, he expressed contempt at what seemed sure to happen the following day. Ford stated that it was a "criminal weakness, without justification or precedent in this country and age to rush her [Mrs. Surratt] to the scaffold and strangle her to haste upon questionable evidence." He implored the commutation or suspension of Mrs. Surratt's sentence until he could speak to President Johnson. He urged that a few days would be enough to establish the truth. "Justice," he said, "would not be balked by a brief delay."[53]

While Ford was burning the midnight oil, in Baltimore, another resident of that city was being made aware of Mary's dilemma. It was nearly midnight when Messrs. Clampitt and Aiken wired Reverdy Johnson for advice. Since no trains were running to Washington at that late hour, Johnson recommended that they apply for a writ of habeas corpus. The writ would be issued on the grounds that Mrs. Surratt was a civilian and should not have been tried by a military court.[54]

The two attorneys drew up the writ and addressed it to President Andrew Johnson and Maj. Gen. W. S. Hancock. They requested that Mrs. Surratt be turned over to the Criminal Court of the District of Columbia at ten o'clock the following morning, July 7.[55]

It was two o'clock the morning of July 7 when Supreme Court Justice Andrew Wylie, for the District of Columbia, was wakened and asked to sign the writ.[56]

After reading and deliberating on it, the judge announced his decision. "I am about to perform an act which, before tomorrow's sun goes down, may consign me to the Old Capitol Prison." With that, the judge signed the writ![57]

The writ was given to a United States marshal at four o'clock in the morning. At eight-thirty, the marshal served it to General Hancock. At ten o'clock, the writ was suspended by President Johnson, the exact time that it had been requested that Mrs. Surratt be handed over to the Criminal Court of the District of Columbia.

The attorneys returned to the prison and gave Mary and the priests the tragic news. At a maximum, there were only four hours left of her life!

Still, there was some hope. John T. Ford arrived in Washington with his letter to President Johnson. Probably believing that someone other than he should deliver the letter, Ford stopped at the home of former postmaster general Montgomery Blair. Since it was an early

hour, Blair was still in bed. Ford left a message with a servant request-
ing that Blair immediately take the letter to the president. Later, Blair
would tell Ford that the letter had been delivered to Johnson.[58]
Nothing came of it.

In spite of Ford's attempt and failure, there was still a chance that
Mrs. Surratt could escape the hangman's noose! Early Friday morning, Father Walter wrote a letter to President Johnson regarding his
interview with Lewis Powell the night before. He said that the prisoner wanted it known "that he believed and was convinced that she was
innocent." The priest said that he believed Powell "as he was now
beyond hope [and] that he would say what he knew about Mrs.
Surratt."[59]

That same morning Lewis Powell reiterated to General Hartranft
what he had told Fathers Walter and Wiget the night before.
Convinced that Powell's near death statement was true, General
Hartranft wrote his own letter to the president stating that he thought
"that Paine [Powell] would state the truth in this matter."[60]

When the general had finished writing, he handed his and Father
Walter's letter to John Brophy, saying: "I will furnish an Army conveyance and swift horses. Take it and drive like mad to the White
House and give the President this note. I will delay the execution until
the last moment or until I hear from you definitely and positively what
the President's answer is."[61]

Anna and Mary Elizabeth Wildman Queen were at the White
House when John Brophy arrived.[62] He found Anna, weeping bitterly,
prostrate on the stairway. Senators King and Lane, in addition to the
soldiers, holding rifles with fixed bayonets, had bared Anna's way to
the president's office on the second floor. She had beseeched everyone she saw to please go to the president and beg for her mother's
life.[63]

The president's daughter happened by while Anna lay agonizing
on the marble steps. "My poor dear," said Martha Johnson Patterson.
"You break my heart, but there is not a thing I can do."[64]

For nearly an hour, John Brophy tried either to see the president
or to find someone who would deliver the messages that he carried.
All the while, Anna was sobbing and choking with grief as she clung
to John Brophy, pleading him to do something more.[65]

Then, suddenly, a fine carriage dashed up to the White House entrance and out of it hurried a richly dressed and strikingly handsome woman. It was Mrs. Stephen A. Douglas![66] Her famous husband had been nominated to run for the presidency in 1860, against Abraham Lincoln.

When Mr. Brophy heard that she had come to try to save Mrs. Surratt, he rushed to Mrs. Douglas and begged her to get him access to the president. She quickly nodded her head, took the letters that he had brought, and rushed the bayonets! Out of respect, the guards lowered their guns.[67]

When a second set of guards tried to stop her, she swept past them, giving them an imperious gesture.[68] Then Mrs. Douglas entered the president's quarters with head and hopes up high. However, when she returned, she shook her head sadly at Anna and John Brophy. Anna was close to hysterics. "Oh, don't give up so," Anna sobbed. "Don't don't! Do go to him again. He won't refuse you! He can't! Do go again!"[69]

Mrs. Douglas turned to try once more.

"Show him General Hartranft's note again," Brophy pleaded. "Ask him if he got the statement I sent him of Weichmann's confession to me. Make another appeal to him, Mrs. Douglas."[70]

"I will," said the dispirited woman. "I will, it is of little use though. I feel it is of no use."[71]

Again, Mrs. Douglas shoved the guards aside and presented herself before the president. And again, he refused to commute the sentence.[72]

It wasn't long before Mrs. Douglas glided solemnly back down the stairs. The forlorn expression on her face told them that all hope was gone.

John Brophy turned to Anna and, with a heart filled with tears, whispered to her, "Come with me if you would see your mother while she lives."[73]

Sadly, Anna, John Brophy, and Elizabeth Queen left the White House and stepped into the army conveyance. Drawn by wild-eyed horses, the carriage dashed down Pennsylvania Avenue and headed back to the penitentiary. The streets were deserted until they drew within a few blocks of the penitentiary. Sightseers were beginning to mass in the streets and on the sidewalks in order to be as near to the execution as possible. The progress of their conveyance slowed until the milling, boisterous mob became impenetrable. Then the carriage stopped and could go no farther. Meanwhile, the minutes were racing by! The deadline for the execution was drawing near![74]

Suddenly, attracting everyone's attention, the sound of clattering horses' hooves and yelling men grew closer. With great effort, the crowd parted and made way for a guard of cavalry that was flanking General Hancock and his carriage. When Hancock and his men rode up, Brophy told the general that their mission had been a failure. Hancock stood in his carriage and loudly ordered the mounted guards to clear the crowd. Then he directed Brophy to follow. The soldiers put spurs to their mounts, drove the crowd out of the way, and led them back to the prison as quickly as possible.[75]

# CHAPTER TWENTY-TWO

## *Finis*

To induce sleep, Mary Surratt was given wine of valerian the night before the execution.[1] Unfortunately, the sedative had had little effect. Throughout the night, she either tossed on her bed or paced the floor. Her female problems had worsened. Excruciating cramps tore at her without cessation.[2] Probably her mind refused to accept the possibility of being hanged the next day. No doubt, it tormented her with the shame that she would bring to her family and their descendants if a reprieve did not materialize. She knew she was innocent. She was sure that her family and friends knew that she was innocent. But what about her progeny? Would they believe that they had descended from a woman who had conspired with others to kill President Lincoln? Would they forever be hounded and haunted because of her?

At such times, Father Walter would have conceivably reminded her that there was still time for a commutation of her sentence. Then he would have rambled on about martyred saints, whom the priest would have described as God's chosen people.

The years of study for the priesthood and the experiences in his life had not prepared the thirty-eight-year-old clergyman for the agonizing

*Reverend Father Jacob A. Walter. The photograph was taken at the approximate time that he was Mary Surratt's confessor. He tried to save her from the gallows. He was with her to the end.*
(Author's Collection)

*Reverend Father Bernardine F. Wiget. He, along with Reverend Walter, accompanied Mary Surratt to the gallows.*
(Courtesy of John Brennan)

night with Mary Surratt in her "Garden of Gethsemane." He would have read her passages from the Bible. He would have encouraged her to repeat the rosary after him, but her concentration would have deserted her. If the priest had spoken the words of Jesus the night before Jesus was arrested, possibly it would have brought her some comfort. Jesus' words would have been fitting for Mary Surratt at this time: "O my Father, if it be possible, let this cup pass from me: nevertheless not as I will but as thou wilt."[3] Then, over and over, the priest and the condemned woman would have repeated the Twenty-Third Psalm: "Yea, though I walk through the valley of the shadow of death, I will fear no evil: for thou art with me; thy rod and thy staff they comfort me. Thou preparest a table before me in the presence of mine enemies: thou anointest my head with oil; my cup runneth over."[4]

Perhaps in time, the wine of valerian would have taken effect and Mary would have fallen into a fitful sleep. She may have been sleeping when the sweet lyrics of a distant mockingbird announced the dawn.

Reverend Dr. A. D. Gillette, of the First Baptist Church, in Washington, D.C., had stayed with Lewis Powell through the night. They conversed freely about religious matters. Dr. Gillette was impressed with the young man's strength. In a sermon that he gave the following Sunday, Dr. Gillette told his congregation that Powell had been "frank and candid, possessing a well cultivated mind." He added that the young man had said that he was ready to meet his God.[5]

George Atzerodt's spiritual advisor, Rev. Dr. Butler, a Lutheran minister, had prayed and preached to the condemned man throughout the night.[6]

Surprisingly, David Herold slept well for several hours. The rest of the time he prayed with the Reverend Mr. Olds of Christ Episcopal Church. David's sisters appeared early in the morning. While they were there, he "partook" of the Sacraments. He said that he was ready to die.

About eleven-thirty the same morning, Christian Rath ordered his men to again test the drops on the gallows. As if rebelling against hanging a woman, Mary Surratt's drop stuck. A carpenter trimmed the edges. At the same time, four chairs were carried by soldiers and placed on the scaffold.[7] The stage was set. The waiting began.

The incessant crashing of the drops falling, and the sound of the carpenter's saw would have reached Mary. The priest would have calmed her as best he could.

Then suddenly, the clatter of the door at the foot of the stairs on the first floor opened and then was pulled shut with a bang. The sound of thumping boots began the long, three-story climb to the courtroom and to Mary's prison room. Then slowly, two soldiers helped her down the interminable steps to the first floor and to cell number 153.[8]

With an agonized groan, Mary collapsed on a mattress that had been placed on the bare brick floor.[9] Then the soldiers left, slamming and locking the cell door behind them. Father Walter, who had followed, along with Father Wiget, who had been waiting in the cell, administered Holy Communion to her. Afterward, the cell was unlocked and John Holohan entered.[10]

Lying on her mattress, Mary barely acknowledged his presence. With her eyes closed and with great effort, she spoke. "Please stay with Annie today. God knows I am innocent but for some cause, I must suffer today. Goodbye. God bless you."[11]

Meanwhile, the day had become increasingly hotter. By nine o'clock it had reached 86.5 degrees.[12] But the extreme heat did not deter the noisy mob that made their way to the arsenal prison. Only those with special passes were allowed to enter through the gate. The others had to find their own vantage points.

In order to see the execution, some of the less favored were relegated to the upper floor windows of the administration building, outside the prison wall. "Grandstand" seats were available to a distinguished few at the windows of the old shoe shop inside the prison wall. Clusters of people stood in the prison yard while others languished under the gallows.[13]

The river steamboats had a rush of business that day. The passengers, however, were due for a disappointment when they found that the eighteen-foot prison wall would block their view of the hanging.[14]

Most of the gusts from the ten-knot wind that blew from the water were usually stopped at the prison wall. On the wall the Sixth Regiment, Veteran Volunteer Infantry, looked down on the scaffold and the assembled crowd. Now and then, a small zephyr leaped the wall, stirred the dust into pirouettes, and teased the hats and the frock coats of the onlookers.[15]

General Hartranft had given Matthew Brady and his assistant permission to photograph the execution. Argus-eyed and completely detached, except for the mechanics of his trade, the renowned photographer set up two cameras. Both cameras faced the gallows. The light was perfect. The cameras would secure the events on photographic plates before and after the drops were sprung.[16]

Soldiers, in full dress uniforms, sweated and complained under the blazing sun. Newspaper reporters, with pads and pencils poised, focused on the door where the condemned would appear. At the same time, the newspaper artists busily roughed-in their sketches. Then those with seemingly no business at all milled around, cursed the heat, and wished to hell the thing were over.[17]

There was one spectator who never failed to attract attention wherever she went. Miss Major Mary Walker, the medical surgeon, who had attended the conspiracy trial in June, was one of the onlookers. Strangely, Mary Surratt and Mary Walker had something in common. One Mary was about to be the first woman hanged by the United States government. Conversely, the other Mary would be the first woman to receive the Congressional Medal of Honor from the same government.[18]

It was shortly after noon when Anna, Eliza Wildman Queen, and John Brophy returned to the prison.[19]

Perhaps it was Brophy who had calmed Anna. Perhaps she was in shock. Whatever the reason, Anna showed unusual control when she walked into her mother's cell and took her into her arms. "Mother, are you resigned?"[20]

"Yes, my child."

"Father, speak to Mother and ask her if she is resigned."

Mary answered, without giving the priest a chance to reply. "Anna, my child, this is no place for you; go to your room."

Later Father Walter described what happened next. He said: "Without a word, this dear child, with broken sobs, left the cell and retired to one of the rooms in the penitentiary."[21]

Another version of the parting of mother and daughter appeared in the *New York Herald*: "Anna took from her bonnet a steel arrow pin and stuck it upon her mother's dress, close to the neck on a bow."[22]

From many accounts, the final parting of Mary and Anna was traumatic, not only for the mother and daughter, but for all who witnessed it. The *Philadelphia Inquirer* reported: "The screams of anguish that burst from the poor girl could be distinctly heard all over the execution ground."[23]

The *Constitutional Union*'s rendition of Anna's grief was described as being "heart-rendering."[24]

It may have been after Anna left the cell that Mary asked John Brophy to try, "at some future time, when the passions of the war are cooled," the task of clearing Mrs. Surratt's name of the crime.[25] This he endeavored to do for the rest of his life.

Then, the time came for friends and relatives of the condemned to leave. It grew quiet when their weeping could no longer be heard. Abruptly, the terrible sound of the cell doors being opened in unison reverberated through that part of the prison.

The two priests helped Mary to her feet and seated her on a chair that had been placed outside the cell. Mary lifted her face to Father Walter. "Father, I wish to say something."[26]

"Well, what is it, child?"[27]

"That I am innocent."[28]

"You may say so if you like, but it will do you no good," Father Walter answered. Later in his presentation before the United States Catholic Historical Society, the priest said: "These words were uttered whilst she stood on the verge of eternity, and were the last confession of an innocent woman."[29]

Rumors were beginning to circulate around the prison yard that a reprieve had been granted Mrs. Surratt. "It is very barbarous to hang a woman," one person said. "Women are very rarely hung in any country and our government will not do it," still another said. Others agreed that Father Wiget held Mrs. Surratt's reprieve in his hand and at the last minute would announce that her life had been spared.[30]

At twelve-fifty, General Hancock posted sentries around the scaffold. At precisely one o'clock, General Hartranft and his staff appeared at the prison door. Reporters and onlookers quickly stepped aside to make an avenue for them to the gallows.[31]

By noon, the temperature had reached 92.3 degrees.[32] When General McCall arrived, he sadly walked to Mary. Gently, he placed her black bonnet with the heavy veil on her head. It would protect her from the sun and the prying eyes of the onlookers.

At a signal, General McCall and an unidentified sergeant gently lifted Mary to her feet. When the procession started to the gallows, the priests began to pray aloud. She rested her eyes on the crucifix

*July 7, 1865–the final hour. From left to right: Mary Surratt, Lewis Powell, David Herold, and George Atzerodt. William Coxhill is leaning against the prop beneath Mary Surratt. D.F. Shoupe is standing behind the second prop.* (Library of Congress)

that one of the clergy held before her. Mary stumbled into the glaring sunlight. She was so unsteady on her feet that the soldiers nearly carried her the thirty paces to the gallows.[33]

Atzerodt followed, trembling with fear as he shambled along between his guards. Dr. Butler and Chaplain Winchester walked slowly behind him.[34]

David Herold came next, supported by his guards. He wore a hat with the brim turned down.[35] Reverend Olds followed in prayer.[36]

All eyes turned to Lewis Powell as he strode indifferently behind the rest. He was dressed in the uniform of a United States Navy sailor, except that the wide turn of the collar was missing. His shirt had the appearance of a tight-fitting undershirt that revealed his muscular frame to advantage. A leghorn hat rode jauntily on his head. With neither fear or shame, his unblinking eyes met the stares of the morbidly curious. When he drew closer to the gallows, he eyed his instrument of death with cool detachment. His obvious bravery in the face of being hanged inspired admiration even from those who despised his crime.[37]

To the terror-stricken and manacled prisoners, the thirteen steps to the platform were a long and laborious climb for all but Lewis Powell. Nonchalantly he climbed the steps with little assistance.[38]

Mary was led to the far left chair on the platform, where she collapsed. There, she suffered with nervous spasms, and leaned her head to alternate sides of her armchair. She moaned audibly when she saw her noose dangling menacingly in front of her. In an attempt to assuage her fears, one of the priests quickly shielded her with his body from the spectacle. From time to time, she would kiss the crucifix on her rosary, while the priests continued their invocations.[39]

All the while, Lewis Powell's thoughts were with Mary. According to Dr. Gillette, Powell kept asking if any word of a reprieve had come for Mrs. Surratt. "She does not deserve to die with us, Doctor," Powell said.[40]

Then, something dislodged Powell's hat. Dr. Gillette bent over, picked it up, and returned it to the young man's head.

"Thank you, Doctor. I won't be needing it much longer," Powell smiled cynically.[41]

George Atzerodt and David Herold shared the same drop. As if in prayer, Herold's lips moved continuously while, at the same time, Reverend Olds leaned over and whispered in Herold's ear.[42]

At the far right of the gallows, Atzerodt slouched in his chair. Ironically, someone had spread a handkerchief on his head to protect him from the sun.[43]

All the while, the nooses hung and occasionally swayed in the sweltering heat.

General Hancock had stationed soldiers on each block from the White House to the penitentiary. The soldiers were under orders to relay an executive reprieve for Mrs. Surratt directly to the general. Full of hope, the general had remained close to the last relay soldier. John Clampitt was there when General Hancock finally appeared empty handed in the prison yard. The two o'clock deadline for the hanging was drawing near.[44]

What transpired next is taken from an interview with John Wesley Clampitt, in 1880, by J. W. Forney, journalist. Prior to the hanging, Clampitt asked Hancock if there was any hope. "General Hancock shook his head slowly and mournfully and, with sort of a gasping catch in his speech, said, 'I am sure there is not. No there is not.'

"He then walked off a bit—and gave some orders to the orderlies and paced about, a moment or two. Returning, he said, 'I have been

*Preparing for the hanging. Mary Surratt's bonnet is being removed while her legs are being bound.* (Library of Congress)

in many a battle and have seen death and moved with it in disaster and in victory. I've been in a living hell of fire, and shell, and grape, but, by God, I'd sooner be there ten thousand times over than to give the order, this day, for the execution of that poor woman. But I am a soldier, sworn to obey, and obey I must.'"[45]

Then General Hancock gave the written order of execution to General Hartranft. All the while, the general and his staff had been waiting for the order while standing on the platform of the gallows. General Hartranft took the order and removed his hat. General R. A. Watts stepped forward and held an umbrella over his superior's head.[46]

In a clear, strong voice, General Hartranft read aloud the written order. At the end, he whispered a few words of religious consolation.[47]

Then Dr. Gillette stepped forward and said that Lewis Thornton Powell, otherwise known as Lewis Paine, wanted to thank General Hartranft and all others who had had charge of him for treating him so well.[48] The doctor followed with a fervent prayer in behalf of Powell. Powell's eyes filled with tears, while, with obvious feeling, he repeated the prayer.[49]

Reverend Olds echoed a similar statement of gratitude on behalf of

*The drop.* (Library of Congress)

David Herold. The minister added that he hoped that David was dying with charity to all men and was at peace with God.[50]

Dr. Butler gave a statement of appreciation for George Atzerodt. The minister followed with an earnest prayer that "God Almighty might have mercy upon this man."[51]

All of the religious invocations had been said for Mary by the priests in her cell, "so as to save her from being too much exposed to the public gaze."[52]

William Coxhill and D. F. Shoupe stood beneath Mary's and Lewis Powell's drop. According to Coxhill, the clergy seemed to talk interminably. The stress and the heat overpowered the young soldier and he became ill. Holding onto the prop, he bent over and vomited.[53]

At a signal, the condemned were made to stand so that their legs could be bound, and the nooses placed around their necks. Then Captain Rath inspected each noose to be sure that they were properly positioned. When he readjusted Powell's noose, Rath told him that he wanted him to die quickly. In reply, the young man answered, "Cap., you know best." Those were Powell's last words.[54]

Powell stood tall and unflinching without support. His spiritual advisor would say later that Lewis Powell, unlike the others, had gone to his death without the aid of drugs. He had said that he wished to die with his mind unclouded.[55]

General McCall had gently removed Mary's bonnet. Her arms were pinioned behind her and her legs were bound over her dress. General McCall's final act for his friend was to slip the noose around her neck and the hangman's hood over her head.[56]

"Don't let me fall," Mary whimpered when she was helped to her feet and led to the drop.[57]

At the same time, David Herold squirmed and protested against the huge knot.[58]

*Finis: Mary Surratt, Lewis Powell, David Herold, and George Atzerodt.* (Library of Congress)

Christian Rath descended the steps from the platform and stationed himself in front of the gallows. Just as he raised both of his hands and was about to give the signal to knock the props, George Atzerodt raised his voice from beneath his hood. In muffled, broken English, he rasped, "Goodbye gentlemen, who are before me now. May we all meet in the other world! God help me now! Oh! Oh! Oh!"[59]

Christian Rath clapped his hands three times. For an instant, there was not a sound. Then, suddenly, the soundlessness was shattered. The drops fell with a deafening crash. George Atzerodt, David Herold, Lewis Powell, and Mary Surratt dropped to eternity with a terrible jolt.

All the while, Anna and Elizabeth Queen were standing at the second floor window in the building where the trial had been held. The same building where she and her mother had stayed together. William E. Doster was standing at the another window. Anna fainted when General McCall placed the noose around her mother's neck.[60]

When the act was done, Captain Rath personally placed Mrs. Surratt in her coffin.[61]

> Her eyes were shut—no motion—not a breath,
> The gentle sufferer was at peace at last.

# *Epilogue*

*Aiken, Frederick A. and Clampitt, John Wesley*—*Philadelphia Inquirer,* July 9, 1866, ". . . The Justice has bound Mr. Aiken over to Court for forging Mr. Clampitt's name to bank checks. The Superintendent of Police has given Mr. Clampitt a certificate that there is nothing involving him in the transaction. The firm was dissolved as soon as Mr. Clampitt discovered Aiken's conduct."

*Jenkins, Elizabeth ("Bessie")*—Mary Surratt's mother converted to Catholicism. She died June 7, 1879. She is buried at St. Ignatius Church, Oxon Hill, Maryland. This is the same church that Mary helped to establish. The epitaph reads, "Mrs. E. A. Webster Jenkins Born 1794 Died 1878."[1]

*Lloyd, John Minchin*—After Mary Surratt's trial and execution, John Lloyd returned to Washington, D.C. There he worked as a bricklayer.

On December 18, 1892, on his sixty-eighth birthday, John Lloyd died from injuries that he sustained when he fell from a building that he was helping to construct.

Ironically, he is buried only fifty yards from Mary Surratt's grave at Mount Olivet Cemetery.[2]

*All that remains of the Old Arsenal Penitentiary. It was on the third floor where the trial of the conspirators was held. Mary Surratt was quartered on the same floor. Currently, the building is used as officers' quarters at what is now Fort Lesley J. McNair, Army War College, Washington, D.C.* (Author's Collection)

*Surratt, Elizabeth Susanna*—After the execution, Anna ran to St. Vincent School at 10th and G Streets. The following is taken from an article that appeared in the *Montgomery County Sentinel*, Rockville, Maryland, August 5, 1948. A young music student witnessed the scene: "I was in the parlor practicing my lesson, watched over by Sister Blanche, when Anna Surratt was announced. She ran into the room weeping uncontrollably. Sister Blanche took her into her arms weeping with her, of course, it was more than I could stand. So I asked the Sister if I might be excused and weeping I left the room."

On June 28, 1867, at the impeachment trial of President Andrew Johnson, Anna testified that she did not know what to do with her mother's former boardinghouse after the government had returned it to her. Then, Eliza Holohan came and offered to help Anna in any way she could. Anna said, "They cleaned up the house and staid [*sic*] with me."

Just two days after her mother's execution, Anna wrote the following letter. It certainly demonstrates Anna's phenomenal character.

Washington D.C.
July 9, 1865


Genl. Hartranft


Genl. Hancock told Mr. Holohan that you had some things that belonged to my poor Ma, which, with my consent you would deliver to him. Don't forget to send the pillow upon which *her head* rested and her prayer beads, if you can find them—these things are dear to me.


Someone told me that you wrote to the President stating that the Prisoner Payne [Powell] had confessed to you the morning of the Execution that Ma was entirely innocent of the President's assassination and had no knowledge of it. Moreover, that he did not think that she had any knowledge of the assassination plot, and that you believed that Payne [Powell] had confessed the truth. I would like to know if you did it because I wish to remember and thank those who did Ma the least act of kindness. I was spurned and treated with the utmost contempt by everyone at the White House.


Remember me to the officers who had charge of Ma and I shall always think kindly of you.


Your Respectfully—
Anna Surratt[3]

*Mt. Olivet Cemetery,*
*Washington, D.C., where*
*Mary Surratt is buried.*
(Author's Collection)

*The plaque below Mary*
*Surratt's headstone. Nearby is*
*a shrine with a bronze plaque*
*that reads: "The souls of the*
*just are in the hands of God,*
*and the torment of malice*
*shall not touch them. In the*
*sight of the unwise they*
*seemed to die, but they are at*
*peace."* (Author's
Collection)

The H Street boardinghouse was lost to creditors on November 13, 1867. The former Surratt House and Tavern met the same fate, on March 11, 1869.[4]

For four years Anna begged for the body of her mother so that it could be accorded a Christian burial. Finally, President Andrew Johnson answered her pleas. On February 8, 1869, Mary Surratt's remains were taken from the burial site at the Old Penitentiary to Mount Olivet Cemetery, Washington, D.C.[5]

The following rather morbid account appeared in *The Washington Chronicle of Yesterday,* February 19, 1869: "The coffin of Mrs. Surratt when lifted, was in tolerable condition, and when opened the remains were found to be in an excellent state of preservation. [Remarkable considering that she was buried more than four years before on a hot July day!] The face though black, was yet perfect in features, and the whole body compact and firm. The dress looked well, and the gaiter shoes appeared not to be the least soiled. Upon the day of her execution her daughter, Annie, who visited her, took from her own bonnet a steel arrow and stuck it upon her mother's dress close up to the neck, and which remained where it had been placed by the daughter." The article continued by saying that Fr. Jacob A. Walter had accompanied the remains to Mount Olivet Cemetery where the body was placed in a handsome walnut coffin.[6]

The following day, Mary Surratt was finally laid to rest. Among those present were John, Isaac, Anna, Honora Fitzpatrick, and Dr. William P. Tonry, Anna's future husband. Father Walter officiated in the service. Father Bernardine Wiget was in Europe, at the time.[7]

Dr. Tonry and Anna were married on June 18, 1869. They were married at St. Patrick's Church, the same church that Anna and her mother had attended. The ceremony was performed by Reverend Father Walter. Zadoc, John, and Isaac were present. Dr. Tonry was a chemist employed by the surgeon general's office.[8] His office was located in the former Ford's Theatre. At that time, the theater was being used as a government office. Dr. Tonry was fired, soon after their marriage, because his bride was the daughter of Mary Surratt. The young couple moved to Baltimore where the doctor established a laboratory of his own. Eventually four children were born to the couple: William, Albert, Reginald, and Clara.[9]

Anna Surratt Tonry was sixty-one years old when she died, October 24, 1904. She is buried beside her mother at Mount Olivet Cemetery.[10]

*Surratt, Isaac Douglas*—On May 4, 1862, Isaac enlisted as a private in Company A, Thirty-Third Regiment, Fourteenth Battalion, Texas Calvary, Captain James Duff's Partisan Rangers in San Antonio, Texas. He was promoted to sergeant on March 1, 1863.[11]

The Thirty-Third Regiment served primarily on the lower Rio Grande. Several companies of the regiment fought in the last battle of the Civil War, at Palmito Ranch on May 13, 1865.[12]

Isaac was paroled from the Confederate service at San Antonio, Texas, September 18, 1865.[13]

According to some accounts, he joined members of his company who fought for the Emperor Maxmillian in Mexico. The company disbanded when the emperor insisted on selecting the officers for the American unit. According to Isaac's obituary, he and the other men went to Europe. Incredibly, and again, according to the obituary, Isaac did not learn of his mother's death until he returned to the United States![14]

Another, more believable, version states that Isaac did not go to Europe. Instead, on October 18, 1865, Gen. Philip H. Sheridan telegraphed Secretary of War Edwin Stanton with a physical description of Isaac. On October 19, Gen. Lafayette Baker, chief of the United States Secret Service, wired Maj. Thomas T. Eckert, aide to Secretary Stanton, that Isaac had been arrested in Baltimore.[15]

Isaac never married. He and his brother, John, were both employed by the "Old Bay Line," a Baltimore steam packet company. Again, according to his obituary, Isaac had been educated as an engineer.

In his later years, he lived with his sister, Anna, and her family.[16] Isaac died at the age of sixty-six on November 3, 1907. He is buried in the Surratt family plot at Mount Olivet Cemetery, Washington, D.C.[17]

*Surratt, John Harrison, Jr.*—After President Lincoln was assassinated, John Surratt tried hard to escape capture. His travels took him to Canada, England, and Rome where he enlisted in the Papal Zouaves as John Watson. Henri Beaumont de Sainte-Marie, a former friend of Louis Weichmann's and an acquaintance of John's, recognized and reported Surratt to the American minister to the Papal States. John was arrested, but escaped to Alexander, Egypt, where he was found and again arrested. He was extradited to the United States to stand trial. He arrived in Washington, D.C., on February 19, 1867.

John Surratt was taken to Old Capitol Prison. He was brought to trial on June 10, 1867. He was tried before the Criminal Court of the District of Columbia. The jury could not reach a verdict and asked for a dismissal. Rather than accept the dismissal, John opted for exoneration and was returned to prison for another trial. On February 4, 1868, he was indicted for treason. But in the case of treason, the law required that the indictment must be found within two years. The two years had elapsed and John Surratt went free.

Now free, John Surratt traveled the lecture circuit telling about his adventurous life. Later, he taught school in Emittsburg and Rockville,

*Surratt House and Tavern, formerly Surrattsville, Maryland, now Clinton, Maryland.* (Author's Collection)

Maryland. Then, like his brother, he secured a position at the "Old Bay Line." In time he rose to auditor and treasurer of the company.

In 1872, John married Mary Victorine Hunter, a second cousin to Francis Scott Key. They resided in Baltimore and had seven children. Only a son and three daughters lived to become adults.

John Surratt died, at the age of seventy-two, on April 21, 1916. He is buried in the New Cathedral Cemetery in Baltimore, Maryland.[18]

*Surratt House and Tavern*—The structure has been restored to its original condition. A lovely private home was acquired to house a museum, gift shop, library, archives, and offices. A memorable twelve-hour bus trip that travels the John Wilkes Booth escape route is offered by the museum. Reservations are needed well in advance. The property is a facility of The Maryland-National Capital Park and Planning Commission. Information may be had by writing: Historian, Surratt House Museum, P.O. Box 427, Clinton, MD 20735 or Tel: (301) 868-1121.

*Weichmann, Louis J.*—Louis Weichmann spent most of the remainder of his life either begging favors from Judge Holt or Secretary Stanton.

According to Weichmann, the Catholic bishop of Philadelphia dismissed his brother from seminary because Weichmann had testified against Mrs. Surratt. Usually, he was treated with insults and ostracized wherever he went.

The trial of the alleged conspirators became an obsession. In an attempt to vindicate himself, Weichmann wrote a book that basically covered his version of the conspiracy and the trial. But out of fear for his life, the book was not published until after Weichmann had died.

On October 25, 1870, Louis Weichmann married Annie Johnson of Philadelphia. The marriage ended without benefit of divorce when Weichmann moved out of the house, leaving his wife to take in boarders. The union produced no children.

After Louis Weichmann lost his government job in 1886, he joined his family in Anderson, Indiana. There he opened a business college. Until his death on June 5, 1902, he lived the life of a haunted man. An obituary of his death appeared in the Muncie, Indiana, *Morning Star,* June 6, 1902. "PROF. LEWIS J. WEICHMANN IS DEAD. WOMAN HANGED ON HIS TESTIMONY." Yet, to the end the unhappy man professed that he had told the truth concerning Mary Surratt at the trial of the alleged conspirators.[19]

# *Notes*

## CHAPTER 1

1. James O. Hall, *The Story of Mary Surratt* (Clinton, MD: Surratt Society Publication, July 1977), p. 4.

2. *The Maryland Genealogical Bulletin,* Baltimore, MD: January 1931 issue. Archibald Jenkins and Elizabeth ("Bessie") Webster were issued a license to marry in Prince George's County, MD, on 4 June 1821.

3. James O. Hall, op. cit.

4. Ibid.

5. Headstone, Mt. Olivet Cemetery, 1800 Bladensburg Rd., NE, Washington, DC.

6. James O. Hall, op. cit.

7. Ibid.

8. Ibid.

9. *The Maryland Genealogical Bulletin,* op. cit.

10. James O. Hall, op. cit.

11. *The Maryland Genealogical Bulletin,* op. cit.

12. Ibid.

13. Ibid.

14. According to Broad Creek Church records, James Gibbs Webster was baptized on 17 April 1768.

15. Transcribed by T. Michael Miller, *Alexandria and Arlington County, Virginia, Virginia Minister Return and Marriage Bonds, 1810-1852,* 1937.

16. A copy of the receipt can be found at the Surratt Society archives in Clinton, MD.

17. Letter from Sister Rose Collins, Daughter of Charity, Cabourne Residence, Los Altos, CA, to John Brennan, dated 30 August 1989.

18. Edward L. Stephens, *One Hundred And Fifty Years For Christ* (Alexandria, VA: pamphlet published by St. Mary's Catholic Church), pp. 29-30.

19. Advertisement for the "Academy for Young Ladies under the direction of the Sisters of Charity," *Alexandria Gazette,* 25 June 1832, p. 3.

20. Death notice of James Webster, son of John Webster, *Alexandria Gazette,* (Friday evening) 18 November 1910. James Webster would eventually serve as a police captain on the Alexandria police force.

21. Ann Elizabeth Ellen Mudd was born 12 February 1817. She died 2 December 1854. Ref: Letter from Frances X. Flaherty-Knox (family genealogist) to the author, dated 5 November 1987.

22. Louis Wright and Elaine W. Fowler, *Everyday Life in the New World, 1787-1860* (New York: G. P. Putnam's Sons, 1972), p. 143.

23. Ibid., p. 133.

24. St. Mary's Catholic Church baptismal record for Henry Randolph Webster, 20 August 1838, p. 57.

25. Edward L. Stephens, op. cit., pp. 30-31.

### CHAPTER 2

1. Laura and Norman H. Sarratt, *Surratt/Sarratt Families 1715-1980* (Fresno, CA: Pioneer Publishing, 1980), pp. 12-13.

2. St. Peter's Catholic Church baptismal record of John Harrison.

Note 2A: For some clarification of Caroline Sarath's last name see John Surratt to the United States, Bond Recorded 21 December 1840, WB 86-PP-100 (Old) or WB-86-93 (New). In the bond, Caroline's last name is stated as being Landersant, Gandusent, or Sanderson. However, according to James O. Hall, author and historian, a man by the name of William Sanderson, who had four daughters, lived near Richard Neale. One daughter was near John Harrison Surratt's age. Mr. Hall obtained this information from the 1830 DC census, p. 40.

3. Marriage license record, District of Columbia, covering the period of 23 December 1811 to August 1858. (James O. Hall research.)

4. Jenkins Family genealogy folder, Surratt Society archives, Clinton, MD.

5. Dr. James Munson, "Signs of the Times," *The Fireside Sentinel,* December 1987, Vol. I, No. 10.

6. Phyllis Luskey Cox, "A Brief Summary of Jenkins, P.G. Co., MD," 2 December 1985.

7. Rambler, *Washington Star,* 29 June 1924, col. 3, page number was not legible.

Note 7A: Henri J. Wiesel's letter to Dr. Richard Mudd, dated 27 November 1954, substantiates the article that appeared in the *Washington Star.* James and Debora Meade Boiseau were the grandparents of Henri Wiesel. In this letter Wiesel claimed that, according to his grandparents, Mary Jenkins and John Surratt were married in the Boiseau home.

8. Rambler, *Washington Star,* 13 October 1912, "With the Rambler, Odd Nooks and Crannies About the City."

9. St. Peter's Catholic Church baptismal record for Isaac Surratt, 13 September 1841.

10. St. Peter's Catholic Church baptismal record for Elizabeth Susanna Surratt, 10 December 1843.

11. From the ledger of John Henry Bayne found by John Walton at the Maryland Hall of Records.

12. *Prince George's County Genealogical Society Bulletin,* Vol. 13, No. 7, March 1982, "The Bayne Family."

13. DC Land Records, Liber WB 98:229-231 and WB 98:232-234, 24 May 1842, Washington National Records Center, Suitland, MD, and James O. Hall, *The Mary Surratt House* (Clinton, MD: The History Division, Maryland-National Capital Park and Planning Commission, 1979), pp. 1-11.

14. St. John's Episcopal Church at Broad Creek marriage register, Vol. III, 1797-1879.

15. James O. Hall, "The Story of Mrs. Surratt," a lecture delivered before the docents of the Surratt House, Clinton, MD, 1976, published August 1977, p. 6.

16. DC Land Records, Liber WB 103:507-510, Washington National Records Center, Suitland, MD (Appendix A). (James O. Hall research.)

17. DC Land Records, Liber WB 107:506-511. Ibid.

18. DC Land Records, Liber WB 139:133-137. Ibid.

19. DC Land Records WB 116:340-341, D.C. Recorder of Deeds Office, Washington, DC (Appendix A).

20. Baptismal record at St. Peter's Catholic Church, baptism of Elizabeth Susanna Surratt.

21. St. Mary's Catholic Church baptismal record 3 June 1845, p. 99. Reverend C. H. Stonestreet officiated. Mary Webster was the sponsor. Margaret Elizabeth was approximately one year five months old at the time of her baptism.

22. Alan Virta, *Prince George's County a pictorial history* (Norfolk, VA: The Donning Company/Publishers, 1984), p. 87.

23. Laura and Norman H. Sarratt, op. cit., p. 13.

24. Seventh Federal Census (1850) District of Columbia, Series M-432, Roll 56, Appendix B, National Archives, Washington, DC.

25. St. Mary's Catholic Church, baptismal record of Sarah Neale, 27 June 1845, p. 53.

26. Dr. Bayne's ledger, op. cit.

27. Laura and Norman H. Sarratt, op. cit., p. 17, 5.1.

## CHAPTER 3

1. Laura and Norman H. Sarratt, *Surratt/Sarratt Families 1715-1980* (Fresno, CA: Pioneer Publishing, 1980), pp. 17-18.

2. Ibid., pp. 17-20.

3. Ibid., p. 11.

4. Ibid.

5. Baptismal record of St. Peter's Catholic Church, Washington, DC, for John Harrison Surratt, Jr., 20 September 1847, Ann Smoot named as sponsor.

6. Woodstock Collection (Letters) 79 (July 1950) 3, p. 236. Special Collections, Georgetown University Library, Washington, DC.

7. Ibid.

8. John Coulson, ed., *The Saints, A Concise Biographical Dictionary* (New York: Hawthorne Books, Inc., 1958), pp. 232-33.

9. Woodstock Collection, op. cit., p. 236.

10. Ibid., p. 237.

11. G. M. Finotti, *Autobiography and Memoirs of Chev. G. M. Finotti* (unpublished), written 1882 and 1883. Transcribed by Beatrice M.

Woodhouse, 1940, p. 9. A copy of the unpublished manuscript was given to the author as a gift from Mrs. Helen Finotti Golembieski, great grandniece of Rev. Joseph M. Finotti.

Note: "Chev." (Chevalier) is the title for both French and Italian knighthood. Gustavus Finotti was awarded the Cross of Knighthood from the Crown of Italy in 1865. Ref: Ibid., p. 4 (outline).

12. Woodstock Collection, op. cit., p. 237.

13. Ibid.

14. Ibid.

15. G. M. Finotti, op. cit., p. 1 (outline).

16. St. Mary's Catholic Church, Alexandria, VA, "Resident Pastors 1818-1945."

17. Authored by St. Ignatius Church, Oxon Hill, MD, *St. Ignatius Church* (White Plains, NY: Monarch Publishing, Inc., 1974), unnumbered p. 14.

18. G. M. Finotti, op. cit., unmarked page 1.

19. Laura and Norman H. Sarratt, op. cit., p. VI.

20. John Coulson, op. cit., pp. 232-33.

21. Woodstock Collection, op. cit., p. 239.

22. St. Ignatius Church, op. cit., unnumbered p. 13.

Note 22A: According to the announcement, the Reverend Charles Stonestreet was given as a reference for the school. Reverend Stonestreet was president of Georgetown College in the years 1851 and 1852. The Reverend George Villager was also given as a reference. Reverend Villager was pastor at St. Mary's Church in Alexandria. He served there from 1852 to 1854. This would indicate that St. Ignatius Female Institute was in operation in 1852. Ref: St. Mary's Catholic Church, Alexandria, VA, "Resident Pastors 1818-1945."

## CHAPTER 4

1. G. M. Finotti, *Autobiography and Memoirs of Chev. G. M. Finotti* (unpublished), written 1882 and 1883. Transcribed by Beatrice M. Woodhouse, 1940, p. 24.

2. Ibid., p. 69.

3. James M. McPherson, *Ordeal by Fire* (New York: Alfred A. Knopf, Inc., 1982), pp. 68,75.

4. The year of the fire is gained from oral history.

Note 4A: In a letter that Mrs. Surratt wrote to Father Finotti on 13 May 1855, she mentioned a "keepsake" that "got burnt up the night of the fire." She requested another. He obliging sent her a book of devotions. The author believes that the original keepsake was a gift of appreciation that the priest had presented to all the parishioners who had helped to make St. Ignatius Catholic Church possible.

5. Calvin Douglas Wilson, "Negroes Who Owned Slaves," *Popular Science Monthly,* November 1912, p. 489.

6. Rambler, *The Evening Star,* 13 October 1912, and *The Sunday Star,* 3 November 1912, "Old Nooks and Crannies: The Surratt Mill."

Note 6A: Anna Jenkins Hoyle was interviewed for the articles. She identified herself as being the daughter of Thomas Jenkins. She mentioned that Mary Surratt and her children had stayed with her family after the fire.

The 1850 Washington, DC, census lists Thomas and Charity Jenkins and their six children. Susana Jenkins, age eleven, was one of the children. The names Susana and Anna or Annie were used interchangeably. It is the opinion of the author that it was Susana who was the Annie Jenkins who later married Samuel Hoyle. Again, according to the 1850 Washington, DC, census, Samuel was nineteen years old at the time. There would have been eight years difference between Susana and Samuel. It is well within the range of possibility that the two were, at one time, husband and wife.

7. Minute Book, 1846-1852, Fairfax County Court, p. 353, dated 18 August 1857.

Note 7A: The Minute Book shows garnishment action against the partnership of John H. Surratt and David Barry for $111.82. (James O. Hall research.) By the author's calculations, Surratt would have been active in this partnership in the summer of 1851 and possibly until April 1852 when the tavern-house was completed.

8. Report from the Office of the Orange and Alexandria Railroad Company, Alexandria, Virginia, to the Board of Public Works, 1 October 1850. Virginia State Library, Richmond, VA.

9. Woodstock Collection, Vol. 14, p. 249. Special Collections, Georgetown University Library, Washington, DC.

10. Johnny Bouquet, *New York Tribune,* 8 May 1881, p. 10, col. 2. ". . . that while her (Mrs. Surratt) husband was yet living an Italian priest who ministered in that part of the country got in such a flirtation with Mrs. Surratt that it raised a commotion that he had to be sent to Boston to get him out of the scandal."

11. G. M. Finotti, op. cit., p. 63.

12. James O. Hall, *The Mary Surratt House* (Clinton, MD: The History Division, Maryland-National Capital Park and Planning Commission, 1979), p. 1-63.

13. Woodstock Collection (Letters), 79 (July 1950) 3, p. 237. Special Collections, Georgetown University Library, Washington, DC.

14. Reverend Joseph Maria Finotti, *Twenty-Six Years a Priest* (unpublished), p. 12.

15. Ibid.

16. James O. Hall, op. cit., p. 1-24.

17. Ibid.

18. H. H. Simms, "Maternal Line of Mrs. Surratt," *The Maryland Genealogical Bulletin,* Baltimore, MD, January 1931.

19. DC Land Records, Liber JAS 57:159 et. seq., Washington National Records Center, Suitland, MD, 10 May 1853.

20. Letter from Mary Surratt to Reverend Joseph Finotti, dated 12 April 1853.

21. Woodstock Collection, Vol. 14, p. 248. Special Collections, Georgetown University Library, Washington, DC.

22. Letter from Mary Surratt to Father Finotti, dated 12 April 1853.

23. Land transfer, dated 10 May 1853.

24. DC Land Records, Liber 70:311, Washington National Records Center, Suitland, MD. (James O. Hall research.)

25. DC Land Records, Liber JAS 70:301-304, and Liber JAS 70:311, et. seq., Ibid. (James O. Hall research.)

26. James O. Hall, op. cit., p. 1-25.

27. The doctors lived less than a mile from the Surratts. Both doctors testified, at the trial of the conspirators, that Mrs. Surratt was a very kind woman. Ref: Benn Pitman, *The Assassination of President Lincoln and the Trial of the Conspirators,* Facsimile Edition (New York: Funk and Wagnalls, reprint 1954, by Philip Van Doren Stern), p. 137, the testimonies of Drs. John T. Hofton and William W. Hofton for the defense.

## CHAPTER 5

1. Undated letter from Mary Surratt to Father Finotti found at the New York Historical Society by Michael W. Kauffman.

2. Ben Perley Poore, *The Conspiracy Trial for the Murder of the President* (Boston: 1865); Reprint Edition (New York: Arno Press Inc., 1972), Vol. II, p. 501, testimony of Anna Surratt.

3. The sisters' headstone at St. Mary's Cemetery, Bryantown, MD.

4. James O. Hall, *The Mary Surratt House* (Clinton, MD: The History

Division, Maryland-National Capital Park and Planning Commission, 1979), pp. 1-29, 1-30.

5. Ibid.

6. Joseph George, Jr., "'A True Childe of Sorrow,' Two Letters of Mary E. Surratt," *Maryland Historical Magazine,* Vol. 80, No. 4, Winter 1985, p. 403. Letter to Father Finotti, dated 15 January 1855.

7. Father Nota's letter to Father Wiget, dated 3 January 1855. Special Collections, Georgetown University Library, Washington, DC.

8. Benn Pitman, *The Assassination of President Lincoln and the Trial of the Conspirators,* Facsimile Edition (New York: Funk and Wagnalls, reprint 1954, by Philip Van Doren Stern), p. 136, testimony of Rev. B. F. Wiget for the defense.

9. Rambler, *Washington Evening Star,* 8 February 1912.

10. Ibid.

11. *The Parish of St. Mary,* Piscataway, MD, a booklet published by the church, unnumbered pages 17-18.

12. *Washington Evening Star,* op. cit.

13. The inscription is located above the front entrance to St. Mary's Catholic Church in Piscataway, MD.

14. Joseph George, Jr., op. cit., p. 403, Mary Surratt's letter to Father Finotti, dated 15 January 1855.

15. Monsignour Alfonso Muzzarelli, *The Month of May Consecrated to the Mother of God* (Boston: Patrick Donahoe, 1854). Mrs. Surratt's book of devotions is on display at the Surratt House and Tavern museum, Clinton, MD.

16. James M. McPherson, *Ordeal By Fire* (New York: Alfred A. Knopf, Inc., 1982), p. 95.

17. Ibid., p. 96.

18. *Planter's Advocate,* 31 December 1856, Enoch Pratt Library, Baltimore, MD.

19. James O. Hall, op. cit., p. 1-33.

20. Ibid., p. 1-35.

## CHAPTER 6

1. Woodstock Collection (Letters), Vol. 60, dated 1916, p. 362. Special Collections, Georgetown University Library, Washington, DC.

2. Ibid.

3. Ibid.

4. Ibid.

5. Helen Jones Campbell, *The Case of Mrs. Surratt* (New York: G. P. Putnam's Son, 1943), pp. 41-42.

6. Mary Surratt's letter to Father Finotti, dated 28 September 1858. The letter was found by Michael W. Kauffman at the New York Historical Society.

7. Louis J. Weichmann, *The True History of the Assassination of Abraham Lincoln and of the Conspiracy of 1865* (New York: Alfred A. Knopf, Inc., 1975), p. 14.

8. George Alfred Townsend, "A Talk with Louis Weichmann," reprinted *Surratt Society News*, 1980.

9. James O. Hall, *The Mary Surratt House* (Clinton, MD: The History Division, Maryland-National Capital Parks and Planning Commission, 1979), p. 1-51.

10. Ibid., p. 1-52.

11. Alice Stone Camallier's letter to Dr. Richard Mudd, dated 5 February 1959. Copy of the letter may be found at the Surratt Society achieves, Clinton, MD.

12. Edited by Alfred Isacsson, (Sidelights) "Some Letters of Anna Surratt," *Maryland Historical Magazine*, September 1959, p. 311.

13. Ibid., p. 312.

14. Letter from Frances X. Flaherty-Knox to Dr. R. D. Mudd, dated 11 August 1987. Also, Frances X. Flaherty-Knox letter to the author, dated 5 November 1987.

15. James M. McPherson, *Ordeal by Fire* (New York: Alfred A. Knopf, Inc., 1982), p. 94.

16. Ibid., p. 114.

17. Harold Holzer, "Raid on Harpers Ferry," *American History* magazine, March 1984, p. 18.

18. Ibid., p. 16.

19. *The Trial of John H. Surratt in the Criminal Court for the District of Columbia* (Washington, DC: Government Printing Office, 1867), p. 695, testimony of Eliza Hawkins (Rachel Seavers).

20. Benn Pitman, *The Assassination of President Lincoln and the Trial of the Conspirators,* Facsimile Edition (New York: Funk and Wagnalls, reprint 1954, by Philip Van Doren Stern), p. 137, testimony of Rachel Semus [*sic*], Seavers (Hawkins) for the defense.

Note 20A: "Rachel Hawkins," *Washington Star,* 21 December 1892. The David Rankin Barbee Collection, Georgetown University Library, Washington, DC.

21. James M. McPherson, op. cit., p. 112.

22. Edward A. Pollard, *Southern History of the War* (New York: Crown Publishers, Inc., 1977), p. 34.

23. Ibid., p. 35

24. Ibid.

25. Ibid., p. 38.

26. Ibid.

27. Ibid., pp. 38,39.

28. Ibid., p. 40.

29. Aunt Rachel Hawkins in an interview with the *Washington Star,* 21 December 1892, tells how fond she was of Mrs. Surratt. She referred to the days with Mary Surratt as being "the good old days."

30. Edited by J. B. McClure, A.M., *Abraham Lincoln's Stories and Speeches* (Chicago: Rhodes & McClure Publishing Co., 1897), p. 406.

31. Benn Pitman, op. cit., p. 130, testimony for the defense of William P. Wood, superintendent of the Old Capitol Prison. "In 1860 and 1861," according to Wood, "Mr. Jenkins was counted as one of the most reliable Union men in that district."

32. Woodstock Collection, Vol. 43. Special Collections, Georgetown University Library, Washington, DC, "The Jesuit Farms in Maryland."

33. Edited by Bayly Ellen Marks and Mark Norton Schatz, *Between North and South* (Cranbury, NJ: Associated University Presses, Inc., 1976), p. 17n.

34. Ibid.

## CHAPTER 7

1. According to Isaac D. Surratt's Confederate Military Record, Isaac joined the Thirty-Third Texas Cavalry on 7 May 1862.

2. Benn Pitman, *The Assassination of President Lincoln and the Trial of the Conspirators,* Facsimile Edition (New York: Funk and Wagnalls, reprint 1954, by Philip Van Doren Stern), p. 130, testimony of William P. Wood for the defense.

3. Bruce Catton, *The Coming Fury* (New York: Doubleday & Company, 1961), p. 283.

4. Ibid., p. 293.

5. Ibid.

6. Ibid., p. 294.

7. Ibid.

8. Ibid., p. 295.

9. Ibid., p. 143.

10. Ibid., p. 306.

11. Ibid., p. 296.

12. Ibid., p. 297.

13. Ibid., p. 308.

14. Ibid.

15. Ibid., p. 311.

16. Ibid.

17. Ibid., p. 324.

18. Daniel D. Hartzler, *Medical Doctors of Maryland in the C.S.A.* (1979), p. 14.

19. Ibid.

20. Bruce Catton, op. cit., p. 341.

21. James O. Hall, "Lincoln and the Baltimore Riots," *Surratt Courier,* May 1989.

22. Edited by Bayly Ellen Marks and Mark Norton Schatz, *Between North and South* (Cranbury, NJ: Associated University Presses, Inc., 1976), p. 24n.

23. Woodstock Collection. Special Collections, Georgetown University Library, Washington, DC, "The Jesuit Farms in Maryland."

24. Edited by Alfred Isacsson, (Sidelights) "Some Letters of Anna Surratt," *Maryland Historical Magazine,* September 1959, p. 312.

25. Rambler, *The Sunday Star,* 3 November 1912. (Fort Snyder was located near the Jenkins home and near what is now St. Elizabeth's Mental Hospital).

26. Ibid., 8 February 1914. Pliny Bryan became an aide-de-camp to General Beauregard. Toward the end of the war, he died of yellow fever. He is buried in Magnolia Cemetery, Savannah, Georgia. Bob Bryan served through the war in the First Maryland Battery, Horse Artillery, C.S.A., attached to Stuart's cavalry. William Pike Bryan served with the Second Maryland Infantry, C.S.A. He lived to an advanced age and is buried in the Bryan plot, St. Mary's Catholic Church cemetery, Piscataway, MD.

27. G. M. Finotti, *Autobiography and Memoirs of Chev. G. M. Finotti* (unpublished), written 1882 and 1883. Transcribed by Beatrice M. Woodhouse, 1940, p. 66.

28. Ibid., p. 67.

29. Rambler, *The Sunday Star,* 8 February 1914.

30. Benn Pitman, op. cit., pp. 137-38, testimony of Rachel Semus.

31. Karen G. Harvey and Ross Stanfield, *A Pictorial History, Alexandria* (Norfolk, VA: Donning Co., Publishers, 1977), p. 136.

## CHAPTER 8

1. Benn Pitman, *The Assassination of President Lincoln and the Trial of the Conspirators,* Facsimile Edition (New York: Funk and Wagnalls, reprint 1954, by Philip Van Doren Stern), p. 130, testimony of William P. Wood for the defense.

2. Harry Wright Newman, *Maryland and the Confederacy* (Annapolis, MD: published by Harry Wright Newman, 1976), p. 110-111.

3. Ibid., p. 111.

4. Ibid.

5. Ibid.

6. Daniel D. Hartzler, *Medical Doctors of Maryland in the C.S.A.* (1979), p. 14.

7. Effie Gwynn Bowie, *Across the Years in Prince George's County* (Richmond, VA: Garrett & Massie Inc., nd), p. 359.

8. Ben Perley Poore, *The Conspiracy Trial for the Murder of the President* (Boston: 1865); Reprint Edition (New York: Arno Press Inc., 1972), p. 501.

9. Harry Wright Newman, op. cit., p. 60.

10. *Prince George's County Genealogical Society Bulletin,* Vol. 13, No. 7, March, 1982, "The Bayne Family History."

11. According to Dr. G. W. Fisher, late private of Company D, Eighty-Fifth Pennsylvania Volunteers, Surratt Society archives, Clinton, MD.

12. Ibid., and *Enquirer-Gazette,* Upper Marlboro, MD, republished June 1956. The David Rankin Barbee Collection, Georgetown University Library, Washington, DC.

13. Rambler, *The Sunday Star,* 15 April 1917.

14. Thomas A. Jones, *J. Wilkes Booth* (Chicago: Laird & Lee Publishers, 1898), p. 23.

15. Ibid., p. 24.

16. Samuel Carter, III, *The Riddle of Dr. Mudd* (New York: G. P. Putnam's Sons, 1974), p. 58.

17. *The Trial of John H. Surratt in the Criminal Court for the District of Columbia* (Washington, DC: Government Printing Office, 1867), p. 892, testimony of John C. Bartlett.

18. Joan Chaconas, "From Our President," *Surratt Society News,* October 1980.

19. Daniel D. Hartzler, op. cit., p. 14.

20. Rambler, *The Sunday Star,* 28 November 1928. In 1865, Col. William P. Wood would become the first chief of the Secret Service

when it became part of the U.S. Treasury Department. Ref: Ibid.

21. Incident narrated in Anna's letter to her friend, Louise Stone, dated 16 September 1862. Ref: Edited by Alfred Isacsson, (Sidelights) "Some Letters of Anna Surratt," *Maryland Historical Magazine,* September 1959, p. 313.

22. Howard B. Farer, *Washington—A Chronological Documentary Handbook.*

23. A quotation from Anna's letter to her friend, Louise Stone, dated 16 September 1862, "to have the banner of Southern liberty unfurled and planted upon the shores of Maryland," was a "long desired" wish of her father. Ref: (Sidelights), op. cit., p. 313.

24. Ibid. According to a letter from Anna Surratt's daughter, Mary Tonry Walsh, to James O. Hall (a copy in the Surratt Society archives): just a year before John Surratt's death, a horse had kicked him. Mrs. Walsh continued by saying that this may have been the cause of her grandfather's death. In addition, Mrs. Walsh stated that a priest had said that John Surratt was almost a Catholic when he died. There have been other accounts that say John Surratt died of apoplexy.

25. Letter to John Brennan, Surratt Society, from Phillip D. Robinson, dated 7 March 1981. According to Robinson, his great-grandfather, William Townsend Robinson, carpenter and undertaker, buried John Surratt, Sr., in the "Catholic churchyard at Piscataway." A copy of the letter is in the Surratt Society archives, Clinton, MD.

26. *Postmaster General's Journal,* Vol. 51, folio 33, National Archives, Washington, DC.

27. James O. Hall, *The Mary Surratt House* (Clinton, MD: The History Division, Maryland-National Capital Park and Planning Commission, 1979), p. 1-56.

28. Ibid., pp. 1-63, 1-66.

29. Benn Pitman, op. cit., p. 130.

30. *The Trial of John H. Surratt,* Vol. I, op. cit., p. 695, testimony of Eliza Hawkins (Rachel Seavers).

31. War Department Files, National Archives, Washington, DC, Series M-599, Reel 6, Frames 0170 through 0200. "Statement of Mrs. Mary E. Surratt—April 28, 1865, Carroll Prison." Mrs. Surratt told Colonel Olcott under questioning that she didn't have a son in the Confederate Army that she knew of. She said the last she had heard from him, he was in Matamoros, Mexico. The statement may be found in the National Archives.

## CHAPTER 9

1. Harry Wright Newman, *Maryland and the Confederacy* (Annapolis, MD: published by Harry Wright Newman, 1976), p. 141.

2. *Harrisonburg Rockingham County Historical Society,* Summer 1986, Vol. 8, # 3.

3. James M. McPherson, *Ordeal by Fire* (New York: Alfred A. Knopf, Inc., 1982), p. 360.

4. Ibid.

5. Ibid.

6. Ibid.

7. Louis J. Weichmann, *The True History of the Assassination of Abraham Lincoln and of the Conspiracy of 1865* (New York: Alfred A. Knopf, Inc., 1975), p. 18.

8. Ibid.

9. Ibid., p. 19.

10. Ibid., p. 18.

11. Ibid., p. 22.

12. Michael W. Kauffman, "David Edgar Herold, The Forgotten Conspirator," *Surratt Society News,* November 1981.

13. Louis J. Weichmann, op. cit.

14. Ibid.

15. Ibid.

16. Ibid., p. 23.

17. Ibid., p. 24.

18. Arthur Barry served with Company B, Ninth Virginia Infantry. Company B was known as the Baltimore Heavy Artillery and fought at Gettysburg. Ref: Daniel D. Hartzler, *Medical Doctors of Maryland in the C.S.A.* (1979), p. 14.

19. A story handed down by the Surratt family.

20. Harry Wright Newman, op. cit., p. 127.

21. "Rebbel [*sic*] Rage in Old Surratts Boded Lincoln's Death," *The Enquirer-Gazette,* Upper Marlboro, MD, June 1956. The David Rankin Barbee Collection, Georgetown University Library, Washington, DC.

22. Helen Jones Campbell, *Confederate Courier* (New York: St. Martin's Press, 1964), p. 30.

23. *The Enquirer-Gazette,* op. cit.

24. James O. Hall, *The Mary Surratt House* (Clinton, MD: The History Division, Maryland-National Capital Park and Planning Commission, 1979), p. 1-56.

25. Mary Anne Surratt, of Washington, Pennsylvania, was first mentioned in Chapter 3.

26. Laura and Norman H. Sarratt, *Surratt/Sarratt Families 1715-1980* (Fresno, CA: Pioneer Publishing, 1980), pp. 10-21.

27. Mrs. Elizabeth Sarratt Irvine's letter to the author, dated July 1986. Mrs. Irvine was the grandniece of Joseph Sarratt.

28. Ibid.

29. *History of Jefferson County*, an unidentified clipping.

30. John Surratt's letter to Belle Seaman, dated 16 December 1863. Surratt Society archives.

31. Laura and Norman H. Sarratt, op. cit., p. 19.

### CHAPTER 10

1. Louis J. Weichmann, *The True History of the Assassination of Abraham Lincoln and of the Conspiracy of 1865* (New York: Alfred A. Knopf, Inc., 1975), p. 26.

2. Ibid.

3. Ibid., p. 27.

4. Edwin W. Beitzell, *Point Lookout Prison Camp for Confederates* (Abell, MD: Edwin W. Beitzell, 1983), pp. 53-54.

5. Louis J. Weichmann, op. cit., p. 27.

6. John P. Brophy's affidavit, items 12 and 13, concerning Louis Weichmann. The David Rankin Barbee Collection, Georgetown University Library, Washington, DC, and Surratt Society archives, Clinton, MD.

7. Letter from John Surratt to Belle Seaman, dated 1 August 1864, Surratt Society archives, Clinton, MD.

8. Ibid.

9. Ibid.

10. Ibid.

11. Ibid.

12. Ibid.

13. G. M. Finotti, *Autobiography and Memoirs of Chev. G. M. Finotti* (unpublished), written 1882 and 1883. Transcribed by Beatrice M. Woodhouse, 1940, pp. 3-4 (outline), p. 69.

14. Edward McPherson, *The Political History of the United States of America During the Great Rebellion* (Washington, DC: 1865), pp. 419-20.

15. Louis J. Weichmann, op. cit., p. 27.

16. Daniel B. Lloyd, *The Lloyds of Southern Maryland* (1971), p. 145.

A copied extraction from the above book found in the Surratt Society archives, Clinton, MD.

17. James M. McPherson, *Ordeal by Fire* (New York: Alfred A. Knopf, Inc., 1982), p. 447.

18. *The Trial of John H. Surratt in the Criminal Court for the District of Columbia* (Washington, DC: Government Printing Office, 1867), p. 693, testimony of Eliza Hawkins (Rachel Seavers).

19. Guy W. Moore, *The Case of Mrs. Surratt* (Norman: University of Oklahoma Press, 1954), p. 5.

20. Harold Wang, "A Visit to the Surratt Boardinghouse, Washington, DC," *Surratt Society News,* August 1982, pp. 5-6.

21. Benn Pitman, *The Assassination of President Lincoln and the Trial of the Conspirators,* Facsimile Edition (New York: Funk and Wagnalls, reprint 1954, by Philip Van Doren Stern), p. 132, testimony of Honora Fitzpatrick for the defense.

22. Guy W. Moore, op. cit., p. 6.

23. By a Lady, *The Old Capitol and Its Inmates* (New York: E. J. Hale & Son, 1867), p. 68 (probably authored by Virginia Lomax). It is generally believed that the "Mary" referred to in the book was Honora Fitzpatrick.

24. Helen Jones Cambell, *Confederate Courier* (New York: St. Martin's Press, 1964), p. 51.

25. Phoebe Yates Pember, *A Southern Woman's Story* (St. Simons Island, GA: Mockingbird Books, Inc., 1980), p. 70.

## CHAPTER 11

1. Louis J. Weichmann, *The True History of the Assassination of Abraham Lincoln and of the Conspiracy of 1865* (New York: Alfred A. Knopf, Inc., 1975), p. 28.

2. Ibid., p. 26.

3. Harry Wright Newman, *Maryland and the Confederacy* (Annapolis, MD: published by Harry Wright Newman, 1976), p. 143.

4. Margaret Leech, *Reveille in Washington* (New York and London: Harper & Brothers Publishers, 1941), p. 251.

5. The David Rankin Barbee Collection, Georgetown University Library, Washington, DC, Amator Justitle, *Trial of Mrs. Surratt; Or, contrasts of the past and present,* Washington, DC, 14 June 1865, p. 2.

6. Guy W. Moore, *The Case of Mrs. Surratt* (Norman: University of Oklahoma Press, 1954), p. 7.

7. Louis J. Weichmann, op. cit., p. 32.

8. Samuel Carter III, *The Riddle of Dr. Mudd* (New York: G. P Putnam's Sons, 1974), pp. 74-77.

9. Ibid., p. 81.

10. Ibid., pp. 88-89.

11. Nettie Mudd, *The Life of Dr. Samuel A. Mudd* (Linden, TN: Continental Book Company, 1975), p. 43.

12. Ibid., p. 44.

13. Louis J. Weichmann, op. cit., p. 33.

14. Nettie Mudd, op. cit., p. 44.

15. Louis J. Weichmann, op. cit., p. 33.

16. Ibid., pp. 33-34.

17. A description of one of Booth's actual outfits.

18. Asia Booth Clark, *The Unlocked Book* (New York: G. P. Putnam's Son, 1938), p. 41.

19. Honora's cat is mentioned in John Surratt's letter to Belle Seaman, dated 6 February 1865.

20. Asia Booth Clark, op. cit., p. 12.

21. Ibid.

22. Asia Booth Clark, op. cit., p. 73.

23. "Hindoo Mother," Ballad, by F. T. Strawinski, published by F. D. Benteen, Baltimore, W. T. Mayo, New Orleans. (Entered according to Act of Congress in the Year 1849 by F. D. Benteen in the Clerks Office of the District Court of Maryland.)

Note 23A: A Hindoo mother is a mother from Negro ancestry.

24. Laurie Verge, "A Portrait of Mary E. Surratt," *Surratt Society News,* May 1981.

25. Louis J. Weichmann, op. cit., p. 70.

26. Laurie Verge, op. cit.

27. Michael W. Kauffmann, "John Wilkes Booth And the Murder of Abraham Lincoln," *Blue and Gray Magazine,* April 1990, p. 19.

28. Louis J. Weichmann, op. cit., pp. 74-75.

## CHAPTER 12

1. Louis J. Weichmann, *The True History of the Assassination of Abraham Lincoln and of the Conspiracy of 1865* (New York: Alfred A. Knopf, Inc., 1975), p. 75.

2. Michael W. Kauffman, "John Wilkes Booth And the Murder of Abraham Lincoln," *Blue and Gray Magazine,* April 1990, p. 19, col 3.

3. Louis J. Weichmann, op. cit., p. 44.

4. Ibid.

5. Champ Clark and the Editors of Time-Life Books, *The Assassination, Death of the President* (Alexandria, VA: Time-Life Books Inc., 1987), pp. 13, 14, 17.

6. Ibid., p. 15.

7. Asia Booth Clark, *The Unlocked Book* (New York: G. P. Putnam's Son, 1938), p. 43.

8. Ibid., p. 42.

9. War Department Files, National Archives, Washington, DC, Series M-599, Reel 16, Frames 0170 through 0200. "Statement of Mrs. Mary E. Surratt—April 28, 1865, Carroll Prison."

Note 9A: The month of early February is from: Michael W. Kauffman, op. cit., p. 22, col. 2.

10. *The Trial of John H. Surratt in the Criminal Court for the District of Columbia* (Washington, DC: Government Printing Office, 1867), p. 669, testimony of John T. Holohan, and p. 688, testimony of Eliza Holohan.

11. John Surratt's letter to Belle Seaman, 6 February 1865, Surratt Society archives, Clinton, MD.

12. James O. Hall, "The Lost Has Been Found," *Surratt Society News,* October 1979.

13. Benn Pitman, *The Assassination of President Lincoln and the Trial of the Conspirators,* Facsimile Edition (New York: Funk and Wagnalls, reprint 1954, by Philip Van Doren Stern), p. 132, testimony of Eliza Holohan for the defense.

14. *Meteorological Observations Made at the U.S. Naval Observatory During the Year 1865.*

15. Guy W. Moore, *The Case of Mrs. Surratt* (Norman: University of Oklahoma Press, 1954), p. 7.

16. James O. Hall, "The Other Boardinghouse Residents—Mary Apollonia Dean and The Holohan Family," *Surratt Society News,* May 1984.

17. *The Trial of John H. Surratt,* op. cit., p. 689, testimony of Eliza Holohan.

18. James O. Hall, "The Saga of Sarah Slater," *Surratt Society News,* February 1982.

19. Ibid.

20. Alexandra Lee Levin, *This Awful Drama* (New York: Vantage Press, 1987), pp. 144-45.

21. James O. Hall, "The Saga of Sarah Slater," op. cit., pp. 2-3, and Alexandra Lee Levin, p. 145.

22. Alexandra Lee Levin, p. 147.

23. James O. Hall, "The Saga of Sarah Slater," op. cit., pp. 2-3.

24. Ibid., p. 3.

25. Benn Pitman, op. cit., pp. 133-34, testimony of Augustus S. Howell for the defense.

26. Louis J. Weichmann, op. cit., p. 84.

27. Ibid.

28. Ibid., pp. 84-85.

29. Ibid., p. 85.

30. Richmond Morcom, "They All Loved Lucy," *American Heritage Magazine,* October 1970, pp. 13,15.

Note 30A: There has never been a consensus of opinion as to whom John Wilkes Booth was engaged. Some believe that it was to Elizabeth Hale, Lucy's sister. Ref: Samuel Carter, III, *The Riddle of Dr. Mudd* (New York: G. P. Putnam's Sons, 1974), p. 78.

31. J. Duane Squires, "Hale, John Parker," *The World Book Encyclopedia,* 1966 ed.

32. C. Vann Woodward, ed., *Mary Chesnut's Civil War* (New Haven and London: Yale University Press, 1981), p. 744.

33. Edited by Bayly Ellen Marks and Mark Norton Schatz, *Between North and South* (Cranbury, NJ: Associated University Presses, Inc., 1976), p. 166.

34. Ibid., p. 172.

35. Ibid.

36. Ibid.

37. Ibid.

38. James O. Hall, "The Saga of Sarah Slater," op. cit., p. 3.

39. Ibid.

40. Benn Pitman, op. cit., p. 119, testimony of Louis Weichmann for the prosecution.

41. James O. Hall, "The Saga of Sarah Slater," op. cit., p. 4.

## CHAPTER 13

1. Louis J. Weichmann, *The True History of the Assassination of Abraham Lincoln and of the Conspiracy of 1865* (New York: Alfred A. Knopf, Inc., 1975), p. 96.

2. Ben Perley Poore, *The Conspiracy Trial for the Murder of the President*

(Boston: 1865); Reprint Edition (New York: Arno Press Inc., 1972), p. 76, testimony of Louis J. Weichmann for the prosecution.

3. Ibid.

4. Ibid., pp. 76-77.

Note 4A: On 12 March 1865, Lewis Powell (Wood or Paine) had beaten a black maid at Branson's boardinghouse in Baltimore. She had him arrested. He was imprisoned and charged as a spy. He was released on 14 March and ordered to the North. At that time he was using the name of Lewis Paine. Ref: *Investigation and Trial Papers Relating to the Assassination of President Lincoln,* National Archives, Washington, DC, Series M-599, RG 393, Register 125, p. 411, 8th Army Corps, Baltimore, MD, LAS File. (James O. Hall research.)

Actually, Lewis Powell, using the name of Lewis Paine, took the Oath of Allegiance in Alexandria, VA, on 13 January 1865. Ref: *Investigation and Trial Papers Relating to the Assassination of President Lincoln,* op. cit., Series M-599, RG 393, Entry, Defenses South of the Potomac, p. 47, LAS File. (James O. Hall research.)

5. Ibid., p. 77.

6. Ibid.

7. Betty Ownsbey, "Lewis Powell Mystery Man of the Conspiracy," *Surratt Society News,* June 1980, p. 5.

8. Ibid.

9. Louis J. Weichmann, op. cit., p. 97.

10. Ben Perley Poore, op. cit., p. 76.

11. Louis J. Weichmann, op. cit., p. 97.

12. Ibid., pp. 97-98.

13. Ibid., p. 98.

14. Ibid., pp. 98,99,100.

15. Ibid., p. 98.

16. Benn Pitman, *The Assassination of President Lincoln and the Trial of the Conspirators,* Facsimile Edition (New York: Funk and Wagnalls, reprint 1954, by Philip Van Doren Stern), p. 131, testimony of Anna E. Surratt for the defense.

17. Ibid., p. 132, testimony of Honora Fitzpatrick for the defense.

18. Louis J. Weichmann, op. cit., p. 99.

19. William Hanchett, "The War Department and Booth's Abduction Plot," *Lincoln Herald,* Winter 1980, Vol. 82, No. 4, p. 499.

20. Ibid., p. 500.

21. Ibid., p. 499.

22. Samuel Bland Arnold, *Defense and Prison Experiences of a Lincoln*

*Conspirator* (Hattiesburg, MS: The Book Farm, 1943), p. 38.

23. David Rankin Barbee, "The Murder of Mrs. Surratt," a paper presented at the Emerson Institute, 25 February 1950. The David Rankin Barbee Collection, Georgetown University Library, Washington, DC.

24. Ibid.

25. Louis J. Weichmann, op. cit., p. 101.

26. "Affidavit of Mr. John Brophy," sworn out against Louis Weichmann that appeared in the *Constitutional Union,* Tuesday afternoon, 11 July 1865, paragraph 10.

Note 26A: The affidavit concerns Louis Weichmann's declaration to John Brophy after the evidence for the defense had closed at the trial of the alleged conspirators. Unfortunately, at the trial, Weichmann did not mention the scene between Mrs. Surratt and her son.

At the time, Brophy was a professor of English at Gonzaga College and a friend of both John Surratt and Louis Weichmann.

The exact day that Mrs. Surratt asked John what was going on, etc., is not known.

27. Louis J. Weichmann, op. cit., p. 470, endnote number 6.

28. Ibid., p. 101.

29. Michael W. Kauffman, "John Wilkes Booth And the Murder of Abraham Lincoln," *Blue and Gray Magazine,* April 1990, p. 24, col. 1.

30. Louis J. Weichmann, op. cit., p. 102.

31. Ibid.

32. Ibid.

33. Benn Pitman, op. cit., p. 85, testimony of John Lloyd for the prosecution.

34. Louis J. Weichmann, op. cit., p. 119.

35. Ibid.

36. It is a basically accepted story among researchers that Lou Weichmann did, in fact, try to kiss Anna Surratt. To partly substantiate the claim, there exists a letter in the National Archives (W409 JAO 1865), written to Weichmann in February 1865, from Mrs. Clara Ritter of New York City. In her letter she wrote: "I hope you will bring dear Miss S——tt with you to call on me. I could love her for *your* sake, & they are all favorably disposed towards you I believe." Ref: Louis J. Weichmann, op. cit., p. 471, endnote 9.

37. Michael W. Kauffman, op. cit., p. 24, col. 2.

38. Benn Pitman, op. cit., p. 131, testimony of Anna Surratt, and p. 132, testimony of Honora Fitzpatrick for the defense.

39. Ibid., p. 131, testimony of Anna Surratt.

40. Ibid.

41. *Daily Constitutional Union,* 7 July 1865.

42. James O. Hall, "The Saga of Sarah Slater," *Surratt Society News,* February 1982, p. 4.

43. Ibid.

44. Ibid.

45. *The Trial of John H. Surratt in the Criminal Court for the District of Columbia* (Washington, DC: Government Printing Office, 1867), p. 752, testimony of David Barry.

46. Ibid., pp. 750-51, testimony of Olivia Jenkins.

47. Ibid.

48. Ibid.

49. Champ Clark and the Editors of Time-Life Books, *The Assassination, Death of the President* (Alexandria, VA: Time-Life Books, 1987), p. 54.

50. Louis J. Weichmann, op. cit., p. 121.

51. Michael W. Kauffman, op. cit., p. 24, col. 2.

52. Ibid.

53. Louis J. Weichmann, op. cit., p. 125.

54. James O. Hall, op. cit., p. 4.

55. Alexandra Lee Levin, *This Awful Drama* (New York: Vantage Press, 1987), p. 152.

## CHAPTER 14

1. James O. Hall, "The Saga of Sarah Slater," *Surratt Society News,* February 1982, p. 5.

2. *The Trial of John H. Surratt in the Criminal Court for the District of Columbia,* (Washington, DC: Government Printing Office, 1867), p. 714, testimony of Honora Fitzpatrick.

3. Ibid., p. 998, testimony of Samuel Jackson.

4. Ibid., p. 713, testimony of Honora Fitzpatrick.

5. James O. Hall, op. cit., p. 5.

6. *The Trial of John Surratt,* op. cit., p. 722, testimony of Honora Fitzpatrick.

7. Ibid.

8. Ibid., p. 721

9. Ibid., p. 722.

10. Louis J. Weichmann, *The True History of the Assassination of*

*Abraham Lincoln and the Conspiracy of 1865* (New York: Alfred A. Knopf, Inc., 1975), p. 129. John Surratt's Rockville, MD, lecture, given 6 December 1870.

11. James O. Hall, op. cit., p. 5.

12. War Department Files, National Archives, Washington, DC, Series M-599, Reel 6, Frames 0233 through 0251. "Statement of Mary Surratt, April 17, 1865."

13. Ibid.

14. Ibid.

15. Ben Perley Poore, *The Conspiracy Trial for the Murder of the President* (Boston: 1865); Reprint Edition (New York: Arno Press Inc., 1972), p. 80, testimony of Louis Weichmann for the prosecution.

16. War Department Files, op. cit., statements of Mary Surratt made on 17 and 28 April 1865.

17. Ibid., "Statement of Mary Surratt, April 17, 1865."

Note 17A: Early on 4 April, John and Sarah Slater left New York. Ref: James O. Hall, op. cit., p. 6.

18. Ibid.

Note 18A: On 6 April 1865, John registered at the St. Lawrence Hall in Montreal, using the name John Harrison. He had arrived from New York by train. Ref: "Report of the Proceedings in Canada," by Special Agent C. W. Taylor, The David Rankin Barbee Collection, Georgetown University Library, Washington, DC.

Note 18B: Also on 6 April, John Surratt met with Edwin Gray Lee, military attaché to the Confederate secretary of state Judah P. Benjamin. It was at that time, when the Confederacy was collapsing, that Surratt turned over important dispatches that he and Sarah Slater had carried from Richmond. These dispatches were from Benjamin to Lee relating to the disposal of Confederate funds that were in the hands of Jacob Thompson.

Thompson was a Confederate emissary stationed in Montreal.* It has often been mistakenly believed that the dispatches were related to the assassination of Abraham Lincoln. It has been satisfactorily proven that the Southern Confederacy was not involved in the assassination. Every effort was made at the trial of the conspirators to prove that President Lincoln's death had been carried out under the direction of the Confederate government. In an effort to establish the Federal government's case against the Confederacy's part in the assassination, Secretary of War Edwin M. Stanton and Judge Joseph Holt looked the other way when men with disreputable reputations perjured themselves in order to help to solidify the government's case against the Confederacy. Ref: *U.S. vs John H. Surratt, 4731, Defendant Affidavit of Proof filed 15 July 1867, National Archives, Washington, DC. Ref: Guy W. Moore, *The Case of Mrs. Surratt* (Norman: University of Oklahoma Press, 1954), pp. 113,114, concerning Southern conspiracy.

19. War Department Files, op. cit., "Statement of Mary Surratt, April 17, 1865."

20. According to the Naval Observatory in Washington, DC, rain began to fall at 9:00 P.M., 9 April 1865.

21. Benn Pitman, *The Assassination of President Lincoln and the Trial of the Conspirators,* Facsimile Edition (New York: Funk and Wagnalls, reprint 1954, by Philip Van Doren Stern), p. 135, testimony of Annie Ward for the defense.

22. Louis J. Weichmann, op. cit., p. 131.

23. Ibid.

24. Ibid.

25. Ibid.

26. Ibid.

27. Ibid., p. 133.

Note 27A: Weichmann claimed that in the morning that they were to leave, Mrs. Surratt asked him to go to the National Hotel and ask Booth to lend them a horse and buggy. Booth said that he had sold them and gave Weichmann ten dollars to hire a rig. The author contends that it would have been logical for Mrs. Surratt to have asked for the use of the horse and buggy when Booth was at the house the night before. Perhaps the reason she didn't ask was because she didn't have as close a relationship to Booth as Weichmann did.

28. Ibid.

29. Poore, op. cit., p. 8, testimony of Louis Weichmann.

30. Otto Eisenschiml, *Why Was Lincoln Murdered?* (Boston: Little, Brown and Company, 1937), p. 281.

Note 30A: For years Emma Offutt had been deeply involved in various Confederate plots to abduct President Lincoln in order to bring the war to an end. There was always talk circulating around Southern Maryland concerning many plans to abduct the president. No one actually knew if any of the plots were sponsored by the Confederate government in Richmond. Ref: An undated letter from Mrs. H. E. Naylor, Jr., to a Mr. Kackley. In the letter, Mrs. Naylor claimed to be related to John Lloyd and privy to family information. The letter is in the archives of the Surratt Society.

Note 30B: John Lloyd testified at the trial of the conspirators that Mrs. Surratt had told him, at their chance meeting in Uniontown, to have "shooting irons" ready, that they would be needed. Ref: Benn Pitman, op. cit., p. 85.

Note 30C: However, in Poore's transcript of the trial, Lloyd said he was not "altogether positive" that Mrs. Surratt had mentioned anything about "shooting irons." Ref: Ben Perley Poore, op. cit., pp. 117, 121.

Note 30D: Strangely, when Mrs. Surratt was questioned at the Old Capitol Prison on 17 April, her interrogator did not ask her if she had spoken to Lloyd about having any "shooting irons" ready! In fact, she wasn't even asked if she had seen Lloyd in Uniontown!

31. Louis J. Weichmann, op. cit., p. 134.

32. *The Trial of John H. Surratt,* op. cit., p. 755, testimony of Capt. Bennett Gwynn.

33. Benn Pitman, op. cit., p. 132, testimony of Honora Fitzpatrick.

34. Approximate date that the little girl was taken back to Virginia.

35. Louis J. Weichmann, op. cit., p. 163.

Note 35A: On 12 April 1865, John Surratt left Montreal for Elmira, New York. Since the Federal prisons were still holding thousands of captured Confederates, Gen. Edwin Lee decided on a bold move. He wanted to free the prisoners in order to reinforce the Confederate States army. It was John Surratt's mission to survey the Federal prison at Elmira for a possible rescue attempt. Ref: Alexandra Lee Levin, *This Awful Drama* (New York: Vantage Press, 1987), p. 153.

36. Benn Pitman, op. cit., p. 126, testimony of George Calvert for the defense.

37. Ibid.

38. Louis J. Weichmann, op. cit., p. 164.

39. Ibid., pp. 164, 165.

40. Benn Pitman, op. cit., p. 116, testimony of Louis Weichmann for the prosecution.

41. According to the *New York World,* 14 November 1868, after Booth left Mrs. Surratt, he went to Ford's Theatre. It was there that he learned that President and Mrs. Lincoln, and General Grant and his wife, would be attending the theater that evening to see the presentation of *Our American Cousin.* Consequently, any assassination plans for that evening had to be made quickly. By then, Mrs. Surratt was on her way to the country. She could not have known that President Lincoln was going to attend Ford's Theatre. Obviously, she could not

have been privy to any plans to kill President Lincoln that night.

That afternoon, Booth wrote a strange letter to the editor of the Washington *Intelligencer*. In the letter, Booth explained how he had, many times, tried to abduct the president but had failed. Now, he had to change his plans. He was sure posterity would justify his actions. He signed the letter, "Men who love their country better than gold or life, J. W. Booth, Paine, Atzerodt, Herold." Notice that neither John Surratt nor his mother's names were mentioned! Later, Booth met John Matthews, a friend and fellow actor, and asked him to deliver his letter to the editor of the *Intelligencer*, at a late hour that night. Matthews became afraid and burned Booth's letter when he heard that President Lincoln had been shot and that Booth may have done the act. Matthews was not allowed to testify in 1865 at the military trial of the conspirators. He did, however, testify about Booth's letter in 1867 at the civil court trial of John H. Surratt.

It wasn't until about eight o'clock that evening when Booth called a meeting of the conspirators at the Herndon House. It was then that the men were given their assignments. Lewis Paine was to kill Secretary Seward; George Atzerodt, the vice president; and of course, Booth, the president. Davey Herold was to guide Paine out of the city after Seward had been murdered.

42. *The Trial of John H. Surratt*, op. cit., p. 759, testimony of J. Z. Jenkins.

43. Louis J. Weichmann, op. cit., p. 168.

44. Benn Pitman, op. cit., p. 125, testimony of Emma Offutt for the defense.

45. James O. Hall, "Why John M. Lloyd Was in Upper Marlboro," *Surratt Society News*, September 1980, p. 5.

46. Ibid.

47. Ibid.

48. Benn Pitman, op. cit., p. 129, testimony of Richard Sweeney for the defense.

49. Ibid., testimony of James Lusby.

50. Ibid., p. 125, testimony of Emma Offutt.

51. *The Trial of John Surratt*, op. cit., p. 755, testimony of Capt. Bennett Gwynn.

52. War Department Files, op. cit., Frames 0170 through 0200. "Statement of Mrs. Mary E. Surratt—April 28, 1865, Carroll Prison."

53. *The Trial of John H. Surratt*, op. cit., p. 755, testimony of Capt. Bennett Gwynn.

54. David Rankin Barbee, "The Murder of Mrs. Surratt," a paper presented at the Emerson Institute, 25 February 1950. The David Rankin Barbee Collection, Georgetown University Library, Washington, DC.

Note 54A: According to John Lloyd's testimony at the trial of the conspirators, he said that Mrs. Surratt personally handed him the package that Booth had given her to deliver to John Lloyd. He said that binoculars were in the package and that she told him at the time to have two bottles of whiskey and "shooting irons" ready for whoever called for them *that night.* Again, the author reminds the reader that Mrs. Surratt could not have been privy to an assassination plot that was to take place that night. Remember, when she saw Booth that morning, he didn't know that the president would be at Ford's Theatre that night. He found that out after he had *left* Mrs. Surratt and had gone to the theater. Many years later, at John Surratt's trial, Lloyd would admit that "whiskey has a very singular effect upon my mind, chiefly, it makes me forget a great many things." Ref: *The Trial of John H. Surratt,* op. cit., p. 298, testimony of John Lloyd.

55. Louis J. Weichmann, op. cit., p. 172.

56. *The Trial of John H. Surratt,* op. cit., p. 691, testimony of John Holohan.

57. Louis J. Weichmann, op. cit., p. 172.

58. *The Trial of John H. Surratt,* op. cit., p. 746, testimony of Olivia ("Lete") Jenkins.

Note 58A: In his book (p. 174), Weichmann would state that the caller at the door was John Wilkes Booth. Historically, his statement has not gone well for Mary, considering that less than two hours later, Booth had shot President Lincoln.

59. Louis J. Weichmann, op. cit., p. 173.

60. *The Trial of John H. Surratt,* op. cit., p. 689, testimony of Eliza Holohan.

Note 60A: Good Friday church services "generally" lasted until ten o'clock in the evening or later. This explains why Mary and Eliza started for church at such a late hour.

61. As it turned out, it wasn't until 11 March 1869, with the settlement of Mary Surratt's estate, that George Calvert was paid. Ref: James O. Hall, *The Mary Surratt House* (Clinton, MD: The History Division, Maryland-National Capital Park and Planning Commission, 1979).

62. Mrs. Lambert, who lived on the south side of H Street between

4th and 5th streets, testified in the John Surratt trial that soldiers did go along H Street yelling that President Lincoln had been shot. This would be the reason why Mary Surratt did not act surprised when detectives came to her house that night and told her that the president had been shot. This was held against her at the trial, since her lack of surprise indicated to the judges that she had known ahead of time that an attempt was going to be made on the president's life. The rest of the news that the detectives gave her concerning her son would have seemed absurd, since she knew that John was in Canada.

63. *The Trial of John H. Surratt*, op. cit., p. 717, testimony of Honora Fitzpatrick.

64. Ibid.

65. Ibid.

66. Ibid.

67. *The Trial of John H. Surratt*, op. cit., p. 696, testimony of John Clarvoe.

68. Ibid.

69. Ibid., p. 698.

70. Ibid.

71. Ibid.

72. Ibid.

73. Ibid.

74. According to Susan Mahoney Jackson's testimony, p. 549, at the John Surratt trial, McDevitt had a red beard.

Note 74A: Around midnight, Booth and his traveling companion, Davey Herold, stopped at Surratt's Tavern (Villa) that was managed by John Lloyd. Lloyd gave them one of the carbines that had been hidden behind the wall, along with a pair of field glasses, that he claimed Mrs. Surratt had given him. Booth had broken his leg when he jumped from the presidential box to the stage below after shooting President Lincoln. Before the pair left Surratt's Tavern, Booth told Lloyd that he had killed the president. By 3:30 A.M, about the time the search party left Mary Surratt's H Street house, Booth was drawing close to Dr. Mudd's residence near Bryantown, Maryland. There, Booth, representing himself as someone else and keeping his face averted from the doctor, received the medical help that he needed.

75. *The Trial of John H. Surratt*, I, op. cit., p. 714, testimony of James A. McDevitt.

Note 75A: As a matter of fact, John Wilkes Booth and David

Herold did stop at the Surratt House and Tavern after Booth had shot the president.

76. *The Trial of John H. Surratt,* op. cit., p. 674, testimony of John Holohan.

77. *Evening Star* newspaper, 15 April 1865.

Note 77A: President Lincoln died at 7:05 A.M. at the Peterson House, across the street from Ford's Theatre.

Note 77B: By the time the Surratt household was at breakfast, Booth and Herold were at Dr. Mudd's.

Note 77C: Weichmann testified that during breakfast, Anna had said that the death of Lincoln was no more than the death of a Negro in the Federal Army. Everyone who was present that morning denied under oath that she had ever said such a thing.

78. *The Trial of John H. Surratt,* op. cit., p. 6, testimony of John Holohan.

Note 78A: "Port Tobacco" or George Atzerodt was under Booth's orders to kill Vice President Andrew Johnson. It is interesting to speculate why Weichmann would suggest that Atzerodt was in a plot to kill anyone. Weichmann would always claim that he knew nothing about any plot either to abduct or to assassinate the president. However, apparently, neither Booth nor Weichmann knew that Atzerodt did not possess enough of the "killer instinct" to assassinate the vice president. All night long, Atzerodt had visited bars and wandered the streets of Washington. He hoped that Booth and Paine would not go through with their ghastly plan. Later, it would be found that it was Lewis Paine-Powell who tried to kill Secretary of State Seward. The next morning, Atzerodt had gotten no farther than the area of the White House when he heard that the president had died. It was probably then that he decided to start on foot to his boyhood home in Germantown, Maryland. Ref: Edward Steers, Jr. *The Escape and Capture of George A. Atzerodt,* privately printed from the research material of James O. Hall.

79. *Washington News,* 9 February 1898.

80. *The Trial of John H. Surratt,* op. cit., p. 675, testimony of John Holohan.

81. Ibid., p. 70, testimony of John Clarvoe.

Note 81A: When Mrs. Surratt moved to Washington, Aunt Rachel Semus (later Hawkins), a former slave, remained at the tavern and worked for John Lloyd. On 21 December 1892, Aunt Rachel was interviewed by the *Washington Star* newspaper. She spoke tenderly of her former mistress. She said that after Mrs. Surratt had moved to Washington, John Wilkes Booth and David Herold used to "come down often, and they and Mr. Lloyd were mighty thick and Mrs. Surratt visited the country home but seldom." Ref: The David Rankin Barbee Collection, Box 7, Folder 359, Georgetown University Library, Washington, DC. Why would Booth visit Lloyd unless the tavern keeper was in the conspiracy to abduct, and later to assassinate the president?

82. From an undated letter to John Brennon, Surratt Society member, from Jennings Clark, Hyattsville, MD. Copy in the Surratt Society archives.

83. War Department Files, op. cit., Frames 0170 through 0200. "Statement of Mrs. Mary E. Surratt—April 28, 1865, Carroll Prison."

84. *The Trial of John H. Surratt,* op. cit., p. 675, testimony of John Holohan.

## CHAPTER 15

1. *The Trial of John H. Surratt in the Criminal Court for the District of Columbia* (Washington, DC: Government Printing Office, 1867), p. 689, testimony of Eliza Holohan.

2. War Department Files, National Archives, Washington, DC, Series M-599, Reel 6, Frames 0233 through 0251. "Statement of Mary Surratt, April 17, 1865."

3. *The Trial of John H. Surratt,* op. cit., p. 676, testimony of John Holohan.

Note 3A: It was approximately three o'clock, the afternoon of 17 April, when detectives Clarvoe, McDevitt, and Bigley of the metropolitan police left Washington, DC, with John Holohan and Louis Weichmann. Their orders were to find John Surratt. Their journey would take them as far as Montreal, Canada. The trip proved unsuccessful, however. Ref: *The Trial of John H. Surratt,* op. cit., pp. 676-87, testimony of John Holohan.

4. Louis J. Weichmann, *The True History of the Assassination of Abraham Lincoln and of the Conspiracy of 1865* (New York: Alfred A. Knopf, Inc., 1975), pp. 183,184.

5. *Investigation and Trial Papers Relating to the Assassination of President Lincoln,* National Archives, Washington, DC, Series M-599, deposition of Maj. H. W. Smith. Mary Surratt's exact words.

6. Ibid., exact words.

7. Ibid., exact words.

Note 7A: It was approximately eight-thirty that evening when Bvt. Maj. H. W. Smith, U.S. Volunteers, received a verbal order from Lt. Col. A. E. King, Army Adjutant General (A.A.G.) to report to Col. H. H. Wells, Provost Marshal General, Defenses South of the Potomac. Wells was in charge of the investigation into the assassination of President Lincoln and the attempt on Secretary Seward's life. Colonel Wells ordered Major Smith to take Captain Wermerskirch, detectives Devoe and Rosch, along with a guard of five soldiers, to search the boardinghouse for any evidence pertinent to the assassination. At the same time he was to "arrest Mrs. Surratt and all in the house." Ref: *Investigation and Trial Papers,* op. cit., deposition of Maj. H. W. Smith.

8. Ibid.
9. Ibid.
10. Ibid.
11. Ibid.
12. Ibid., exact words.
13. Ibid.
14. *The Trial of John H. Surratt,* op. cit., p. 718, testimony of Honora Fitzpatrick, referring to where Anna was actually sitting.
15. *Investigation and Trial Papers,* op. cit., deposition of Maj. H. W. Smith, exact words.
16. *The Trial of John H. Surratt,* op. cit., p. 718, testimony of Honora Fitzpatrick, referring to where Olivia ("Lete") and Honora were actually sitting.
17. *Investigation and Trial Papers,* op. cit., deposition of Maj. H. W. Smith.
18. Ibid.
19. Ibid., exact words.
20. Ibid., exact words.
21. Ibid.
22. Ibid., exact words.
23. Ibid., exact words.
24. Ibid.

Note 24A: According to the meteorological observations made at the U.S. Naval Observatory, Washington, DC, at nine o'clock that evening, it was clear and forty-seven degrees.

25. *Investigation and Trial Papers,* op. cit., deposition of Maj. H. W. Smith.
26. Ibid., exact words.

27. Ibid., exact word.

28. Ibid.

29. Ibid.

30. Ibid.

31. Ibid., exact words.

32. Ibid.

33. Ibid., exact words.

34. Ibid., exact words.

35. Ibid., exact words.

36. Ibid., exact words.

37. Ibid., exact words.

38. Ibid.

39. Ibid.

Note 39A: As it turned out, the stranger was Lewis Powell, alias Lewis Paine and Reverend Wood, better known as Lewis Paine.

Note 39B: It is interesting to note that Detective Sampson in his deposition claimed to have questioned Powell, but he said that the man had told him that he had come to dig *a garden*, not a gutter. Powell's reason for coming late was that he didn't know what time it was. Ref: Department of War Records, National Archives, Washington DC, 19 April 1865, LAS-2 #1077, "Statement of Officer Sampson."

40. Benn Pitman, *The Assassination of President Lincoln and the Trial of the Conspirators,* Facsimile Edition (New York: Funk and Wagnalls, reprint 1954, by Philip Van Doren Stern) p. 121, testimony of Maj. H. W. Smith for the prosecution, exact words.

41. Ibid., exact words.

42. War Department Files, op. cit., Mrs. Surratt's exact words when she was questioned at General Augur's headquarters, 17 April 1865.

Note 42A: It is interesting to note that Mrs. Surratt's eyesight was so poor that she probably mistook the pickaxe for a carbine. To her, it probably looked like a rifle since Powell held it to his side with the pick head resting on the floor.

43. Benn Pitman, op. cit., p. 122, the testimony of Maj. H. W. Smith for the prosecution.

Note 43A: Honora Fitzpatrick, who, as far as was known, had perfect eyesight, admitted that she did not recognize Powell when she passed him in the hall on her way out of the house that night. Ref: Benn Pitman, op. cit., p. 132, testimony of Honora Fitzpatrick.

44. War Department Files, op. cit., Mary Surratt's exact words of 17 April 1865, at General Augur's headquarters, when she quoted Anna.

45. *Investigation and Trial Papers,* op. cit., deposition of Maj. H. W. Smith, Smith's exact words.

Note 45A: At this point it is important to disclose what led to Mrs. Surratt's arrest. On Saturday night, 15 April 1865, Susan Mahoney, a colored servant girl of Mrs. Surratt's, while feigning sleep, claimed to have overheard and witnessed certain transactions at Mrs. Surratt's house that would prove that the inmates at the boarding-house were involved in the assassination of President Lincoln. The next day she told her aunt, Mary Ann Griffin, a colored woman in the employ of John H. Kimball, what she had seen and heard. The following day Mrs. Griffin told Kimball what her niece had told her. He in turn reported the information to General Augur. Ref: 39th Congress, lst Session, House of Representatives, Report 99, *Reward for the Capture of Booth,* to accompany H.R. No. 801, July 24, 1866—ordered to be printed.

It was later discovered that Susan Mahoney Jackson's observations were unfounded. Nevertheless, Susan Mahoney Jackson and Mary Ann Griffin were rewarded $250 each and Mr. Kimball received $500. The rewards were felt justified since the information, though incorrect, did lead to the arrest of Lewis Powell.

46. It was during the search of the boardinghouse that the photographs of the Southern notables, Davis, Stephens, Beauregard, and Stonewall Jackson, and the Northern notables, generals McClellan, Grant, and Hooker, were found. A photograph of Booth was found behind the picture *Morning, Noon, and Night* that Lou Weichmann had given Anna. She had hidden Booth's photograph there when her brother John had told her to get rid of it.

At the trial of the conspirators, it would be the photographs of Booth and the Southern notables that would be used to prove Anna's disloyalty to the United States government.

It was alleged that a bullet mold was found in Mrs. Surratt's room. It was the type of mold that could have been used to make the bullets for the gun that John Wilkes Booth used to assassinate the president. There are those who believe that Mrs. Surratt was indeed making bullets for Booth. The author finds this assertion unfounded. If Mrs. Surratt had been making bullets for the assassin, why didn't the authorities find other evidence, such as ingots of lead, a melting pot, and the ladle to pour the lead into the mold? All of these items were necessary to make bullets.

47. The description was derived from an actual photograph of the general.

48. War Department Files, op. cit. All information and quotations came from the statement of Mary Surratt made on 17 April 1865, while at General Augur's headquarters.

49. Benn Pitman, op. cit., p. 132, testimony of Honora Fitzpatrick for the defense. Honora was quoting Anna.

Note 49A: According to the testimony of Honora Fitzpatrick, she didn't recognize the man as Paine (Powell) until she saw him at General Augur's headquarters when he was no longer wearing his cap. We must remember that the last time that she had seen him, Powell was immaculately dressed as a minister.

50. According to David Rankin Barbee, Mrs. Surratt recognized Lewis Powell at this time. If she recognized him with her poor eyesight, no doubt the others did, as well. Ref: David Rankin Barbee, "The Murder of Mrs. Surratt," a paper presented at the Emerson Institute, 25 February 1950. The David Rankin Barbee Collection, Georgetown University Library, Washington, DC.

Of course, it must be remembered that if Mrs. Surratt and the others recognized Powell at General Augur's headquarters, they would not have known that Powell had tried to kill Secretary Seward.

Note 50A: Again according to Barbee, Lewis Powell had been hiding in a tree in the outskirts of Washington ever since Powell had attacked the secretary of state. It seems that Powell's horse had thrown him into a pool of mud, which accounted for his unsightly appearance. After he had inadvertently left his hat at Secretary Seward's, Powell covered his head with the sleeve from an undershirt.

51. War Department Files, op. cit., "Statement of Mary Surratt, April 17, 1865."

52. Ibid.

53. Added information.

Note 53A: Mrs. Surratt, the young ladies, and Lewis Powell were not the only ones arrested on April 17. Ned Spangler, one of the stagehands at Ford's Theatre, had been arrested that afternoon. Someone had identified Spangler as one of John Wilkes Booth's cronies who had helped Booth escape from the theater.

In addition, Sam Arnold and Michael O'Laughlin were captured the same afternoon. They had helped Booth in the plot to abduct the president, but they had nothing to do with the assassination. Ref: Samuel Carter, III, *The Riddle of Dr. Mudd* (New York: G. P. Putnam's Sons, 1974), p. 138.

54. Louis J. Weichmann, op. cit., pp. 186-87.

## CHAPTER 16

1. By a Lady, *The Old Capitol and Its Inmates* (New York: E. J. Hale & Son, 1867), p. 13 (probably authored by Virginia Lomax), and Samuel Carter, III, *The Riddle of Dr. Mudd* (New York: G. P. Putnam's Sons, 1974), p. 151.

2. Ishbel Ross, *Rebel Rose, Life of Rose O'Neal Greenhow, Confederate Spy* (New York: Harper Brothers, 1954), p. 193.

3. Ibid.

4. Colonel Wood was described as a large man with twinkling eyes and graying hair. Ref: By a Lady (Virginia Lomax), op. cit., p. 16.

Note 4A: Colonel W. P. Wood, who ruled Capitol Prison, would become the first chief of the Secret Service when it became part of the U.S. Treasury Department. Ref: Rambler, *Washington Star,* 28 November 1928, Vol. 4-123.

5. R.G. 22nd Army Corps, DC, Book 331a.

6. By a Lady (Virginia Lomax), op. cit., p. 85.

7. *Philadelphia Weekly Times,* "The Annals of the War" (The Times Publishing Co., 1878), reprint (Dayton: Morningside, 1988), p. 502.

8. Ishbel Ross, op. cit., pp. 123-24.

9. The description of Old Capitol Prison was obtained from: By a Lady (Virginia Lomax), op. cit., passim. Also Ishbel Ross, op. cit., passim.

10. By a Lady (Virginia Lomax), op. cit., p. 75.

11. Ibid., p. 76.

12. Ibid.

Note 12A: Virginia Baxley was a brave and humorous woman whom Virginia Lomax often referred to in her book as Mrs. Johnson. Virginia Baxley and Virginia Lomax were both serving time at Old Capitol Prison, Carroll Annex, when Mrs. Surratt, Honora, Anna, and Lete were there.

13. Ishbel Ross, op. cit., p. 206.

14. Mrs. Greenhow did not return Mrs. Baxley's affection. She considered her an obnoxious troublemaker. Ref: Margaret Leech, *Reveille in Washington, 1860-1865* (New York: Harper & Brothers Publishers, 1941), pp. 140,150.

15. Luna Lambert, "Spy or Patriot? The Story of Rose O'Neal Greenhow," *The International Confederate Magazine,* Wiltshire, UK, Summer 1989, p. 11.

16. By a Lady (Virginia Lomax), op. cit., p. 142.

17. Ibid., p. 73.

18. *Daily Morning Chronicle,* Washington, DC, 21 May 1865, p. 1.

19. That same day, 18 April, John Holohan and Lou Weichmann were enlisted to go to Montreal in order to identify John Surratt, if he were found. The expedition proved unsuccessful. Ref: "Report of Proceedings in Canada," by C. W. Taylor, Sec. Agt., 24th District (War Department, Washington, DC).

20. By a Lady (Virginia Lomax), op. cit., p. 74.

21. Ibid., p. 73.

22. Thomas A. Jones, *J. Wilkes Booth* (Chicago: Laird and Lee Publishers, 1893), p. 122.

23. David Rankin Barbee, "The Murder of Mrs. Surratt," a paper presented at the Emerson Institute, 25 February 1950. The David Rankin Barbee Collection, Georgetown University Library, Washington, DC.

24. John T. Ford, "Behind the Curtain of a Conspiracy," *The North American Review,* 1889, p. 485.

   Notes 24A: John Lloyd was paid three dollars a day, for every day of the trial, which lasted fifty days. Ref: A receipt from the Comptroller General, The David Rankin Barbee Collection, Georgetown University Library, Washington, DC.

   Note 24B: Louis Weichmann received $150 in January 1867, $40 in March 1867, and $150 in April 1867 from the War Department as "necessary expenses" for "government witness," according to Judge Advocate Joseph Holt. Ref: Professor Joseph George, "'The Days are Yet Dark,' L. J. Weichmann's Life After the Lincoln Conspiracy Trials," a paper read at the American Catholic Historical Association, 13 April 1984, at Villanova University.

   Note 24C: During the early days of Anna Surratt's imprisonment, Arthur Barry was discharged from the Confederate army and attempted to return to Surrattsville. Because of the assassination, he was not allowed to enter Southern Maryland. The young doctor went to Texas. He and Anna never saw each other again. Ref: Daniel D. Hartzler, *Medical Doctors of Maryland in the C.S.A.* (1979), p. 14.

25. By a Lady (Virginia Lomax), op. cit., p. 85.

26. Benn Pitman, *The Assassination of President Lincoln and the Trial of the Conspirators,* Facsimile Edition (New York: Funk and Wagnalls, reprint 1954, by Philip Van Doren Stern), p. 153, testimony of Hartman Richter for the defense.

27. James O. Hall, "John Wilkes Booth Escape Route," *Surratt Society News,* 1984, p. 12. Also Steven G. Miller, "Roll Call For The

Garrett's Farm Patrol," *Surratt Courier,* September 1994, p. 4.

28. Guy W. Moore, *The Case of Mrs. Surratt* (Norman: University of Oklahoma Press, 1954), p. 72.

29. Benn Pitman, op. cit., p. 87, testimony of Alexander Lovett for the prosecution.

30. By a Lady (Virginia Lomax), op. cit., pp. 146-48.

31. Ibid., p. 67.

Note 31A: In her book, Virginia Lomax referred to Honora as Mary. Mrs. Lomax referred to herself as Maria Miller. Ref: Ibid., p. 69.

32. Clarence V. Joerndt, "St. Ignatius Church Linked With Lincoln Assassination." *The AEGIS,* Bel Air, MD, Thursday, 16 March 1967.

33. The Reverend J. A. Walter, "The Surratt Case," *Church News,* Washington, DC, 16 August 1891, also read before the U.S. Catholic Historical Society, Washington, DC, 25 May 1891. Ref: Tonry Collection, E 457 .5 .S985 No. 1, Surratt Society Archives, Clinton, MD.

Note 33A: It is not known if Anna Surratt received the following letter from Belle Seaman. The letter was written from Washington, PA, 20 April 1865. Ref: National Archives, Washington, DC, microfilm LAS 599, Reel 3, frames 0749 through 0751.

My dear Anna,

It was with feelings of deep regret that we heard the rumors of Cousin John being accused of the assassination of Mr. Lincoln. I was rejoiced to receive a letter from him written from Montreal. It was written on the 10th, mailed the 11th, and came here the 17th, which was just sufficient in my mind to clear him from all suspicion. The Provost Marshal, hearing I had it, came and demanded it. A copy of which is now in the hands of the authorities in Washington. Write at the earliest convenience, as we are all interested in your welfare. Love is yours and the assurance of the sincere love of,

Your cousin,
Belle Seaman

34. Margaret Leech, op. cit., p. 147.

35. Ibid.

36. War Department Files, National Archives, Washington DC, "Statements Made by the Alleged Lincoln Conspirators Under Examination, 1865," M-599, Reel 6, 0170 through 0200.

37. Benn Pitman, op. cit., p. 86, col. 2, testimony of John Lloyd for the prosecution.

38. Colonel Olcott's report, The David Rankin Barbee Collection, Georgetown University Library, Washington, DC.

39. *The Trial of John H. Surratt in the Criminal Court for the District of Columbia* (Washington, DC: Government Printing Office, 1867), p. 998, testimony of Samuel L. Jackson.

40. Brevet Lieutenant Colonel Richard A. Watts, "The Trial of the Lincoln Conspirators," reprint *Surratt Courier,* October 1985, p. 6.

41. *The Evening Star* newspaper, Washington, DC, Saturday, (date unknown) 1865.

42. By a Lady (Virginia Lomax), op. cit., p. 134.

43. Ibid.

44. Ibid., p. 135.

45. Ibid.

46. Ibid.

47. Ibid.

48. Ibid.

49. Ibid., pp. 136-37.

50. Report of Col. William P. Wood, superintendent of Old Capitol Prison, on Louis J. Weichmann. Bureau of Military Justice Records, National Archives.

51. David Rankin Barbee, op. cit., p. 17.

Note 51A: The following is Item 2 in an affidavit sworn to by John Brophy. Brophy was, at the time, professor of English at Gonzaga College, and a one-time friend of John Surratt and Louis J. Weichmann. After the trial and before Mrs. Surratt was executed, Weichmann went to Brophy and told him "that he [Weichmann] was arrested as a conspirator and threatened with death by Mr. Stanton and Mr. Burnett, unless he would reveal all about the assassination—[Stanton and Burnett] alleging that he [Weichmann] knew all about it."

In Item 7 of the affidavit Brophy said "that a short time before the assassination, he [Weichmann] introduced Atzerodt to me as a particular friend of his; and that the same day he and Atzerodt were riding on Booth's horses." Ref: Affidavit of John Brophy, *Constitutional Union,* 11 July 1865. The David Rankin Barbee Collection, Georgetown University Library, Washington, DC.

In an effort to save Mrs. Surratt, Brophy sent the original affidavit to President Andrew Johnson. The president did not respond to the affidavit, and Mrs. Surratt was hanged. After she was executed, Brophy gave a copy of the affidavit, for publication, to the *Constitutional Union.*

52. By a Lady (Virginia Lomax), op. cit., pp. 172,173. The description of Mrs. Surratt's departure from Old Capitol Prison was taken from the Lomax book.

53. Richard E. Sloan, "The Contents of Mrs. Surratt's Pockets," *Surratt Society News,* September, 1984.

54. By a Lady (Virginia Lomax), op. cit., pp. 173-76.

## CHAPTER 17

1. David K. Sullivan, "Behind Prison Walls: The Operation of the District Penitentiary, 1831-1862," paper given to the Columbia Historical Society, 15 February 1972, p. 247.

2. Benn Pitman, *The Assassination of President Lincoln and the Trial of the Conspirators,* Facsimile Edition (New York: Funk and Wagnalls, reprint 1954, by Philip Van Doren Stern), p. 17.

3. Ibid.

4. Ibid., p. 18.

5. Ibid., p. 17, biographical sketch by Michael W. Kauffman.

6. Ibid.

7. Ibid.

8. Ibid.

9. Ibid.

10. Ibid.

11. Ibid.

12. Ibid.

13. Ibid.

14. General John Hartranft's letter, dated 5 May 1865, to Gen. Winfred Scott Hancock, commanding Middle Military Division, DC.

Note 14A: The ledger with all of General Hartranft's letters to General Hancock was found by Betty J. Ownsbey at Gettysburg College Library, Gettysburg, PA. Betty Ownsbey is a Surratt Society member and the author of *Alias "Paine" Lewis Thornton Powell, the Mystery Man of the Lincoln Conspiracy* (Jefferson, NC, and London: McFarland & Company, Inc., 1993).

15. David Rankin Barbee, "The Murder of Mrs. Surratt," a paper presented at the Emerson Institute, Washington, DC, 25 February 1950, p. 21. The David Rankin Barbee Collection, Georgetown University Library, Washington, DC.

16. Ibid.

17. Ibid.

18. General Hartranft's letter, dated 9 May 1865, to Major General Hancock.

19. Benn Pitman, op. cit., p. 20.

20. Champ Clark and the Editors of Time-Life Books, *The Assassination, Death of the President* (Alexandria, VA: Time-Life Books, 1987), p. 148.

21. *Daily Constitutional Union,* September 1868.

22. Joan L. Chaconas, "The Detectives," *Surratt Society News,* March 1979.

23. Colonel Julian E. Raymond, *A Country Requires a Capital,* unpublished book manuscript, Fort Leslie J. McNair, Washington, DC, p. 13. That portion of the building still remains that was the courtroom and Mary Surratt's room on the third floor. The building is now used for married officers' quarters at Fort Lesley J. McNair, Washington, DC.

24. Ibid., p. 57.

25. Ibid.

26. Ibid.

27. By a Lady, *Old Capitol Prison and Its Inmates* (New York: E. J. Hale & Son, 1867), p. 206 (probably authored by Virginia Lomax).

28. There has always been a controversy as to whether Mrs. Surratt was manacled or not. Here are some observations:

"This unfortunate woman like other prisoners is in irons. A bar of about 10" in length passes from one ankle to the other and is there attached to an iron band that encircles each leg." Ref: *New York Times,* 15 May 1865.

Frederick A. Aiken, one of Mrs. Surratt's attorneys, said that she was not manacled. Ref: *Washington Daily Morning Chronicle,* 19 September 1873, p. 4.

Mrs. Jane Swisshelm asserted in a letter to the *New York Tribune,* 16 September 1873, that "Mrs. Surratt was in irons."

Benn Pitman, one of the court reporters, claimed that Mrs. Surratt was "fettered by manacles on her feet, but without the ball." Ref: Benn Pitman, "Some Facts of the Assassination," unpublished, handwritten account, p. 3, New York Public Library.

29. General Hartranft's letter, dated 10 May 1865, to General Hancock.

30. David Miller DeWitt, *The Judicial Murder of Mary E. Surratt* (Baltimore, MD: John Murphy, 1885), p. 28.

31. *Philadelphia Inquirer,* Saturday, 13 May 1865.

32. *Washington Evening Star,* 9 May 1865.

33. William E. Doster, *Lincoln and Episodes of the Civil War* (New York

& London: G. B. Putnam's Sons, The Knickerbocker Press, 1915), Ch. XI, 12 May 1865.

34. *Washington Post,* 24 December 1878, p. 2.

35. Aiken's letter was found by James O. Hall and Mike Musick in the National Archives, Washington, DC.

36. Champ Clark, p. 148, op. cit.

37. *Washington Post,* 24 December 1878, p. 2.

38. Ibid.

39. Michael W. Kauffman research.

40. Benn Pitman, op. cit., p. 22.

41. Ibid.

42. Champ Clark, op. cit., p. 140.

43. Ibid.

44. William E. Doster, op. cit., Ch. XI, 12 May 1865.

45. Ibid.

46. Ibid.

47. Ibid.

48. *War of the Rebellion, Official Records of the Union and Confederate Armies,* Series I, Vol. XLIX, Part II, pp. 566-67.

49. Benn Pitman, op. cit., p. 38, testimony of Henry Von Steinacker for the prosecution.

50. Champ Clark, op. cit., pp. 149-50.

51. Ibid.

52. Ibid.

53. Benn Pitman, op. cit., p. 24, testimony of Richard Montgomery for the prosecution.

54. Champ Clark, op. cit., p. 150.

55. Ibid.

56. Benn Pitman, op. cit., pp. 28-29, testimony of Sanford Conover for the prosecution.

57. Champ Clark, op. cit., p. 151.

58. Louis J. Weichmann, *The True History of the Assassination of Abraham Lincoln and of the Conspiracy of 1865* (New York: Alfred A. Knopf, Inc., 1975), p. 320.

59. Ben Perley Poore, *The Conspiracy Trial for the Murder of the President* (Boston: 1865); Reprint Edition (New York: Arno Press Inc., 1972), Louis Weichmann's testimony for the prosecution, pp. 69-110.

60. Samuel Carter, III, *The Riddle of Dr. Mudd* (New York: G. P. Putnam's Sons, 1974), p. 171.

61. Ben Perley Poore, op. cit., pp. 94-101, testimony of Louis Weichmann.

62. Benn Pitman, op. cit., p. 117, col. 1, and Ben Perley Poore, op. cit., p. 94.

Note 62A: However, on page 53 in Louis Weichmann's book, which he wrote years later, he refers to the date as December 23, 1864. Guy Moore, in *The Case of Mrs. Surratt,* (page 10), agrees that the meeting date was December 23, 1864. David Rankin Barbee in his presentation, "The Murder of Mrs. Surratt," which he gave at the Emerson Institute, agreed that December 23, 1864, was the date that Dr. Mudd introduced John Wilkes Booth to John Surratt. It has been established that John Wilkes Booth first visited the Surratt H Street boardinghouse on January 1, 1865. Therefore, it would seem that Dr. Mudd, did, in fact, introduce John Wilkes Booth to John Surratt on December 23, 1864.

63. Ben Perley Poore, p. 105.

64. Ibid., p. 114.

65. Ibid., p. 117, testimony of John Lloyd.

66. Ibid., p. 118.

67. War Department Files, National Archives, Washington DC, Series M-599, Reel 4, Frame 0442 through Frame 0485. "Statement of Mrs. Mary E. Surratt—April 28, 1865, Carroll Prison."

68. Ben Perley Poore, op. cit., p. 119, testimony of John Lloyd.

69. David Rankin Barbee, op. cit.

## CHAPTER 18

1. General August V. Kautz, "At the Trial of the Lincoln Conspirators, The Reminiscences of General August V. Kautz," edited by Charles F. Cooney, *Civil War Times Illustrated,* Vol. XII, No. 5, August 1973.

2. Charles M. Snyder, *Union County Pennsylvania, a Bicentennial History,* p. 229.

3. Benn Pitman, *The Assassination of President Lincoln and the Trial of the Conspirators,* Facsimile Edition (New York: Funk and Wagnalls, reprint 1954, by Philip Van Doren Stern), p. 121, testimony of Emma Offutt for the prosecution.

4. Mrs. H. E. Naylor's letter to Mr. Kackley. Mrs. Naylor claimed to have been a descendant of John Lloyd's. Surratt Society archives, Clinton, MD.

5. Benn Pitman, op. cit., p. 118, testimony of Louis J. Weichmann for the prosecution.

6. Ben Perley Poore, *The Conspiracy Trial for the Murder of the President*

(Boston: 1865); Reprint Edition (New York: Arno Press Inc., 1972), p. 136, testimony of Louis J. Weichmann for the prosecution.

7. Benn Pitman, op. cit., p. 119, testimony of Louis J. Weichmann for the prosecution.

8. Ibid., p. 119.

9. Louis J. Weichmann, *The True History of the Assassination of Abraham Lincoln and of the Conspiracy of 1865* (New York: Alfred A. Knopf, Inc., 1975), p. 86.

10. Ibid.

11. Ibid., p. 75.

12. Ibid.

13. Benn Pitman, op. cit., p. 133, testimony of Augustus S. Howell for the defense.

14. Ibid., pp. 122-23, testimony of R. C. Morgan for the prosecution.

15. Ibid.

16. Ibid., pp. 121-22, testimony of Maj. H. W. Smith for the prosecution.

17. Ibid., p. 128, testimony of Capt. W. M. Wermerskirch for the prosecution.

Note 17A: Jerome B. Stillson, *New York World*, 14 November 1868, ran the following item: "Payne [Powell] himself declared in prison that he went to Mrs. Surratt's only because he knew but two or three houses in Washington, and because he knew John H. Surratt so well. He had no opportunity of making any communication to Mrs. Surratt at all. He presented himself at a most unfortunate moment for him, and was nabbed by the officers before Mrs. Surratt came through the parlor door. He felt himself to be hunted from behind, and flew to this place for refuge, to find himself in the lion's mouth. 'If I had two lives,' said Payne [*sic*] at one time to General Hartranft, 'I would be given them both to save that woman.'" The David Rankin Barbee Collection, Georgetown University Library, Washington, DC.

18. Benn Pitman, op. cit., p. 121, testimony of Honora Fitzpatrick for the prosecution.

19. The *Washington Chronicle*, 23 May 1865, The David Rankin Barbee Collection, Georgetown University Library, Washington, DC.

20. James M. McPherson, *Ordeal by Fire* (New York: Alfred A. Knopf, Inc., 1982), p. 455.

21. Mrs. Jane G. Swisshelm, *The Pittsburgh Daily Commercial*, Monday, 10 July 1865, The David Rankin Barbee Collection, Georgetown University Library, Washington, DC.

22. Mrs. Jane G. Swisshelm's letter to Maj. Gen. David Hunter, dated 20 May 1865.

## CHAPTER 19

1. *Meteorological Observations Made at the U.S. Naval Observatory During the Year 1865.*

2. Benn Pitman, *The Assassination of President Lincoln and the Trial of the Conspirators,* Facsimile Edition (New York: Funk and Wagnalls, reprint 1954, by Philip Van Doren Stern), p. 132, testimony of Honora Fitzpatrick for the defense.

3. Ibid., pp. 132-33, testimony of Eliza Holohan for the defense.

4. Ibid., p. 136, testimony of the Reverend B. F. Wiget for the defense.

5. Ibid., testimony of the Reverend Francis E. Boyle for the defense.

6. Ibid., testimony of the Reverend Charles Stonestreet for the defense.

7. Ibid., p. 126, testimony of George H. Calvert for the defense.

8. Ibid.

9. Ibid., testimony of B. F. Gwynn for the defense.

10. Ibid.

11. Ibid., p. 124, testimony of George Cottingham for the defense.

12. Ibid.

13. Ibid.

14. Ibid.

15. Ibid.

16. Ibid., p. 125, testimony of Emma Offutt for the defense.

17. Ibid.

18. Ibid.

19. Ibid., p. 126.

20. Ibid., testimony of John Nothey for the defense.

21. Ibid., p. 136, testimony of the Reverend Peter Lanihan for the defense.

22. Ibid.

23. Ibid., testimony of the Reverend N. D. Young for the defense.

24. General Hartranft's ledger book, Gettysburg College, Gettysburg, PA. Copy of the ledger may be found in the Surratt Society archives.

25. Benn Pitman, op. cit., pp. 126-27, testimony of Joseph T. Nott [*sic*] for the defense. (The transcriber at the trial misspelled Knott's name.)

26. Ibid., p. 127, testimony of J. Z. Jenkins for the defense.

27. Ibid.

28. Ibid., p. 128.

29. Ibid.

30. Ibid.

31. Ibid.

32. *Boston Daily Advertiser,* 31 May 1865.

33. *The Pittsburgh Daily Commercial,* 10 July 1865.

34. *Boston Daily Advertizer,* op. cit.

35. Benn Pitman, op. cit., p. 130, testimony of Anna E. Surratt for the defense.

Note 35A: According to Virginia Lomax, in her book, By a Lady, *Old Capitol Prison and Its Inmates* (New York: E. J. Hale & Son, 1867), p. 206, Anna Surratt was released from prison when the trial of the conspirators commenced.

36. Ibid.

37. *The Trial of John H. Surratt in the Criminal Court for the District of Columbia* (Washington, DC: Government Printing Office, 1867), pp. 669-70, testimony of John Holohan.

38. Benn Pitman, op. cit., p. 131, testimony of Anna E. Surratt for the defense.

39. Ibid.

40. Ibid.

41. Ibid.

42. Ibid.

43. Ibid.

44. Ibid.

45. Ibid.

46. Henry Kyde Douglas, *I Rode with Stonewall* (Chapel Hill: University of North Carolina Press, 1940), p. 347.

47. *Philadelphia Inquirer,* 3 May 1865 (Washington, Wednesday, 1 May 1865).

48. *New York Times,* 3 June 1865 (Washington, Friday, 2 June 1865).

49. *Washington Evening Star,* June 1865, Third Edition, 3:00 P.M., "The Conspiracy Trial, Proceedings Today." Complete date is unknown. Betty Ownsbey, *Surratt Society News,* 1 July 1981.

50. Ibid.

## CHAPTER 20

1. "Hangman of President Lincoln's Assassins Tells His Story," *The New York Press,* 4 September 1898.

2. Benn Pitman, *The Assassination of President Lincoln and the Trial of*

*the Conspirators,* Facsimile Edition (New York: Funk and Wagnalls, reprint 1954, by Philip Van Doren Stern), p. 132.

3. Ibid.

4. Ibid., p. 130, testimony of William P. Wood for the defense.

5. Ibid.

6. Ibid., testimonies of J. B. Blanford and J. C. Thompson for the defense.

7. Ibid., p. 139, testimony of John Holohan for the prosecution.

8. Ibid.

9. *The Trial of John H. Surratt in the Criminal Court for the District of Columbia* (Washington, DC: Government Printing Office, 1867), p. 669.

10. Benn Pitman, op. cit., p. 139, testimony of John Holohan for the prosecution.

11. Ibid., p. 140.

12. Ibid.

13. Ibid.

14. Ibid.

15. Ibid., testimony of James McDevitt for the prosecution.

16. Ibid., p. 141, testimony of Andrew Kallenbach for the prosecution.

17. Ibid.

18. General Hartranft's ledger, letter to General Hancock, dated 8 June 1865, Surratt Society archives.

19. *Meteorological Observations Made at the U. S. Naval Observatory During the Year 1865.*

20. Benn Pitman, op. cit., p. 247, testimony of Henry Hawkins for the defense.

21. Ibid.

22. Ibid., pp. 137-38, testimony of Rachel Semus for the defense.

Note 22A: On 21 December 1892, Rachel Semus Hawkins was interviewed by the *Washington Star.* Below is part of that interview:

"Aunt Rachel Hawkins was a slave in the Surratt family. She lives now on I Street, near F southwest. The house is neat and cozy. It is as clean as a pin is said to be. The rooms are large and with order. In one of them Aunt Rachel lies buried in a white featherbed. She is 'pretty low.' She divides her time between reminiscent talks and telling of her prayer beads. She is a devout Catholic. She likes to be addressed as aunty. It sounds like 'old times.'

"She propped herself up in the pillows for a chat, for Aunt Rachel is never so happy as when to an attentive listener she is recounting the incidents of the, 'good old days.' She teems with them. Her memory is vigorous and although a little off on dates she is usually able to indicate the time by associating it with some prominent event.

"Aunt Rachel was born, 'why bless yo' heart, honey, de lawd on'y knows w'en!' She first belonged to the family of Cornelius Wildman and subsequently to that of Sylvester Boone. In the year that John Brown was hung, she began her servitude with Mrs. Surratt.

"She speaks tenderly of her former mistress, and says that Mrs. Surratt always treated her like one of the children. Mrs. Surratt was, 'kind-hearted and wouldn't do hurt to no soul.'

"The kitchen where she was most employed adjoined the pantry where the guns were afterwards found, and she had several times heard Booth and Lloyd in there, but did not know what for.

"Nobody could persuade Aunt Rachel but that Mrs. Surratt was innocent of the crime for which she was hanged. Any suggestion of that sort, is apt to arouse her ire." Ref: The David Rankin Barbee Collection, Georgetown University Library, Washington, DC.

23. Ibid., p. 137, testimonies of John T. Hoxton and William W. Hoxton for the defense.

24. *Philadelphia Inquirer,* 7 June 1865.

25. Benn Pitman, op. cit., pp. 251-62, argument of Reverdy Johnson.

26. Ibid.

27. Ibid., p. 262.

28. Ibid., pp. 289-99, argument of Frederick Aiken.

29. Ibid.

30. Ibid.

31. Ibid.

32. General Hartranft's ledger, op. cit., letter to Hancock, 18 June 1865.

33. William E. Doster, *Lincoln and Episodes of the Civil War* (New York and London: G. P. Putnam's Sons, The Knickerbocker Press, 1915), pp. 265-66.

34. General Hartranft's ledger, op. cit., letter to Hancock, 2 June 1865.

35. William E. Doster, op. cit., pp. 266-67.

36. Ibid., pp. 267-68.

37. General Hartranft's ledger, op. cit., letter to Hancock, dated 19 June 1865.

38. Ibid.

39. Ibid., 20 June 1865.

40. *Meteorological Observations Made at the U.S. Naval Observatory During the Year 1865.*

41. Mrs. Burton Harrison, *Recollections Grave and Gay* (New York: Charles Scribner's Sons, 1911).

42. Colonel Julian E. Raymond, *A Country Requires a Capital,* unpublished book manuscript, pp. 19-24, Fort Leslie J. McNair, Washington, DC.

43. Ibid., p. 54.

44. Anna Surratt's letter to General Hartranft, dated 9 July 1865.

45. General Hartranft's ledger, op. cit., letter to Hancock, 21 June 1865.

46. Henry Kyde Douglas, *I Rode With Stonewall* (Chapel Hill: University of North Carolina Press, 1940), p. 328.

47. Brevet Lieutenant Colonel Richard A. Watts, report of "The Trial of the Lincoln Conspirators," *Surratt Society News,* November 1985.

48. Benn Pitman, op. cit., pp. 308-09, argument of General Doster.

49. Ibid., p. 309.

50. Ibid., p. 311.

51. Ibid.

52. Ibid.

53. Ibid., pp. 300-307, excerpt from the "Argument in Defense of George A. Atzerodt by W. E. Doster, Esq."

54. Ibid., p. 307, excerpt from "Statement by George A. Atzerodt, Read by his counsel, W. E. Doster, Esq."

55. Ibid., pp. 268-75, excerpt from "Argument in Defense of David E. Herold by Frederick Stone, Esq."

56. *Alexandria Gazette,* 21 June 1865.

57. Benn Pitman, op. cit., p. 265, excerpt from "Argument On The Plea To The Military Commission By Thomas Ewing, Jr."

58. Ibid.

59. Ibid., pp. 264-65.

60. Ibid., p. 264.

61. William E. Doster, op. cit., p. 281.

62. Brevet Lieutenant Colonel Richard A. Watts, op. cit., *Surratt Society News,* November 1985.

63. Benn Pitman, op. cit., p. 359, "Argument of John A. Bingham."

64. Ibid., p. 369.

65. Ibid.

66. Ibid., p. 392.

67. Ibid., Bingham's exact words.

68. *Alexandria Gazette,* 29 June 1865.

Note 68A: On February 12, 1993, the University of Richmond T. C. Williams Law School held an appeal for Dr. Samuel Mudd, in a moot courtroom. Counsel for the petitioner, Dr. Mudd, was a well-known attorney. The other attorney was the great-great-granddaughter of Gen. Thomas Ewing, who, in 1865, defended Dr. Mudd in the trial of the conspirators.

The decision of the mock trial, a three-judge panel, decided unanimously that Dr. Mudd should not have been tried by a military tribunal, but instead by a civilian court, and that Dr. Mudd's conviction should be set aside.

It is the belief of the author based on the above decision, that all of the convictions in this case should be set aside.

## CHAPTER 21

1. R. A. Watts (acting assistant adjutant general under Judge Advocate Holt), "The Trial and Execution of the Lincoln Conspirators," *Michigan History Magazine,* Vol. VI, No. 1, 1922, p. 99.

2. Ibid.

3. Ibid.

4. Ibid., pp. 99-100.

5. "An Interview with Colonel J. W. Clampitt," *Chicago Times Herald,* 23 March 1895.

Note 5A: For the names of the five men on the commission who signed the plea for clemency, in behalf of Mrs. Surratt, see Chapter 17.

6. Ibid.

7. Ibid.

8. *The Trial of John H. Surratt in the Criminal Court for the District of Columbia* (Washington, DC: Government Printing Office, 1867), p. 1207.

9. *Investigation and Trial Papers Relating to the Assassination of President Lincoln,* National Archives, Washington, DC, Series M-599, Reel 15.

10. Ibid., Reel 14.

11. Samuel Carter, III, *The Riddle of Dr. Mudd* (New York: G. P. Putnam's Sons, 1974), p. 214.

Note 11A: Orders were later changed and Dr. Mudd, Arnold, Spangler, and O'Laughlin were sent to the prison at Fort Jefferson,

Dry Tortugas, Florida. O'Laughlin died of yellow fever. The others were released on 8 March 1869. Ref: Ibid., p. 337.

The following important statements appeared in *Century Magazine,* 1890, concerning the plea for clemency:

"*Judge Bingham says*: 'Before the President had acted on the case, I deemed it my duty to call the attention of Secretary Stanton to the petition for the commutation of the sentence of Mrs. Surratt, I did call his attention to it before the final action of the President. . . . After the execution I called upon Secretaries Stanton and Seward and asked if this petition had been presented to the President before the death sentence was approved by him, and was answered by each of those gentlemen that the petition was presented to the President and was duly considered by him and his advisers before the death sentence upon Mrs. Surratt was approved, and that the *President and the Cabinet,* upon such consideration, were a unit in denying the prayer of the petition; Mr. Seward and Mr. Stanton stating that they were present.'"

*Attorney General James Speed* was quoted in the same article in *Century Magazine* as saying that he saw the record of the case in the president's office. Attached to it was the plea signed by "some members of the commission recommending that the sentence against Mrs. Surratt be commuted to imprisonment for life."

*James Harlan, secretary of the interior,* did not agree with Judge Bingham's assessment. He said that he did not remember hearing "in *Cabinet* meeting any part of the record of the trial or *the recommendation of clemency.*" He stated further that he had been told that the case had been examined by the attorney general and the secretary of war, the two cabinet members who were more concerned with the case. (Emphases by author.)

*General R. D. Mussey, President Johnson's private secretary,* said that the president had told him that the court had "recommended Mrs. Surratt to mercy on the grounds of her sex (and age, I believe). But that he said the grounds urged insufficient, and that he had refused to interfere; that if she were guilty at all, her sex did not make her any the less guilty; that he, about the time of her execution, *justified it*; that he told me that there had not been '*women enough hanged in this war*'" (Emphases by author.) Ref: Joseph Holt Papers, Vol. 67 by R. D. Mussey to Holt, 19 August 1873, Special Collections, Georgetown University Library, Washington, DC.

12. "Hangman of President Lincoln's Assassins Tells His Story," an

interview with Christian Rath, *The New York Press,* 4 September 1898.

13. Ibid.

14. Ibid.

15. The Reverend J. A. Walter, "The Surratt Case," *Church News,* Washington, DC, 16 August 1891, also read before the U.S. Catholic Historical Society, 25 May 1891. Ref: Tonry Collection, E457 .5 .S985 No. 1, Surratt Society archives, Clinton, MD.

16. Harlow Randall Hoyt, "William Coxhill's Recollections," *Town Hall Tonight* (Englewood Cliffs, NJ: Prentice Hall, Inc., 1955), pp. 148-52. Also, *Surratt Courier,* September 1986. All of the dialogue between Rath and the men of the Invalid Corps is accurate.

Note 16A: Prentice Hall, a division of Simon and Schuster, granted the author permission to refer to the recollections of William Coxhill in this book on Mary Surratt only. All other notes that refer to the William Coxhill's recollections hereafter referred to either as op. cit. or ibid. have been covered with this same permission.

17. Ibid.

18. Ibid.

19. Ibid.

20. Edward F. Smith, "Jackson Officer Was Lincoln Conspirators' Hangman," *Jackson Citizen Patriot,* Jackson, MI, 21 January 1962.

21. Harlow Randall Hoyt, op. cit.

22. Ibid.

23. Colonel Julian E. Raymond, *A Country Requires a Capital,* unpublished book manuscript, Fort Lesley J. McNair, Washington, DC, p. 72.

24. Harlow Randall Hoyt, op. cit.

25. The Reverend J. A. Walter, op. cit.

26. Ibid.

27. *The AEGIS,* Bel Air, MD, 16 March 1967.

28. The Reverend J. A. Walter, op. cit., Rev. Walter's exact words.

29. Ibid.

30. Ibid.

31. General Hartranft's unpublished ledger, 8 July 1865, p. 87, Gettysburg College, Gettysburg, PA.

32. *Washington Evening Star,* 7 July 1865.

33. *Surratt Courier,* March 1987, and *Saturday News,* Lewisburg, PA, 6 February 1909.

34. *New York Times,* 6 July 1865.

35. Otto Eisenschiml, *In the Shadow of Lincoln's Death* (New York: Wilfred Funk, Inc., 1940), p. 185.

36. The Reverend J. A. Walter, op. cit., Congressman Thomas Florence's exact words according to Rev. J. A. Walter.

37. Ibid.

38. Ibid.

39. John Brophy's affidavit, *Washington Constitutional Union,* 11 July 1865.

40. Ibid.

41. Samuel Carter, III, op. cit., p. 216.

42. J. W. Clampitt, "The Trial of Mrs. Surratt," *North American Review,* September 1880, p. 234.

43. Ibid., p. 235.

44. Ibid.

45. Ibid.

Note 45A: According to William Wilkins Glen in his diary for 7 July 1865, "President Johnson has been too ill for more than a week to receive anyone. This gives rise to surmises. Some say he has succumbed to his old weakness and been in a state of intoxication." Ref: Edited by Bayly Ellen Marks and Mark Norton Schatz, *Between North and South* (Cranbury, NJ: Associated University Presses, Inc., 1976), p. 231.

46. *Baltimore Sun,* 8 July 1865.

47. *Evening Star,* Washington, DC, 7 July 1865.

48. "Hangman of President Lincoln's Assassins Tells His Story," op. cit.

49. Ibid.

50. Ibid.

51. *Follansbee Review,* WV, Catherine Dodd's obituary. Date of the article is missing. Mrs. Dodd died 18 May 1916. Researched by Joan Chaconas and James O. Hall of the Surratt Society, Clinton, MD.

52. R. A. Watts, op. cit.

53. John T. Ford, "Behind the Curtain of a Conspiracy," *North American Review,* Vol. CXLVII, April 1889, p. 485.

54. J. W. Clampitt, op. cit.

55. Ibid.

56. Ibid.

57. Ibid.

58. John T. Ford, op. cit.

59. Reverend Walter's letter to the president, National Archives, RG 153, JAO, Box 3, unnumbered item.

60. Ibid.

Note 60A: In September 1978, Joan Chaconas, former president of the Surratt Society, met the great-grandson of Gen. W. E. Doster. General Doster was the defense attorney for Lewis Powell and George Atzerodt. At the meeting, Mrs. Chaconas was allowed to go through the general's papers. While examining them, she found a statement that presumably had been made by George Atzerodt. The statement was given to Provost Marshal McPhail in the presence of John L. Smith on the night of 1 May 1865. Ref: A copy of the statement is in the Surratt Society archives, Clinton, MD.

After reading the statement, one has to wonder if the statement was made under duress, as John Lloyd's and Louis Weichmann's testimonies had been made. Or perhaps the government struck a faithless deal, that if Atzerodt agreed to make the statement, he would not have to stand trial. Consequently, Atzerodt's incentive in making the statement is not known. What follows are extractions from that statement that refer to Mrs. Surratt and Atzerodt's part in the conspiracy.

According to George Atzerodt, Booth told him that "Mrs. Surratt went to Surrattsville to get out the guns [two carbines] which had been taken to that place by David Herold. This was Friday." A little farther on, Atzerodt said, "Booth never said until the last night [Friday] that he intended to kill the President." That would have been after Mrs. Surratt had gone to Surrattsville; therefore, she would not have known that Booth's intentions were to kill the president. Booth had no plans for the president when Booth gave Mrs. Surratt the package to take to Surrattsville. It was not until Booth went to Ford's Theatre that he learned that the president would be attending the theater that night. It was only then that Booth began to formulate a plan to kill the president. Consequently, Booth could not have told Mrs. Surratt to tell Lloyd to have (according to May 13 trial testimony of Lloyd) "those shooting arms ready that night, there would be parties who would call for them." Therefore, Atzerodt's indictment of Mrs. Surratt was no indictment, after all.

Farther on in the statement, Atzerodt said: "I repeat, I never knew anything about the murder. I was intended to give assistance to the kidnapping." At the beginning of that same paragraph, Atzerodt had said that Herold "came to the Kirkwood House same evening [Friday, April 14] for me to go to see Booth. [Booth was at the Herndon House.] I went with Herold and saw Booth. He then said he was going to kill the President and Wood [Lewis Powell] the Secretary of State. I did not believe him." Atzerodt failed to include himself in the statement that he, Atzerodt, had been given orders by Booth to kill Vice President Johnson.

George Atzerodt was frightened. He would have said anything to save himself from the hangman's noose. Lewis Powell had nothing to lose and told the truth when he said that Mrs. Surratt was innocent of the plan to kill the president.

61. *The Sun,* Baltimore, MD, Sunday, 7 July 1901, dialogue obtained from the article.

62. Most accounts merely mention that Anna was with a friend at the White House on the morning of 7 July. According to Mrs. Helmas Jenson, granddaughter of Mary Elizabeth Wildman Queen, her grandmother attended Mrs. Surratt's hanging and "escorted the daughter home afterwards." Mary Elizabeth Queen is the only female friend documented to have been with Anna on that fateful day. Ref: Mrs. Jenson's undated letter, the Surratt Society archives, Clinton, MD.

63. *The Sun,* op. cit.

64. Ibid., exact dialogue from the article.

65. Ibid.

66. Ibid.

67. Ibid.

68. Ibid.

69. Ibid., exact dialogue from the article.

70. Ibid., exact dialogue from the article.

Note 70A: Soon after the trial of the conspirators had ended, John Brophy and Louis Carland, a former customer at Ford's Theatre, and Louis Weichmann had taken a walk. Weichmann was filled with guilt for the way he had testified. When Brophy asked Mrs. Douglas to ask the president if he had received his (Brophy's) statement, Brophy was referring to the statement that he had written telling the president what Weichmann had told him and Carland on that walk. Weichmann had claimed that when he was arrested, he had been arrested as one of the conspirators. Both Stanton and Burnett had threatened him with death unless he revealed all about the assassination. Weichmann declared "that he would rather be hooted at as a spy and informer, and do anything rather than be tried as a conspirator . . . ." Weichmann then admitted that he had lied on the witness stand. This is what was in the statement that Brophy had sent to the president. The president thought it "wholly without weight" and refused to interfere in the hanging.

On the day of the execution, John Brophy swore out an affidavit in which he disclosed Weichmann's statements above. On 11 July 1865, the Washington *Constitution Union* published the sensational affidavit.

During the trial of John Surratt in 1867, Louis J. Carland gave testimony concerning Louis Weichmann.

Carland testified that he had taken a walk with Louis J. Weichmann and John Brophy, in the spring or summer of 1865, that it was after Weichmann had testified before the Military Commission. At that time Weichmann said that his conscience was troubling him about the testimony he had given at the trial. He wanted to go to St. Aloysius Church to make a confession in order to relieve his conscience. Carland testified that he told Weichmann to go to a magistrate and make a statement under oath. Weichmann said that he would, but he was afraid of being indicted for perjury. According to Carland, Weichmann said that had he been allowed to give his statement as he wanted, things would be a lot different for Mrs. Surratt. Weichmann said that he had to swear to a statement that had been prepared for him by those in charge of the Military Commission. Weichmann said that if he did not swear to the statement he would be prosecuted as one of the conspirators. Ref: *The Trial of John H. Surratt,* op. cit., Vol. 2, p. 814.

On another occasion Colonel William P. Wood, the superintendent of Old Capitol Prison, sent for John T. Ford. When Ford arrived, Junius Booth, brother of John Wilkes, and Asia's husband, John Sleeper Clarke, were present. Wood spoke freely about the trial, particularly the trial of Mrs. Surratt, whom Wood believed innocent. John Ford asked Colonel Wood what he thought of Weichmann. "He is a lying son of a bitch," was the colonel's reply. Ref: David Rankin Barbee, "The Murder of Mrs. Surratt," p. 19, a paper given at the Emerson Institute, Washington, DC, 25 February 1950.

71. Ibid., exact dialogue according to the article.

72. Ibid.

73. Ibid., exact dialogue according to the article.

74. Ibid.

75. Ibid.

Note 75A: The following concerns an interview that W. Scott Smith, newspaper correspondent, had with former president Andrew Johnson. It appeared in the *Philadelphia Press,* 12 December 1881:

"Talking of this matter of the Lincoln assassination, I remember asking Andrew Johnson, one day, when we were traveling through East

Tennessee, at a time when he was running for congressman-at-large against Horace Maynard and Frank Cheatham, why it was he did not pardon Mrs. Surratt. He was in a communicative mood and said: 'The true history of that case has never been told. It was represented in the papers that I refused to see Annie Surratt when she came to the White House the morning of the execution, asking for the pardon of her mother. The fact is that I never knew it was Miss Surratt, because a man named Mussey, who had general charge of the White House, came to me and said that a crazy woman was downstairs and wanted to get in to see me, and she would not give her name, but was crying and tearing her hair, and exhibiting all the evidence of insanity.'"

Interesting, when one remembers that Mrs. Douglas had twice tried to see President Johnson on behalf of Mrs. Surratt and her daughter. It would seem that she would have told him that Anna was downstairs. Furthermore, wouldn't the president have believed his own daughter when she probably told him that she had seen Anna Surratt agonizing on the stairs?

The man to whom former president Johnson referred to as Mussey was none other than General Mussey, the president's private secretary. He is the one, who, early in the author's notes, said the president had stated, whether guilty or not, Mrs. Surratt's execution was *justified*, since there had not been "*women enough hanged in this war.*" (Emphasis by author.)

## CHAPTER 22

1. Helen Jones Campbell, *The Case for Mrs. Surratt* (New York: G. P. Putnam's Sons, 1943), p. 268.

2. *The Evening Star,* Washington, DC, 7 July 1865.

3. *The Holy Bible,* King James Version, Matthew 26:39.

4. Ibid., Psalm 23:4,5.

5. *New York World,* 11 July 1865, Gillette's exact words taken from the newspaper account.

6. *The Evening Star,* op. cit.

7. Ibid.

8. *Trial of the Assassins and Conspirators for the Murder of Abraham Lincoln* (Philadelphia: Barclay and Company, 1865), re-issued by James L. Barbour (Port Tobacco, MD: 1981), p. 99.

9. The Reverend J. A. Walter, "The Surratt Case," *Church News,*

Washington, DC, 16 August 1891, also read before the U.S. Catholic Historical Society, 25 May 1891. Ref: Tonry Collection, E457 .5 .S985 No. 1, Surratt Society archives, Clinton, MD.

10. General Hartranft's unpublished ledger, 8 July 1865, p. 87, Gettysburg College, Gettysburg, PA.

11. The dialogue was taken from an alleged note that Mrs. Surratt possibly wrote either to Eliza Holohan or Eliza Wildman Queen. Due to ink blots and a poor pen, the note is barely legible. Ref: Manuscript Division, Library of Congress, AC. 2670.

12. *Meteorological Observations Made at the U. S. Naval Observatory, During the Year 1865.*

13. Colonel Julian E. Raymond, *A Country Requires a Capital,* unpublished book manuscript, Fort Lesley J. McNair, Washington, DC, p. 72, and D. F. Landon, Lieutenant Colonel, Company G, Fourteenth Indiana Regiment, letter published in the *Indiana Magazine of History,* 1939, Georgetown University Library, Washington, D.C.

14. Ibid.

15. Landon's letter, op. cit.

16. Roy Meredith, *Mr. Lincoln's Camera Man* (New York: Charles Scribner's Sons, 1946), p. 205.

17. Inspired by: *The Constitutional Union,* 2nd Edition, 7 July 1865.

18. Allison Lockwood, "Pantsuited Pioneer of Women's Lib., Dr. Mary Walker," *Smithsonian Magazine,* March 1977.

19. *Daily Morning Chronicle,* 8 July 1865.

20. Reverend J. A. Walter, op. cit., Anna's exact words according to Father Walter.

21. Ibid.

22. *New York Herald,* — 1867—. The day and month of the article were not legible.

23. *Philadelphia Inquirer,* 7 July 1865.

24. *The Constitutional Union,* 7 July 1865.

25. Guy W. Moore, *The Case of Mrs. Surratt* (Norman: University of Oklahoma Press, 1954), p. 70, Mrs. Surratt's exact words according to Moore's book.

26. Reverend J. A. Walter, op. cit., Mrs. Surratt's exact words, according to the priest.

27. Ibid., Reverend Walter's exact words.

28. Ibid., Mrs. Surratt's exact words.

29. Ibid.

30. *Trial of the Assassins and Conspirators,* op. cit.

31. Ibid.

32. *Meteorological Observations Made at the U.S. Naval Observatory During the Year 1865.*

33. *The Constitutional Union,* 7 July 1865, and *Daily Morning Chronicle,* 8 July 1865.

34. *The Evening Star,* 7 July 1865.

35. *New York Times Weekly Tribune,* 15 July 1865.

36. Ibid.

37. Ibid.

38. *Philadelphia Public Ledger,* 10 July 1865, and *The Constitutional Union,* 7 July 1865.

39. Ibid.

40. Amy Gillette Bassett, *Red Cross Reveries* (Harrisburg, PA: Stackpole Co., 1960), p. 90, Powell's exact words according to Mrs. Bassett, daughter of Dr. Gillette. (Research courtesy of James O. Hall.)

41. Ibid., Powell's exact words.

42. *The Sun,* Baltimore, MD, 8 July 1865.

43. Ibid.

44. Colonel Julian E. Raymond's manuscript, op. cit., p. 78

45. Forney's interview with Clampitt, 1880, exact words according to the interview. Ref: The David Rankin Barbee Collection, Georgetown University Library, Washington, D.C.

46. R. A. Watts (Judge), "The Trial and Execution of the Lincoln Conspirators," *Michigan History Magazine,* Vol. VI, No. 1, 1922, p. 102.

47. *The Sun,* Baltimore, MD, 8 July 1865.

48. Ibid.

49. Ibid.

50. Ibid.

51. Ibid., Dr. Butler's exact words.

52. Reverend J. A. Walter, op. cit., exact quotation from Father Walter's article that appeared in the *Church News.*

53. Harlow Randall Hoyt, "William Coxhill's Recollections," *Town Hall Tonight* (Englewood Cliffs, NJ: Prentice Hall, Inc., 1955), pp. 148-52, and *Surratt Courier,* September 1986.

Note 53A: Prentice Hall, a division of Simon and Schuster, granted the author permission to refer to the recollections of William Coxhill for her book on Mary Surratt only.

54. Edward F. Smith, "Jackson Officer Was Lincoln Conspirators' Hangman," *Jackson Citizen Patriot,* Jackson, MI, 21 January 1962.

55. *New York Times Weekly Tribune,* 15 July 1865.

56. *The Trial of the Assassins and Conspirators for the Murder of President Lincoln* (Philadelphia: T. B. Peterson and Brothers, 1865), p. 207.

57. Reverend J. A. Walter, op. cit., Mrs. Surratt's exact words.

58. Colonel Julian E. Raymond's manuscript, op. cit., p. 78.

59. *The Sun,* Baltimore, MD, 8 July 1865, Atzerodt's exact words.

60. William E. Doster, *Lincoln and Episodes of the Civil War* (New York and London: G. P. Putnam's Sons, The Knickerbocker Press, 1915), p. 276.

61. Edward F. Smith, op. cit.

## EPILOGUE

1. John C. Brennan letter to Dr. Joseph George, Jr., dated 29 June 1983.

2. Laurie Verge, "That Man Lloyd," *Surratt Courier,* April 1988, p. 3.

3. From the files of General Hartranft from Gerald S. Brinton to John C. Brennan.

4. Laurie Verge, "What Happened to the Children?" *Surratt Society News,* August 1984, p. 4.

5. Timothy Cwiek, "The Plight of Anna Surratt," *Surratt Society News,* October 1981.

6. The David Rankin Barbee Collection, Georgetown University Library, Washington, DC.

7. *Washington Star,* 9 February 1869. The David Rankin Barbee Collection, Georgetown University Library, Washington, DC.

Note 7A: The *Star* article mentions that Mrs. Surratt's body had decomposed. That would seem more logical.

8. *Baltimore Sun,* June 18, 1869.

9. *Biographical Encyclopedia,* Surratt Society archives, Clinton, MD, p. 177.

10. *Surratt Society News,* February 1979.

11. Isaac Surratt's Confederate military records.

12. Compiled by Brig. Gen. Marcus J. Wright, C.S.A., edited by Col. Harold B. Simpson, U.S.A.F., *Texas in the War, 1861-1865* (The Hill Junior College Press, nd), p. 121. My thanks to Michael R. Green, reference archivist, Texas State Archives, Texas State Library, Austin, Texas.

13. Isaac Surratt's Confederate military records.

14. *Baltimore News,* 4 November 1907, obituary of Isaac D. Surratt.

15. Laurie Verge, "Where Was Isaac?" *Surratt Courier,* August 1986.

16. Alfred Isacsson, "An Update on Mary Surratt and Her Offsprings Anna and Isaac," *Surratt Courier,* May 1986, p. 4.

17. Laurie Verge, "Mrs. Surratt's Other Son," *Surratt Society News,* August 1977.

18. The material on John Surratt was obtained from two sources:

1. *Surratt Courier,* July 1993.

2. Reverend William Madden's dissertation sent to John Brennan from Reverend Alfred Isacsson, 28 October 1986.

19. Joseph George, Jr., "The Days Are Yet Dark," a paper read on April 13, 1984, at Villanova University, Villanova, PA, and Louis J. Weichmann, *The True History of the Assassination of Abraham Lincoln and of the Conspiracy of 1865* (New York: Alfred A. Knopf, Inc., 1975), p. 405—Appendix.

# *Author's Note*

In the name of justice, it is the sincere wish of the author that the United States government pardon Mary Elizabeth Surratt and issue an apology to her descendants. I believe that President Lincoln would have it so, if he could speak to us today. A woman was unjustly hanged and, because of this injustice, her descendants have suffered ever since. Thank you.

Elizabeth Steger Trindal

# Index